Goal Focused Positive Psychotherapy

Goal Focused Positive Psychotherapy

Psychotherapy

A Strengths-Based Approach

COLLIE W. CONOLEY

AND

MICHAEL J. SCHEEL

OXFORD
UNIVERSITY PRESS

OXFORD
UNIVERSITY PRESS

Oxford University Press is a department of the University of Oxford. It furthers
the University's objective of excellence in research, scholarship, and education
by publishing worldwide. Oxford is a registered trade mark of Oxford University
Press in the UK and certain other countries.

Published in the United States of America by Oxford University Press
198 Madison Avenue, New York, NY 10016, United States of America.

© Oxford University Press 2018

Library of Congress Cataloging-in-Publication Data
Names: Conoley, Collie W. (Collie Wyatt), 1949– author. | Scheel, Michael J., author.
Title: Goal focused positive psychotherapy : a strengths-based approach /
Collie W. Conoley and Michael J. Scheel.
Description: Oxford ; New York : Oxford University Press, [2018] |
Includes bibliographical references and index.
Identifiers: LCCN 2017022821 (print) | LCCN 2017023056 (ebook) |
ISBN 9780190681739 (updf) | ISBN 9780190681746 (epub) |
ISBN 9780190681722 (paperback)
Subjects: LCSH: Psychotherapy. | Positive psychology. | BISAC: PSYCHOLOGY /
Clinical Psychology. | PSYCHOLOGY / Psychotherapy / General.
Classification: LCC RC475 (ebook) | LCC RC475 .C66 2018 (print) |
DDC 616.89/14—dc23
LC record available at https://lccn.loc.gov/2017022821

9 8 7 6 5 4 3 2 1

Printed by Webcom, Inc., Canada

CONTENTS

We believe Goal Focused Positive Psychotherapy (GFPP) opens psychotherapy to a revolutionary new path that diverges from the therapeutic methods now in practice. We regard GFPP as an exciting and unique approach to helping people find happiness while diminishing feelings of distress. We strive to convey the paradigm shift within GFPP through the mechanism of change employed (i.e., Broaden-and-Build) and the focus upon well-being rather than pathology. Our aim was to provide a method that helps people lead happier, more satisfying lives despite the inevitable problems of life that all people encounter. The enhancement of people's lives above a focus on problems and symptom alleviation is the priority. Through increasing positive emotions and hope, GFPP makes psychotherapy more enjoyable for clients while decreasing or making more manageable clients' problems and symptoms.

GFPP is a very teachable therapeutic method based on four processes: (1) the identification and enhancement of client strengths, (2) the promotion of positive emotions, (3) the formation of approach goals, and (4) engendering hope. These four GFPP hallmarks are interconnected and interrelated as they unfold in therapy. GFPP requires the therapist to embrace an authentic belief in the benefits of a psychotherapy that prizes strengths rather than highlighting pathology; moves from extrinsically oriented avoidant goals to intrinsically oriented approach goals; shifts from fearing negative emotions and problems to feeling confident about experiencing negative emotions because positive emotions become more accessible; and moves from tendencies to avoid past memories and future fears to embracing the present by fully experiencing life, and eagerly anticipating a more meaningful and happier future.

In this book, we write about several advantages of GFPP over traditional, more problem-focused therapies. We also provide empirical evidence for GFPP positive outcomes and its superiority in motivating clients to be engaged in therapy. Clients are more accepting of therapy and feel less stigmatized by GFPP due to helping clients attend to the best parts of themselves. Strengths and positive emotions create an enjoyable therapy experience for clients to embrace new possibilities and hope for their futures. We see the GFPP process as a transcendent experience for clients through their discovery of new ways of being defined by strengths, desired life goals, hope and empowerment for the future, and experiencing human beings' ultimate goal—happiness; not by their problems or pathology.

GFPP's therapeutic goal focuses on increasing well-being to increase clients' ability to deal with their problems. GFPP includes tools to support happier, healthier, and more meaningful lives. The science of positive psychology reveals that growth and flourishing occur under known conditions: involvement in meaningful activities; experiencing supportive, caring relationships; feeling competent; having goals; and experiencing positive emotions frequently. GFPP is designed to help individuals gain each of these desired, therapeutic states.

GFPP creates a welcoming, heartening process for people who seek help through therapy. GFPP does not require individuals to focus on past bad behavior or experiences. Effort is not devoted to affixing blame or responsibility for past problems and transgressions. Instead clients are invited to find the intersection of meaning, strengths, and goals that make them happier and experience a more fulfilling life. The depression and anxiety that clients bring to therapy are viewed as natural parts of life that distract from focusing on a meaningful life. The philosophy conveyed through GFPP is that the more individuals attend to negative emotions, states, and experiences, the more distracted they become from meaning. Through GFPP, we encourage both therapists and clients to listen to what depression and anxiety might be communicating to us. We teach therapists to help clients realize the desired states that are embedded in a juxtaposition to the negative emotions of depression and anxiety. The GFPP process reorients the client's focus toward what is meaningful.

We choose to adopt a positive view of human nature through GFPP that human beings under the right conditions tend toward actualization; that people have a natural affinity to be virtuous and when individuals experience virtue in their lives, well-being is enhanced. Thus, GFPP taps into the virtuous parts of individuals. When individuals are able to feel worthy, honorable, and true to themselves they are able to flourish in their lives.

We are extremely grateful to a number of people in our lives that have contributed more than they know to this book. Our life partners, Jane Close Conoley and Joan Bangert Scheel, have taught us to pay attention to the best parts of who we are. Through their encouragement and belief in us, we have been able to write this book. They have guided us through their caring and loving relationships to us. We also recognize their patience in waiting for us to find our virtuous selves. Jane and Joan also have made it possible for us to experience virtue through the love we feel toward them, the greatest contributor to our happiness.

We would also like to express our gratitude to our children and grandchildren who give our lives meaning. Thank you, Timothy, Jaime, Kara, Brian, Colleen, Collin, Beth, Greg, Samantha, Michael, Haley, Jack, Declan, and Nola.

Goal Focused Positive Psychotherapy

Introducing Goal Focused
Positive Psychotherapy

Welcome to Goal Focused Positive Psychotherapy (GFPP), an exciting, important advancement in the field of psychotherapy. GFPP promotes client strengths, hope, and positive emotions in order to assist clients in accomplishing what they desire in life (i.e., the client's approach goals). Positive psychology research and theory have developed sufficiently in recent years to form the basis of this comprehensive psychotherapeutic approach with the goal of optimizing well-being while diminishing the effects of psychological distress.

We see GFPP as the fifth force in psychotherapy: an approach that profoundly embraces and enhances a client's resources for experiencing happiness, in contrast to the more traditional clinical approaches that focus almost exclusively on reducing client pathology. Proclaiming that our approach is the fifth force may seem presumptuous in comparison to the four other forces: psychoanalytic/psychodynamic, behavioral/cognitive-behavioral, humanistic/experiential, and multicultural. We see GFPP as revolutionary in its departure from the previous four paths because GFPP prioritizes well-being, happiness, hope, strengths, and positive emotions, as well as a change process based on positive emotions.

GFPP helps clients understand what they want in life and opens the horizons to involvement in activities that are meaningful to the client via frequent positive emotions. Goals for a lifetime are sought and affirmed throughout therapy, providing an inspirational "best possible self" for the future. As a GFPP therapist, you will communicate that virtuous, meaningful goals lead to happiness AND that accomplishing goals by harnessing positive emotions and personal strengths can contribute to an enjoyable, satisfying life, moving a person incrementally toward lifelong aspirations.

At the same time, the therapist explains to clients that their problems—typically the reasons clients seek therapy—will be addressed using a positive, strength-oriented focus. The rationale is that as clients find better, more enjoyable, and more meaningful lives, the effects from their initial problems diminish and their ability to cope with the inevitable challenges of life expands. Through therapy, positive states such as hope, optimism, gratitude, and self-compassion are generated, allowing clients to move toward more enjoyable and meaningful lives. The burden of the initial problems and their accompanying symptoms are alleviated through a generative method that produces those positive emotions and uplifting experiences associated with enhanced well-being.

A HAPPY LIFE

The ultimate outcome goal of GFPP is increased happiness or subjective well-being.[1] Philosophers and researchers alike have championed happiness as an ultimate goal for a meaningful life. Aristotle and the Dalai Lama agree that the meaning of life is centered on happiness; that is, living well or flourishing (Garfield, 2011).[2] Arguments attributed to Aristotle may best express the rationale: happiness is reasoned to be the highest goal in life because happiness is the final-good. In other words, when reflecting upon what your specific motivation is for a particular action, you may often find that the action is a means to an end. The initial activity is a way to achieve a secondary, greater purpose: the "final-good," or ultimate purpose, is not typically contained within the initial action. In contrast, Aristotle's "final-good," or highest goal, is done only for itself, not in order to accomplish something further. As the final-good, happiness is both the ends and the means.

For example, why do you strive for money? Money is not a final purpose. We usually seek money to accomplish a subsequent, associated goal. Perhaps that associated goal is security, and the next is peace of mind, and so on, until reaching the ultimate goal of happiness, at which point there is no farther to go, for what else could a person wish that would not be contained within the wish for happiness? Happiness can be argued to be the final goal because we do not seek happiness to accomplish another goal.

Another of Aristotle's arguments for the worth of happiness is based upon self-sufficiency (Garfield, 2011). That is, if you have happiness, then you want for nothing else. For example, wealth or honor can be considered very important. However, even having wealth or honor, you could still long for happiness. Having happiness is so marvelous that you need nothing else. Happiness is sufficient— and necessary— for a good life.

To accept the argument of final good or self-sufficiency, happiness must be defined carefully. Defining happiness has historically been a challenge. For Aristotle, happiness consists of an evaluation of one's life as a whole, not just the experience of the present moment. The positive psychology literature uses the construct of life-satisfaction to describe the evaluation of life overall. If people believe that their lives are ideal and contain almost no regrets, then they have high life-satisfaction (Diener, 1984). In positive psychology, happiness or subjective well-being is defined as a person experiencing (a) life-satisfaction or a satisfying life overall, (b) frequent positive emotions, and (c) infrequent negative emotions (Diener, 1984). Later, we will more clearly define what contributes to happiness as the outcome goal for GFPP. As a psychological construct, happiness can be defined relatively clearly, while at the individual level, happiness is almost always idiosyncratic. For example, research unequivocally demonstrates that cultivating social relationships contributes to happiness. But the specific types of relationships and the characteristics of the people in those relationships that produce happiness will vary significantly from client to client. The client's context, worldview, and personal priorities must be honored when considering the constituents of happiness.

IS HAPPINESS TOO SELFISH?

People's first reaction to happiness as a life goal is often repulsion: "How selfish! This is just the problem with the world today!" However, as you may guess we, the authors, have changed our initially negative opinion. The next few paragraphs are included to win you over to happiness as a worthy goal if at first reading you are feeling skeptical.

While GFPP has nothing to do with religion, religious beliefs may be viewed as conflicting with the goal of happiness. We offer a brief account of our prior struggles reconciling religion and positive psychology in hope that our journey may provide a perspective that helps readers to integrate their particular religious beliefs and the goals of GFPP. Growing up in a small-town Presbyterian church (the first author) and a Catholic church (the second author), we believed that sacrifice for others was the goal of life. How does happiness fit in this worldview? Our early belief was that one should be suffering in order to live a good life, that experiencing happiness was actually *antithetical* to living a good life. Our personal understanding of religion was that engaging in meaningful acts that better the lives of others would not make us happy, but virtuous acts would make us good people. Furthermore, many religious beliefs dictate that happiness will not be attained until after death, and upon going to heaven.

Our resolution of the happiness issue came through several discoveries. For us, religion has been about how to be good people. Studying psychology--and especially positive psychology--has been an awakening. By experiencing the effects of practicing positive psychology, we have come to a realization that happiness can be a worthwhile goal. Research reveals that virtuous acts lead to happiness (Buschor, Proyer & Ruch, 2013).

Apart from religion, consider altruism. Altruism is the motivation to help others even at personal loss (Bateson, 2011). Some argue that altruistic behaviors are actually performed for personal gain, while others believe that some acts are certainly self-sacrifice. It is difficult to argue with the common experience that acts of kindness toward others are personally reinforcing, because often the outcome is feeling happy. Research indicates that experiences of increased health and subjective well-being accompany altruistic behavior (Miller, Kahle, & Hastings, 2015): virtuous acts create happiness. (The research supporting virtues will be presented in Chapter 2.)

Therefore, the eternal argument about whether a virtuous action is performed for the sake of another or to make us happy becomes a moot point. Acting altruistically leads to happiness automatically when engaging in a virtuous act. Acting in ways that reflect individual meaning creates happiness whether or not one believes that virtue creates happiness. Being virtuous is a good way to live life!

Consider heaven or reincarnation as the ultimate goal in life. Aristotle's question of the final-good could be phrased as "Why do you want to go to heaven?" The desire to go to heaven (i.e., the goal of Christianity) is to be happy. The final-good is then to be happy.

Perhaps you, the reader, found happiness an easy goal to accept from the beginning. Great! Sorry to waste your reading time with an unnecessary, persuasively oriented section. Probably every psychotherapy theory has the implicit outcome goal of helping the client experience greater happiness anyway. However, if you are still having difficulty accepting happiness as a worthy life goal, please keep an open mind to being happy and helping others be happy! We have more research evidence that is especially persuasive. In addition, if you are having trouble accepting our philosophical arguments for happiness as a life goal, we will also have some very pragmatic ones in support of happiness as the goal of therapy. To pique your curiosity here, we offer the observation that it is very difficult, if not impossible, for a person to be both happy and unhappy at the same time, and happy people are better equipped to overcome hardships and difficult circumstances than those who are unhappily preoccupied with problems and dissatisfaction. Systems theory informs us that when one component of a system changes, other corresponding components change as well. The conditions of happiness affect one's state of unhappiness. More reasoning and research will follow in later chapters to offer support for happiness as the goal of therapy. Next, we move to introducing our GFPP therapy model.

CLIENTS AND GOALS

The issue of goals is central to GFPP and significant in several ways. One very important issue surrounding goals is the way in which goals become confused with problems. As we have already mentioned, the initial motivation for therapy often resides in the desire to decrease or eliminate a problem. Reorienting the client to think differently and more expansively is often difficult. Clients have often lived so long with a problem such as depression or anxiety that all they can think of is to be rid of the negative experiences and conditions. The goal of ceasing to have a problem is an *avoidance goal*. Avoidance goals emphasize escaping negative outcomes, such as conflict, rejection, or resentment (Gable, 2006). What to replace the negative feelings *with* often seems unimportant initially to the client. However, the goal of simply avoiding feared experiences leaves clients entangled with their feared experiences and thus continuously troubled by them, no matter how hard they try to reduce their exposure to and awareness of the avoided experiences.

On the other hand, moving toward a goal that is meaningful and virtuous typically increases the client's happiness. Goals that focus upon a desirable end-state are *approach goals* (Gable, 2006). The client decides on approach goals with the encouragement and guidance of the therapist. Incredibly, the establishment of approach goals can be the most difficult accomplishment of therapy, and once they are established, the client sometimes needs little or no help in accomplishing them. However, to continue with the explanation of the importance of goals, let us assume that suitable goals have already been established before moving to the next phase of progression toward the goals.

As clients progress toward significant approach goals, problems that brought them to seek therapy often change. Some problems disappear because they are outgrown. For example, the experience of depression that is heavily influenced by loneliness can be outgrown as the client enjoys the benefits of an intimate friendship or partner. Outgrowing a problem happens in the best circumstance. However, some life problems must be faced and accepted because some of life's problems cannot be outgrown or solved. Everyone experiences sadness and loss in life; such experiences cannot be avoided and should not be denied as important life occurrences. The major way in which GFPP contributes to clients' ability to face and accept life's losses and unchangeable difficulties is by increasing clients' subjective well-being. Coping is enhanced when clients experience confidence that despite life's difficulties, they can still experience happiness. The realities of life's losses and suffering do not fundamentally negate life's meaningfulness and happiness, although they often temporarily make the meaning and happiness feel less accessible or potent. The inevitability of suffering and loss in life heightens the importance of learning the skills to embrace the joy in life, be it meager or bountiful.

A visual representation of a client's experience may communicate more clearly the influence of increased well-being. Figure 1-1 represents the experience of a client entering psychotherapy. The size of life's problems is perceived as larger than the client's experience of well-being. The client experiences an inability to effectively deal with such large problems with the available resources. After successfully increasing well-being, Figure 1-2 represents the client's perception of the same-sized problem from the perspective of greatly enhanced well-being. The problems that were experienced as initially overwhelming loom less threatening in the new perspective that contrasts problems and well-being. Well-being brings many resources to counter despair.

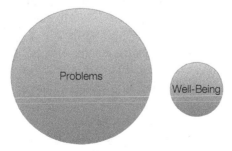

Figure 1-1 A client's perspective of feeling overwhelmed by the size of problems in the context of resources to deal with the problems at the beginning of therapy.

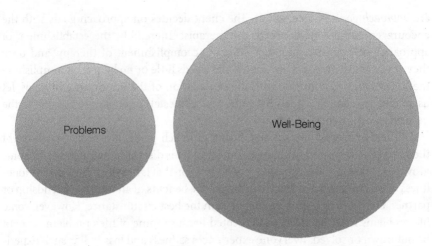

Figure 1-2 A client's perspective of feeling empowered by the enhanced size of well-being with the same problems that were debilitating.

PSYCHOLOGICAL VERSUS PHYSICAL SCIENCES METAPHOR

Fundamentally GFPP approaches psychological problems from a different perspective than most previous methods (e.g., psychodynamic therapy, cognitive-behavioral therapy). The difference in perspective can be understood through the metaphors that either explicitly or implicitly guide the logic of psychotherapy. We believe that the physical sciences metaphor,[3] the historical framework for understanding psychotherapy, actually constrains and somewhat misdirects most psychotherapy theories. The physical sciences metaphor refers to expecting the general rules of physics to fit psychotherapy.

A fundamental assertion in physics is that every effect has a specific cause. The functioning of a car provides an appropriate application of the physical sciences paradigm. For example, when the engine of a car does not start, the most important step is to identify the source of the problem. Why is the car broken? What is the specific cause or critical part that is failing? Identifying the cause of the car's malfunction is essential. The mechanic should not change the spark plugs if the car is out of gas! After diagnosing the cause of the problem, a specific intervention is applied that will cause the car to function again. For a car, the specific intervention consists of replacing or fixing a dysfunctional part. The car functions once again just as it did before! Cause-and-effect reasoning—the linchpin of the physical sciences paradigm—works splendidly for machines.

In psychotherapy, too often the corresponding belief prevails that understanding the cause of a problem will reveal its cure. Even when physics does not apply, the physical sciences metaphor is assumed. Perhaps you have heard or experienced the statement, "At least I know what I'm dealing with now." Presumably, if the cure is not known, the physical sciences metaphor offers reassurance because knowing the problem is the first step toward solving the problem. Or "We need to get at the root of the problem." Similarly, the statement assumes that the actual cause can be known—and indeed must be known—in order to create an effective solution.

The physical sciences metaphor creates difficulty because a person's psychological processes do not operate according to the laws of physical sciences. Perhaps the most cogent example is that diagnosing a client does not lead to a specific or unique psychotherapy treatment (Lopez, Edwards, Pedrotti, et al., 2006; Wampold, 2007; Wampold & Imel, 2015).

To further explain the point, we will define mechanization as the opposite of anthropomorphism. Anthropomorphism involves attributing human characteristics to nonhumans. Problems occur when expecting the nonhuman to behave as a human would. For example, "That chair fell over while I was sitting in it, so I kicked it! Now it will behave." Nonsensical, eh? On the other hand, mechanization can be defined as regarding something mechanical that is not mechanical, like a human's psychological functioning: "The person does not work adequately; therefore, the person is defective. The person must be fixed." A central difference is how change typically occurs. Something specific inside a machine is changed to make it function. However, a person's way of thinking or acting is changed through perception or context, rather than by replacing or adjusting a single "defective" internal component. Both ideas of change occur from outside of the person to influence the person to act, think, or feel differently. However, the person is less likely to feel "pathologized" when what is seen as needing alteration is the perception or the context instead of something internal.

Too often the physical sciences metaphor is forced to fit psychotherapy. For example, the first pillar of physics is cause and effect. If the cause is found, then the effect can be altered. Translated to psychotherapy, this might lead us to search for the singular cause of a person's problem. For example, the client's problem could be relationship difficulties, and eventually the therapist may find that the primary parent was often intrusive and sometimes distant. The therapist might conclude that the root problem is that the client as a child could not count on a supportive parent. Attachment theory would support that that problematic parenting style causes the client's anxiety, insecurity, and poor relational skills. Now the cause of the client's problem becomes clear. But wait: is insecure attachment the real cause? Perhaps the parents functioned well enough as parents. Could the real cause be the client's terrible childhood friends? Or could the cause be that there were no good role models for relationships? Or could it also be that the client just went through a terrible divorce? Or is the cause a recent sexual trauma? Which cause is the real cause that needs treatment? If the real cause is not identifiable in the physical sciences model, treatment cannot work.

After identifying a list of probable causes for the client's problem, the second issue with following a physical sciences metaphor occurs when fixing the problem. How does the treatment change based upon the cause? The ability to be free of a haunting past, and learning how to have good relationships, may not be contingent on the cause of the problem. The interventions that support clients' growth in dealing with scary, intrusive memories as well as having the confidence in and knowledge about relationships will be what will help them make progress in treatment, regardless of the sources of the problem.

Another significant concern in using the physical sciences metaphor in psychotherapy theory is that the outcome goal of therapy becomes implicitly or explicitly achieving the no-symptom or no-problem level of functioning. Two concerns become obvious with a no-symptom outcome goal. First, psychotherapy outcome goals that aspire to benefits beyond the goal of "no problem" or maintenance of a status quo are more ethical because of beneficence (i.e., what creates the greater good). A central goal of GFPP and positive psychology is based upon moving beyond a symptom/problem focus. GFPP focuses on creating meaningful life-long goals that are pursued with as much enjoyment as possible. Investigating the meaningful goals and paths for experiencing happiness, fulfillment, and flourishing are our lofty, transformative purpose. Goals such as increasing an individual's successful experiences in love, vocation, friendship, and forgiveness are typical meaningful goals.

The second concern in focusing upon a goal of attaining a "no problem" outcome for psychotherapy is that the goal is impossible. Life presents us with problems every day! Psychotherapy cannot promise the existence of a life without problems. To promise an existence of being fixed, meaning the individual has no problems, creates false expectations. Promising false expectations is unethical in that it causes maleficence. Depression, anxiety, loss, and loneliness, to name but a few human challenges, are an inevitable part of life. Psychotherapists can never promise to help the client attain a life without anxiety, depression, or loss.

Rather than contorting the physical sciences metaphor in an attempt to understand psychological processes, we propose a simple, elegant shift: use a psychological metaphor to describe psychotherapy. After all of the years of practice and research, surely there could be some fitting metaphors for our field. As you probably guessed, we have a metaphor to suggest!

A PSYCHOLOGICAL METAPHOR

Our psychological metaphor is based on two issues:

- First, the goal of psychotherapy is to facilitate the client's subjective well-being.
- Second, influence is the closest psychological equivalent of causality.

The research cited throughout this book underscores the central goal of well-being. Research describes the endpoints and the more distal waypoints along the routes to well-being. However, the individual client decides the values that form the realities of life that supply the details of well-being. The second point is installing influence as a psychological replacement for the physical science term of cause and effect or simply causality. The individual client perceives, processes, interprets, and decides as a human, thus making all actions upon the individual *mediated* rather than *direct*. That is, the individual thinks and feels. The predictable cause and effect does not occur because a human does not simply react when acted upon. The term *influence* means that change occurs in psychotherapy because of the client and only indirectly through the therapist. GFPP focuses on the influence of the relationship in therapy and the client's positive emotions.

The psychological metaphor facilitates increased clarity of direction (goals) and facilitates movement (change) toward thriving based upon the "ingredients" discovered via research, while also being informed by the client's specific desires and idiosyncrasies.[4] By this we are referring to those things that the client wants in each of the categories that contribute to a happy life or subjective well-being. When people experience higher states of subjective well-being, they increase their opportunities for effectively addressing challenges and accomplishing fulfilling lives. Whatever the life issues are—typical developmental issues or traumatic unpredictable occurrences—a higher state of well-being[5] allows clients both to live with unresolvable problems more easily and to resolve manageable issues with greater ability.

One way to understand the benefit of achieving higher well-being is the attainment of a position of strength: using all possible capabilities to deal with problems rather than ignoring or avoiding them. An analogous common experience provides an example of how high well-being assists in the change process. Consider how having a good night's sleep contributes to dealing with or accepting an issue. Sleep does not typically make a problem go away. However, viewing an issue from a rested, fully capable state can make a problem seem less difficult to deal with or to accept. Creativity, confidence, determination, and many other helpful personal strengths are more readily available when we are rested, even though the problem may still be present. Sleep, like a high level of well-being, provides a psychological context for dealing with life more effectively. Cause and effect of problems is not relevant in this more accurate rendering: sleep does not cause the creation of a solution, nor does it cause acceptance of an insoluble problem. Additionally, we bet that you did not say to yourself, "Oh, sleep only works if the problem is about relationships" or "Everyone knows that sleep never works when dealing with job problems." That is because the diagnosis or cause of the problem becomes unimportant when the remedy is universal. Sleep helps bring forth more psychological resources when compared to being tired. Sleep was not prescribed for a specific problem.

The psychological metaphor we propose borrows heavily from humanistic psychology and positive psychology. Carl Rogers (1951), a founder of the humanistic psychology movement, asserted and researched the value of supportive relationships that facilitated clients' growth toward their life goals. He theorized that people innately grow toward self-actualization or flourishing when in a supportive environment. In a similar vein, positive psychology research expands our knowledge about supportive environments that facilitates our inclination to grow toward high subjective well-being or thriving. We borrow heavily from the work of Carol Ryff (1989) and Kristen Neff (2012) in this assertion, because their research demonstrates that psychological well-being and self-compassion predict subjective well-being.

More specifically, helping people with the following goals and processes facilitates their subjective well-being. The goals of life include relationships, work, play/hobbies/interests, and meaningful involvement. The attainment of subjective well-being has research supporting universal importance, even though the importance of the components (i.e., life satisfaction, positive affect, and negative affect) in contributing to subjective well-being can differ (Diener, Oishi, & Ryan, 2013). Similarly, a great deal of research supports our selection of general goals fitting into a multicultural context, which is detailed in a subsequent chapter. The individual client specifies how the goal is defined. For example, while you, as the therapist, urge multiple high-quality relationships based upon the theory, whom a relationship is with and what type of a relationship will be determined by the client, not by you or GFPP.

Additionally, how a person accomplishes goals or lives life while moving toward goals matters. How we live our life matters. The processes endorsed by GFPP, which are to be maximized when pursuing life goals, include feeling effective, involved, mindful, autonomously motivated, and engaged. Ideally, the process of achieving goals is also supported by the desire to be virtuous, as well as the experience of frequent positive feelings, enduring hope, and persistent self-compassion. The details of the research supporting these goals and processes will be outlined in the following chapters.

THE PROCESS OF CHANGE

Growth, change, and learning are ways to describe the process of moving toward goals. When the process of moving toward goals is painful, it is human nature to tend to avoid the goals. A friend put it clearly when I explained our commitment to having big life goals. My friend said, "Oh, you want me to have another reason to beat myself up!" He was correct by inferring that promoting lofty goals without considering the larger context could be anti-therapeutic. Too often motivation for achieving a goal comes from the threat of a negative outcome like shame, embarrassment, or guilt. For example, "I know that one of my big goals in life is to have a loving family. I am such a selfish, thoughtless, inconsiderate, poor excuse of a person for not being in contact with my brother. If I do not call my brother today, then I will feel even worse. I had better call today or it will prove how worthless I am." Sadly, such self-flagellations work well, but at a cost. Probably I will not enjoy speaking with my brother and my sour, guilty mood might spoil the conversation for him too. The ultimate goal of creating a loving family might be unintentionally undermined.

Lofty goals are facilitated by a client enlisting kind ways to facilitate growth and engage in self-evaluation. In facilitating change, GFPP enlists the client's positive emotions, strengths, self-compassion, hope, and mindfulness, which can buffer against the pain of change. Additionally, the process of change is viewed as an incremental process to counter the typical client belief in all-or-nothing polarities. While clients do at times make very large changes immediately, GFPP suggests change to the client in small increments that are noticeable and defined by the client.

Growth can be painful or enjoyable. Every person experiences both. Learning to purposefully employ enjoyable methods of change in therapy is highly ethical as well as functional. Subsequent chapters will more clearly present the research and procedures for facilitating change, including the central importance of the Broaden-and-Build Theory (Fredrickson, 2001).

THE CASE STUDY OF GEORGE

This case example provides an illustration of GFPP. The case is a good example of GFPP because it concerns a client, whom we will refer to as "George," coming to therapy with what others had defined as his problem, and a diagnosis given by a previous clinician who did not possess an acceptable treatment course. The lack of autonomous client motivation is an important issue in this real case that makes the case very difficult, yet especially illuminating of GFPP.

George was a 50-year-old male retired from the military after an extensive combat history that included multiple wounds in battle and several experiences of seeing "my buddies gone" and then "gaining revenge" from the enemy. George reported symptoms corresponding to posttraumatic stress disorder (PTSD) that included nightmares, insomnia, suicidal ideation, and flashbacks. He had arrived at therapy because his partner threatened to leave him if he did not get help for what she described as his problems with anger. George disagreed, denying feeling anger or any other emotions. He stated, "I don't feel. I just am here skating along feeling nothing one way or another." George explained his presence in therapy as being a means of appeasing his partner.

In previous referrals to other agencies, George had been unwilling to cooperate with the evidence-supported treatment fitting his diagnosis. Similarly, this time he came into therapy committed to proving to the current therapist and to himself the futility of any therapeutic method that directly addressed the problem or its symptoms as previously defined by others. He was fully committed to thwarting any attempts at problem resolution. In the first session he reported that he had become an expert in frustrating previous therapists who had diagnosed him with PTSD and treated him through the corresponding treatments. His previous treatments at the Veterans Administration (VA) hospital had consisted of exposure-oriented methods to process the trauma and the use of selective serotonin reuptake inhibitors (SSRIs). George bragged that none of the treatments had been effective. He expressed resignation to live his life out as it was at that moment, and predicted that it would be "a short ride from here." He also reported constant suicidal ideation but denied current plans to act on his suicidal thoughts. However, he proclaimed that if he did decide to commit suicide, he would not let the therapist or anyone else know ahead of time.

As might be imagined, this caused considerable consternation and concern. Consequently, the therapist acted to ensure George would be safe from suicide by—after some wrestling back and forth—convincing George of the need to agree to inform the therapist if he started to move closer to acting on his suicidal thoughts. The therapist reasoned with George that giving fair warning would help to ensure George's safety, and without some level of assurance from George, the therapist explained that he would not be able to move beyond the issue of suicide to the process of assisting George in creating a better life.

This discussion and its resulting information were carried out through a traditional intake interview. Invoking GFPP's emphasis on client-centered positive goal formation, the therapist asked George to describe what he would like better than his current situation, what his desired state was, and how it would be possible for him to lead a satisfying life. This was the therapist's initial attempt to move toward forming approach goals. In response, George demonstrated his desire to maintain control in therapy by stating that a satisfying and desirable life was impossible for him.

George's one request of the therapist was to judge whether or not he was currently "sane." He would ask every session for the therapist's opinion about his sanity. Without answering the question, the therapist would reframe by praising George for wanting to understand what normality was after so many years of living under the abnormal conditions of war. A continuing theme that George communicated to the therapist in a number of ways was that "you need to deal with me and where I am at." George explained that the therapist should "pay attention to my problems even though you cannot help me with them." The therapist validated George's horrific experiences in combat and during an abusive childhood. The therapist demonstrated traditional empathy by depicting these experiences as "internal struggles." Using positive empathy,[6] the therapist tentatively suggested the goal of George freeing himself from his past. George was unwilling to describe his combat experiences as "struggles" and was more willing to talk about his childhood living with an abusive mother. George found it easier to accept the empathy the therapist showed for George's experiences as a child. He viewed his childhood abuse as indicating his "toughness and hard life." George consistently revealed fantastic stories of danger in the military, near-death experiences, and multiple events of being shot or stabbed while in combat. The horrific stories were perhaps offered as evidence that life could never again be good.

The therapist invariably communicated unconditional acceptance for all that George revealed and celebrated his positive experiences, emotions, and strengths (e.g., being a hard worker; caring deeply about his daughter; demonstrating great resiliency and perseverance; possessing a heroic attitude) that George identified through the process of talking about his life. The therapist used what Harlene Anderson (1995) terms the "not knowing" stance. The "not knowing" stance means accepting the client where he or she is attitudinally and emotionally, not doubting as real or true what the client talks about. By doing this, the therapist is acknowledging that the client's constructed reality is what is important, not a reconstructed conceptualization based on diagnostic categories and symptoms of the diagnosis. The therapist listened carefully and vigilantly for George's expression of emotion, both positive and negative. The therapist accentuated positive emotions and events during the session.

Over the course of eight sessions, the therapist uncovered and reported back to George several strengths the therapist had observed through their interactions. These included George's sense of humor; resilience; good-naturedness (per his descriptions, donations, and other caring and altruistic actions); creative and entertaining storytelling (the therapist highlighted the power of George's life narratives); the use of metaphors (e.g., "our therapeutic dance," "the box where the client's emotions were held"); and George's penchant for philosophical interpretations of his life (e.g., "life is somewhat a self-fulfilling prophecy;" "life is what you make of it"). Overall, the therapist was successful in communicating to George the therapist's appreciation for him as a worthwhile person, authentically demonstrating to George both the therapist's hope and affinity for him as a person with much to contribute to others. The therapist continually accentuated George's reported acts of kindness toward his daughter, his partner, and countless experiences of helping homeless veterans on the street. Over the course of treatment George softened his stance toward the therapist and therapy.

Overall, multiple strengths, positive experiences, and emotions were identified during therapy. George was able to acknowledge his growing appreciation and positive feelings toward the therapist. His growing engagement and investment in therapy was also noted. George stated that he saw the therapist as "different," and as an exception to other "shrinks." The therapist also complimented George in taking pride in being able to relate honestly to others, as exemplified by his relationship to his daughter, his partner, animals, and the therapist. George's progress was noted in feeling unburdened from the blame he had previously carried concerning his childhood abusive episodes. George's heroism and selflessness--exemplified by episodes of saving the lives of others during his military tours--was also emphasized. His heroism was generalized to current acts of kindness toward others. A goal was formed for George to find meaning and healing through his acts of kindness toward others.

The therapist did not attempt to focus directly on George's suffering, although multiple times he expressed his desire that George find a less painful and more healthy way to live his life. Concern for George's lack of sleep and his hopelessness about the future were expressed. George initially pushed away statements of traditional empathy, but was able to more readily accept statements of positive empathy such as "you would like to see a future for yourself," and "you would like to move forward instead of feeling stuck due to your past." When George did show emotions, both negative and positive, the therapist framed them as "opening up the box." George seemed to appreciate when the therapist identified progress denoted by demonstrations of emotion.

Progressively, George became more invested and engaged in the therapeutic process, as demonstrated by his consistent attendance and his willingness to stay for the whole session, something he had found difficult to do in early sessions. In the first sessions, when George was feeling tense about a topic that had come up marked by the emergence of an emotion, he would leave, using the excuse that he needed a smoke, and not return. The therapist would then call to encourage George to come back for the next session.

Eventually, George was willing to talk about what he wanted to be different in his life. The approach goals that he identified (prompted by the therapist) were as follows: creating more meaningful relationships/supports; engendering a stronger sense of optimism and hope for the future; and deepening his self-awareness and insight about what he was feeling. George eventually was able to expand upon the initial goals that the therapist and he had developed. He desired to deepen his ability to recognize, tap into, and acknowledge his emotional states; and to feel safe in sharing his emotional states with others (e.g., partner; daughter) in more honest and vulnerable ways.

After 15 sessions, George suggested stopping, saying that he had obtained what he needed from the experience. He also told the therapist that he would miss him, indicating caring and appreciation for his therapist, a relational state that initially had seemed a very distant possibility. The outcomes noted and acknowledged by the therapist and George included feeling more hopeful (as indicated by the emergence of immediate and future goals for George's life with clear pathways and motivation to work to accomplish the goals); sleeping through the night for the first time in over 20 years; and expressing positive feelings toward the therapist and generalizing this change to other important people in his life, such as his daughter and partner. Over the course of therapy, George rather suddenly opened up in revealing both positive and negative emotions that he was experiencing. He seemed to discover the relief that accompanied letting the emotions out of his metaphorical box. Consequently, he expressed relief from the burden that he had been carrying around for so long. Regarding hopefulness, George was able to predict a long life and a vision for his future.

All this was accomplished without directly addressing George's suicidal ideation, problems with sleep, the trauma from combat, or the apparent and unacknowledged anger he was experiencing.

In the case example, the therapist helped George achieve change through building a therapeutic context based upon client strengths and the creation of positive emotions. Approach goals were formed as a result of the principles and techniques of GFPP described in this book. Therapy was concentrated on the in vivo experiences of validation, authenticity, and consistent concentration on what was right about the client, and how his life could be different. The client's process during the course of therapy included broadening in which he became less guarded, more open to the therapist's suggestions, and more able to expand his own cognitive set. The promotion of the client's autonomous motivation in therapy was an important ingredient in the success of the process. Overall, George was able to move to the realization that future happiness and well-being were possible, because he had experienced brief examples of feeling happy that were highlighted during therapy.

Examples make theories come alive. However, no single example provides enough supportive evidence for a psychotherapy model. This case example provides a taste of how GFPP can be applied. Moving beyond our personal clinical experience, the following section provides our rationale for why we believe GFPP is helpful to clients.

RESEARCH SUPPORT FOR GFPP

The Contextual Perspective

Bruce Wampold and his associates have championed the Contextual Model as a psychological meta-model that obviates the grip of the physical sciences model or the medical model on psychotherapy, observing that "the medical model is too seductive and often we succumb to its allure, unaware of our implicit approval of a model that cannot, in the long run, advance our specialty" (Wampold, Ahn & Coleman, 2001, p. 268). The following is a summary of Wampold's arguments, as well as germane clinical research evidence providing support for the GFPP model.[7]

Research supports that psychotherapy works (Lambert & Bergin, 1994)! Furthermore, Wampold asserts that any psychotherapy meeting the requirements of the Contextual Model will be effective, but no more effective than any other model of psychotherapy. Fortunately, GFPP meets the criteria for the Contextual Model. The criteria are as follows:

a. Treatments need to appear to the patients to be efficacious, and the rationale needs to be cogent and acceptable;
b. The therapists have to have confidence in the treatment and believe, to some extent, that the treatment is legitimate (e.g., not a sham);
c. The treatment has to be delivered in a manner consistent with the rationale provided and contain actions that induce the patient to participate in therapeutic actions that reasonably address his or her problems; and
d. The treatment has to be delivered in a healing context (Wampold & Imel, 2015, Kindle Locations 2727–2733).

Meta-analysis results support the contention that treatments that include the specifications listed in the Contextual Model are not statistically different from one another in helping clients accomplish their outcome goal (e.g., Wampold et al., 1997).

For our purposes in presenting GFPP, the significance of Wampold's research supporting the Contextual Model is twofold. First, Wampold provides a strong and eloquent argument supporting our concerns about the physical science model, and he promotes a psychological metaphor for change. In arguing against the physical science model, Wampold asserts that the specific actions of the therapist are not significant if they are not consistent with the *beliefs* of the client and the therapist. A physical sciences model is based upon cause and effect. That is, specific actions should lead to a specific effect even when the therapist and client believe that the physical science treatment will not work. If a therapist follows an empirically based treatment manual closely, the physical science model predicts a specific outcome. However, evidence supports the importance of both the therapist and client needing to believe the treatment will work for the predicted results to occur (Messer & Wampold, 2002). The idea that belief is the key variable rather than precise actions clearly contrasts a psychological versus a physical sciences metaphor for psychotherapy.

We go one step further than Wampold's assertion by naming a specific belief about the therapeutic interventions that facilitates success. In GFPP, we view *hope* as central. The client as well as the therapist must have hope that the therapy will lead to successful outcomes. Without a therapist's hope for the process—that is, if the therapist does not believe that the therapy plans can be effective—surely the process is doomed to failure. Furthermore, without the benefit of the therapist's authentic hope, why would the client be hopeful? Hopefulness is persuasive and breeds commitment to a process of therapeutic change. Frank and Frank (1991), in their seminal work *Persuasion and Healing,* put forward the Contextual Model and support the importance of engendering hope in therapy. In fact, they assert that the central purpose of therapy is client re-moralization (i.e., facilitating the creation of client hope for change).

The second reason for presenting Wampold's thesis is that Wampold provides a data-driven argument that supports the outcome effectiveness of GFPP. The good news is that psychotherapy helps! The statistical magnitude when comparing psychotherapy to a placebo is very large, and the magnitude when comparing psychotherapy to no treatment is even larger (i.e., the effect sizes are .48 and .82 respectively; Lambert & Bergin, 1994). However, comparing the outcomes of two or more psychotherapies meeting the criteria of the Contextual Model results in no difference or an effect size that dwindles to zero (Wampold et al., 1997). In essence, this means that there is statistically no difference in outcomes between psychotherapy approaches. There are many implications of these rather startling results. Our implication is that GFPP should do as well as any other therapy that fits the criteria of the Contextual Model.

Before you put down the book because you have decided that it really makes no difference what you do as a therapist, WAIT! There is more to the story! Remember the four criteria for the Contextual Model. Several of the criteria make a big difference in outcome success, and they are not as simple as initially thought. The variable that makes the biggest difference in client change according to the extant research is the therapist (Wampold & Imel, 2015). Did you see that coming? So this book will help you become the therapist you want to be!

The two primary results supporting the importance of the therapist in psychotherapy center on the therapist's ability to create a therapeutic relationship with the client and the therapist's belief in the treatment (i.e., allegiance). The next section discusses the evidence that the GFPP model is superior at facilitating the therapeutic alliance and specifically the therapeutic relationship!

Summary of the Three-Year Study of GFPP

The effectiveness of the GFPP model as an integrated psychotherapy treatment is based upon a three-year treatment comparison study. The purpose of the research was to examine the therapeutic effectiveness of GFPP compared to empirically supported psychotherapy as performed in a clinic. The three-year effectiveness study examined what the clients thought of the psychotherapy sessions (i.e., the process) and how effective the psychotherapy was (i.e., the outcome). The results of this initial evaluation of GFPP are quite favorable. The hypothesized non-difference between the GFPP and treatment-as-usual clients on the outcome measures was correct: GFPP was not better or worse in reducing client symptoms than previously empirically supported treatments. The outcome results match the decades of research on therapy outcome that find similar outcomes when comparing complete psychotherapy models that are performed by therapists who believe in their psychotherapy model (Wampold & Imel, 2015). The GFPP three-year study substantiates that GFPP performs as well as the empirically supported psychotherapies.

The reason you should use GFPP is because the GFPP clients rated their therapy sessions more positively than the treatment-as-usual clients. The clients reported that they liked the relationship with the therapist, the goals discussed and the topics talked about in the session, and the approach the therapist used in GFPP more than the treatment-as-usual sessions. The heart of our argument for using the GFPP is that clients rate the therapy sessions and the therapist higher. That is, clients like the process of focusing upon their strengths, positive emotions, and goals as described in the GFPP model.

Research indicates that the therapist, not the client, makes a larger difference in whether a client rates the therapeutic alliance as high or low (Baldwin, Wampold & Imel, 2007). Certain therapists consistently receive higher scores from their clients regarding the therapeutic alliance, while other therapists consistently receive lower alliance scores. GFPP facilitates a higher therapeutic alliance. The therapeutic alliance is a central psychotherapy process that consists of developing a relationship bond between the therapist and client, as well as agreeing upon the goals and tasks to be pursued in a therapy session (Hatcher & Barends, 2006; Horvath & Bedi, 2002). Research consistently reveals that a higher therapeutic alliance predicts client success (Del Re, Flückiger, Horvath, Symonds, & Wampold, 2012) and reduced client dropout (Sharf, Primavera, & Diener, 2010). The therapeutic alliance reveals clients who generally benefit less from psychotherapy. For example, clients with lower educational levels tend to benefit less from therapy and also report a lower therapeutic alliance (Sharf, Primavera, & Diener, 2010). Since clients rate GFPP higher in therapeutic alliance than treatment as usual, GFPP should help groups of people who have historically benefitted less from traditional psychotherapy.

The authors attribute the higher therapeutic alliance scores for the GFPP compared to treatment as usual to be a result of the GFPP techniques that promote the therapists' expression of the characteristics and techniques that the literature describes as facilitative of the alliance. A literature review by Ackerman and Hilsenroth (2003) specified the therapist attributes and techniques that have contributed to strong alliances. The techniques they identified include exploration, reflection, supportive statements, noting past therapy success, accurate interpretation, facilitating expression of affect, actively affirming, understanding, attending to clients' experiences, and interpreting what the clients want. The therapist's personal attributes include being flexible, respectful, trustworthy, interested, friendly, warm, and open. The GFPP model structures most of the techniques and characteristics known for facilitating therapeutic alliance into the process of therapy. Although not enumerated by Ackerman and Hilsenroth, GFPP adds techniques that identify strengths, positive emotions, and approach goals that surely enhance the therapeutic alliance. We contend that GFPP elicits the characteristics of the therapist that clients value through the GFPP-promoted therapeutic techniques and attitudes.

In conclusion, the first effectiveness study of GFPP supported the theory's benefits when compared to treatment as usual. GFPP was as good at producing the client outcome scores as treatment as usual and was better at achieving a higher therapeutic alliance. The three-year GFPP study is presented in detail in Chapter 6. Wampold and Imel's (2015) meta-analyses remind us that therapies meeting the contextual definition are not different from one another in helping clients change. However, GFPP was superior to treatment as usual in client ratings of the therapeutic alliance. The superiority of GFPP in the formation of the therapeutic alliance makes sense. The therapeutic intention of GFPP therapists is to focus on client strengths, increase in-session as well as out-of-session positive emotions, increase hope, and establish goals toward well-being. When clients experience hope and belief in their own abilities that the GFPP therapist has identified and emphasized, then good session ratings should occur. We believe that future research will reveal that the greater enjoyment of the GFPP sessions will predict increased client attendance and a healthier client self-definition, and even enhance the lives of therapists using GFPP. GFPP therapists have reported that they enjoy life and therapy more after a year of training!

CONCLUSION

In the first chapter, we have introduced you to GFPP—its philosophy, foundational premises, and initial empirical support. In doing so, we have promoted subjective well-being as the overall goal of therapy by offering a philosophical and pragmatic argument for why well-being is a worthwhile goal of therapy. We have also explained how GFPP differs from traditional psychotherapy by focusing on positive emotions, client strengths, the formation of approach goals, and the instillation of hope as the central foci of therapy. Finally, we have described some of the advantages of GFPP:

- GFPP is ethical by virtue of promoting beneficence while protecting against maleficence;
- GFPP uses a psychological metaphor that is more fitting with psychotherapy than the physical sciences metaphor;
- GFPP is at least as efficacious as traditional therapy;
- GFPP enhances the therapeutic alliance significantly more than traditional therapy;
- GFPP attends to the client and the client's context at least as much as the client's problems; and
- GFPP focuses on positive emotions to create change.

We have also presented a case that demonstrates the therapeutic process of GFPP. The process is based in positive psychology as well as humanistic psychology and is grounded in facilitating clients to discover a more virtuous and meaningful life, which in turn equips them to fend off the debilitating effects of life's inevitable problems. In the next chapter, we go into more detail of the theoretical grounding and research supporting the four hallmarks of GFPP: creating approach goals, identifying strengths, promoting positive emotions, and engendering hope.

The Foundational Constructs of Goal Focused Positive Psychotherapy

Goal Focused Positive Psychotherapy (GFPP) strives to facilitate clients' thriving. Our dream is that psychotherapy becomes an attractive process for a lifetime of growth. Growth toward each client's meaningful, virtuous goals through an enjoyable process embodies our aspiration. Because we are human, life includes death and pain: life can never be completely enjoyable. Begrudgingly we acknowledge that death and pain profoundly contribute to the meaning of life and happiness. Every person shares the experiences of depression, anxiety, loss, guilt, and a multitude of other human negative experiences. We are presenting our psychotherapy theory about the best we can do. Our approach is a recipe for change that emphasizes positive processes. Life is a process. GFPP seeks to support clients' learning to live life growing toward worthy goals in the kindest way to themselves and others.

Our presentation of GFPP describes a process for helping clients experience the good life, which translates to experiencing subjective well-being and meaning. Remember the two pairs of circles in Figures 1-1 and 1-2 in Chapter 1 that represent the size of a person's problem and amount of well-being. In the first figure, the well-being circle is much smaller than the problem circle and represents an individual's incapacity to deal with or accept life's challenges. In the second pair of circles, the size of the problem circle remains the same, but the well-being circle is twice as large. Symbolically the shift in size represents that the problem becomes less intimidating and experientially easier to address. In maximizing the client's perseverance and resources through more enjoyable growth, the well-being circle enlarges to the point that the individual can work more effectively through or accept problems, and, thus, flourish (i.e., lead the good life).

PSYCHOTHERAPY ROOTS OF GFPP

GFPP combines elements from positive psychology and traditional psychotherapy. The combination creates an approach that builds upon an individual's personal and contextual strengths fueled by positive emotions. The growth in positive emotions incrementally moves the client toward self-selected approach goals that enhance well-being and meaning in life. While our model has some unique aspects for a psychotherapy theory, the method is based upon extant research. This chapter presents the theoretical basis for GFPP and empirical support for the theoretical constructs.

The positive psychology elements in GFPP are directly related to Steve de Shazer and Insoo Kim Berg's Solution Focused Therapy as well as Carl Rogers's and Abraham Maslow's Humanistic Psychotherapy. Their foundational work in positive psychology (before it was called positive psychology) provides the bedrock assumption that humans have many strengths, and when nurtured, we grow in fulfilling, healthy ways. Additionally, Rollo May and Viktor Frankl's existential psychology highlights the importance of meaning to the human experience and offers the insight that positive meaning can be created even in a living hell. Permeating our theory and interventions are the contributions of Jean Piaget and George Kelly in their development of constructivism, as well as Humberto Maturana and Kenneth Gergen's social constructivism: meaning and reality are created individually and interactively.

We also have the advantage of a great many theoreticians and researchers in positive psychology such as Martin Seligman, Sonja Lyubomirsky, Barbara Fredrickson, Shelly Gable, Shane Lopez, Carol Dweck, and many more cited throughout this volume. While we cannot name all of those who deserve credit, we do want to thank our scholarly forebears and colleagues upon whose shoulders we attempt to stand.

THE SCIENCE AND PRACTICE OF POSITIVE PSYCHOLOGY

> Positive psychology is the study of the conditions and processes that contribute to the flourishing or optimal functioning of people, groups, and institutions.
>
> GABLE & HAIDT, *2005, p. 104*

Helping individuals identify and engage in processes that contribute to optimal functioning and flourishing is an ideal addition to psychotherapy. Every individual can embrace wanting to function optimally through meaningful activities and experiencing frequent positive emotions to fuel the activities. Flourishing is thought to be the central component of complete mental health. Keyes (2005) identifies 13 dimensions of flourishing within the categories of emotional well-being, psychological well-being, and social well-being:

- Emotional well-being includes positive affect and avowed quality of life;
- Psychological well-being includes self-acceptance, personal growth, purpose of life, environmental mastery, autonomy, and positive relations with others; and
- Social well-being includes social acceptance, social actualization, social contribution, social coherence, and social integration (Keyes, 2007).

The World Health Organization (2004) has defined mental health as "a state of well-being in which the individual realizes his or her own abilities, can cope with normal stresses of life, can work productively and fruitfully, and is able to make a contribution to his or her community" (p. 12). The overall aim of GFPP is to assist individuals to realize the good life. Thus, individuals living the good life experience high levels of mental health by flourishing. Even individuals who flourish, however, do experience life's problems. Scholars have emphasized that mental health and mental illness exist simultaneously in one individual (Keyes, 2007; Keyes & Lopez, 2002). We posit that individuals are better equipped to address life's problems effectively when they also possess a high level of well-being.

The current research in positive psychology provides new vigor to the intersection of research in psychotherapy and optimal human functioning. Some of the exciting concepts developing via positive psychology research highlight the benefits of positive emotions and meaningful activities, as well as personal strengths and virtues that contribute to functioning well psychologically (Fredrickson, 2001; Lyubermirsky, 2007; Sheldon & King, 2001).

At the phenomenological level, positive psychology research focuses upon valued experiences from the past (e.g., contentment and satisfaction with life), for the future (e.g., hope and optimism), and occurring in the present moment (e.g., mindfulness, flow, and positive emotions). Within a more objective framework, positive psychology examines an individual's activities that facilitate these valued subjective states (e.g., Self Determination Theory, psychological well-being, and virtues). Happiness in life consists of frequent, brief encounters with positive emotional experiences and more enduring experiences of meaningful activities. Hope and optimism provide a confidence that happiness can be achieved often and consistently, and that negative emotions and experiences will not overwhelm an individual with fear or ruminations. Confidence in our ability to achieve happiness again and again enhances our ability to face life's problems and losses, courageously again and again.

THEORY IS KEY

There is nothing so practical as a good theory.

LEWIN, *1951, p. 169*

GFPP is a comprehensive psychotherapy theory that includes therapy processes, as well as a theory of change. Theory in psychotherapy, by necessity, oversimplifies the client's world. A theory helps the therapist know which issues deserve attention, exploration, and building upon, because they will lead toward establishing and accomplishing therapeutic goals. We ascribe to the belief that there are many helpful theories that lead to therapeutic growth. However, theory consistency is important. We worry about the confusion of combining theories or using self-developed theories, especially for early career psychotherapists.

The first film of psychotherapy, *Three Psychotherapies*,[1] provides an ideal example of expert use of theory. The same brave woman, Gloria, served as the client for the three most prominent and distinctively different therapists of her time. Each therapist "found" the issues that his theory hypothesized would occur in Gloria and used interventions distinctive to the theories to move toward goals associated with the particular theory. Gloria reported that she could gain from each of the approaches even though they were very different. However, what if one therapist used all three approaches based upon what Gloria talked about during a session? The triple theory therapist could use each theory expertly; however, what would the client understand? We fear the client would be confused with multiple approaches that change as the topic discussed in therapy changes. The client could feel frustrated, leading to greater hopelessness. We endeavor to present the client with experiences and information that consistently support growth from a particular perspective. We hope you will too!

AN OVERVIEW OF GFPP THEORY

In the next paragraph we provide an overview of the GFPP model that describes the purpose of the major GFPP constructs and their relationship to one another. A psychotherapy model describes how change occurs, what appropriate goals are, and what processes are used to engage the change mechanism in order to accomplish the goals. A psychotherapy model does not describe how a person got into the predicament. Theories about psychological development or developmental psychopathology describe the circumstances of development. The way a person attains a problem does not dictate how to resolve a problem. (See Chapter 1 for more on the physical science metaphor.) GFPP is designed to facilitate change toward a better life regardless of the client's past path. Each of the constructs used in the next paragraph will be described in detail later in the chapter with references. You may have to refer back and forth to fully understand the following paragraph. Also, the description portrays psychotherapy in a deceptively simple manner. The case presentations of Chapter 5 will help clarify the complexity. Enough caveats! The abbreviated statement of theory follows.

Most central to psychotherapy is the mechanism of change—that is, what specifically occurs that facilitates the client's ability to change. *The mechanism of change in GFPP is the influence of momentary positive emotions within the client as described by the Broaden-and-Build Theory.* Many of GFPP's therapeutic techniques seek to facilitate the client's ability to experience momentary positive emotions to support change. A second central issue in a psychotherapy model is describing the goal of the psychotherapy. *The broadest goals of GFPP are facilitating the client's achieving well-being and a meaningful life.* The client decides how to live life in order to seek this broad goal. To help guide the client and therapist toward the broad goal, Self Determination Theory assists the therapist in helping the client recognize goals that facilitate experiencing competence, relatedness, and autonomy. Further, research on goals reveals that the most helpful type of goal is an intrinsic approach goal. Finally, the third central issue in the model is *to help the client identify strengths and build hope as the major processes facilitating the positive emotions* that fuel the Broaden-and-Build model.

The rest of Chapter 2 will explicate the constructs referred to in the preceding paragraph. Then Chapter 3 will describe the therapeutic techniques for accomplishing GFPP.

THE GFPP CHANGE THEORY: BROADEN-AND-BUILD

The Broaden-and-Build Theory describes how change occurs in GFPP. Barbara Fredrickson's (2001) Broaden-and-Build Theory of positive emotions posits that brief positive emotions create long-term beneficial changes as well as more positive emotions in the future. A positive emotion initiates the initial stage of change that *broadens* a person's thoughts and actions. The *broadened* thoughts and behaviors then facilitate the *building* of personal resources. Personal resources include lasting abilities, knowledge, and social bonds. The lasting resources create circumstances for more positive emotions that can begin the Broaden-and-Build cycle again. Well-being occurs through the building of meaningful personal resources that increase the probability of more frequent positive emotions, which engages the broadening again (Cohn, Fredrickson, Brown, Mikels, & Conway, 2009). Broaden-and-Build Theory is supported by a large body of research that underscores the value of frequent, small experiences of positive emotion to create well-being (see Fredrickson [2013b] for a review).

The first step of Broaden-and-Build Theory is the broadening experience following a brief positive emotion. The broadening phase describes the client's experience of becoming more psychologically and physiologically open to a wider scope of involvement, greater flexibility, and increased creativity. Upon experiencing a positive emotion such as joy, interest, contentment, pride, or love, a person experiences an increased openness to noticing, seeking, and accepting new thoughts and behaviors that can *build* personal assets. Building resources can occur in many ways. When a person broadens by engaging another person, the conversation may lead to an acquaintanceship or perhaps a friendship. By investigating an idea, the client might understand a new meaning. The positive emotion that opens a person to trying an activity may lead to a new hobby or occupation. Positive emotions can provide a momentary openness to change.

Positive emotions function differently than negative emotions. Negative emotions narrow attention, cognition, and physiology to cope with an immediate threat or problem (Cosmides & Tooby, 2000). Negative emotions facilitate predictable, quick reactions that are not well thought out and function best for a momentary survival action: fight or flight. Positive emotions provoke a more general action tendency that facilitates longer-term survival and thriving (Fredrickson, 2013a). For example, experiencing joy generally activates a person toward many actions such as engaging with another person, trying a new behavior, or being creative at work (Frijda, 1986). Feeling interested leads to broadening from the general urge to explore, learn, and have new experiences (Csikszentmihalyi, 1990; Izard, 1977; Ryan & Deci, 2000; Tomkins, 1962). On a physiological level positive emotions literally broaden our visual attention (Rowe, Hirsh, & Anderson, 2007; Wadlinger & Isaacowitz, 2006). Functional magnetic resonance imaging (fMRI) technology reveals that the physical encoding of perceptions expands during positive emotions (Schmitz, De Rosa, & Anderson, 2009). Noticing, opening up, understanding, and engaging within a therapy session lay the groundwork for changes that could be small or large in facilitating a client's well-being.

Helping a client access positive emotions to facilitate Broadening-and-Building typically requires therapist skill in understanding the client. Initially, clients are not accessing positive emotions easily. One positive emotion that can often be accessed is pride. When feeling proud, a client experiences the general urge to share other accomplishments and envision future achievements (Lewis, 1993). To access pride, as the therapist, you can ask clients about their hobbies or favorite activities. If they report on healthy activities (i.e., strengths), then momentary experiences of pride may occur that lead clients to experience openness. You can then use the openness to ask about more interests or relationships. If clients are particularly open, they might explore desires (i.e., goals, values, meaning). The enduring resource that might be *built* is clients' increased clarity of goals, values, and meaning.

In Chapter 3 we present therapy skills or techniques that facilitate positive emotions in therapy sessions to benefit the client. Additionally we present, from the current positive psychology research literature, several multistep interventions that facilitate the expression of positive emotions. Most of the multistep interventions have been used successfully in a group setting or via the internet to increase well-being. Research supports that people can purposefully engage in activities that increase their positive emotions and grow from the experience (Fredrickson, Cohn, Coffey, Pek, & Finkel, 2008). Depending upon the client, the purposeful pursuit of positive emotions can be learned by the client outside the traditional individual therapy office hour.

In summary, Broaden-and-Build Theory asserts that fostering the client's momentary positive emotions supports the appearance of openness to new perspectives and insights that lead to increased personal resources (Fredrickson, 2001). Because therapy is a complex interaction that demands openness to new perspectives and the development of resources, therapeutic interventions help when they support experiences of positive emotions. Therefore, positive emotions are an important part of both the process and the end-state (i.e., well-being) of GFPP.

GOALS

Goals are the cognitive representations of what people wish to attain and avoid in life (Elliot & Niesta, 2009). Goals provide direction in life based upon values and personal meaning. When asked about life goals, the topic of what makes a happy, meaningful life inevitably emerges (Emmons, 2003). Goals contribute to a meaningful life by thoughtfully aligning personal values into an intentional life. In forming goals, two dimensions are central in the research literature: the goal orientation (i.e., approach or avoidant goals) and the meaning reflected in the goal's content (i.e., what is pursued). Both dimensions of describing goals influence a client's well-being.

Goal Orientation

An approach goal, the favored goal orientation, orients a client toward a desirable end-state: what the client wants. The cognitive representation that a person focuses upon is the preferred circumstances when using an approach goal. The less favored goal orientation, an avoidant goal, refers to evading or stopping an undesired outcome: what the client does not want. A wealth of research supports the advantages of employing approach goals over avoidant goals (e.g., see Elliot [2008] for a review).

Examples of approach goals include having more friends, more intimacy in a relationship, better grades, better work habits, or a healthier lifestyle. Conversely, avoidance goals emphasize escaping negative outcomes, such as wanting less conflict, avoiding rejection, or escaping sadness (Gable, 2006). Unfortunately most clients seek therapy because of the pain caused by a problem. Understandably therapy often begins with the initial goal of ceasing a problem, which is an avoidance goal. For example, a common problem that brings a person to therapy is depression. Most often a client will state a goal of being rid of depression, an avoidant goal. The client's wisdom is that the depression is problematic. The client is correct and insightful. Asking clients to expand their wisdom in ways fitting with their values and culture is considered building on their abundant strengths.

Through the process of therapy, an approach *goal* is developed. Clients decide what is desired (i.e., the approach goal) rather than what is not desired (i.e., the avoidant goal). Moving from avoidant goals of stopping the negative state of depression to approach goals may be a quick, easy therapeutic accomplishment or it may be lengthy and difficult. Initial approach goals often need refinement. Clients may state that happiness is their approach goal. While happiness is an approach goal, therapists strive for specificity that reveals the client's idiosyncratic values within a goal. For example, an approach goal that could facilitate happiness might be, "I want to have friends to do something with on the weekends." GFPP supports the client's development of several approach goals that are congruent with the client's values and lead to a meaningful life. The client's culture and personal experiences influence the decisions surrounding values and meaning that make up the content of an approach goal.

Approach goals are more helpful than avoidant goals in several ways central to the process of successful therapy. Research reveals that approach goals lead to more novel and creative solutions (Friedman & Forster, 2001), as well as increased motivation, persistence, and openness to attempting challenging activities (Sideridis & Kaplan, 2011), when compared to avoidant goals. Therapy relies upon clients' openness to new, often scary circumstances, as well as their determination to work toward accomplishing goals. Approach goals facilitate therapy success by employing client strengths.

Approach goals have a logical link to facilitating change as described by the Broaden-and-Build Theory. Research indicates that an advantage of approach goals is that when achieving an approach goal, good feelings are generated (Carver, 2004; Elliot & Church, 2002; Higgins, Shah, & Friedman, 1997). However, when accomplishing an avoidant goal, at best a person feels relief about avoiding a problem and can immediately begin feeling anxious about the next time (Dweck, 1999; Lench & Levine, 2008). The positive emotions generated via accomplishing an approach goal can fuel the broadening of the Broaden-and-Build process for change. For example, a client may have the avoidant goal of not being a misfit at a friend's party. After a successful evening of not spilling a drink, not being laughed at, and not being rejected, the client may feel relief but begin worrying about the next party. Accomplishing the avoidant goal of not feeling foolish can provide only a feeling of relief upon avoidance of the problem but does not contribute to a more functional self-definition. Becoming better at avoidance (i.e., fight or flight) in the context of social occasions does not have long-term client benefits.

However, accomplishing an approach goal consisting of wanting to meet new people at a party would lead to a happy feeling. Upon success, the client could be more eager to meet new interesting people. The new orientation toward people can create a new self-definition of a person who has social abilities. The positive feeling accompanying competence when moving toward a desired goal opens the client to be able to *build* the psychological resource of confidence and *build* the social skills of relating well with others. The changes can lead to more opportunities for brief positive emotions that fuel the Broaden-and-Build cycle of growth as well as a more functional sense of self.

The *motive*, the reason why a person has an approach goal, needs to be explored with a client. The definition of approach and avoidant motives parallels the definition of approach and avoidant goals. The most beneficial motive is an approach motive that fuels the approach goal. An example of an approach motive with an approach goal is "I want to have more friends [approach goal] because I believe that would make me enjoy life more [approach motive]." Unfortunately at times an avoidant motive can support an approach goal—for example, "I want to have more friends [approach goal] because I do not want be alone [avoidant motive]." Another example is the goal of success in school or business, which can sound on the surface like an approach goal with an unstated approach motive. However, the motive could be an unfortunate avoidant motive: "I want to make good grades [approach goal] so that I won't feel ashamed of myself [avoidant motive]." Helping the client find an approach motive to fuel the approach goal would be an important therapeutic task.

The approach orientation facilitates growth. Our initial and as yet unpublished research into goals shows that generally people have a negative emotional reaction to setting goals. Clients who are experiencing low confidence may not be willing to set meaningful approach goals initially. Wisely, clients may recognize a personal pattern of being punishing toward themselves to supply motivation for accomplishing a goal, and for failing to accomplish a goal. Often therapists will need skill and patience to help clients identify approach goals based upon approach motives, as well as to help clients learn self-compassion and incremental change approaches.[2] The other important issue in identifying goals is the content of the approach goal.

The Goal's Content

Goals contribute more to a person's well-being over a longer period of time when personally valued goals focus upon intrinsic goal contents rather than extrinsic goal contents (Kasser & Ryan, 1996). *Intrinsic goals* are generally categorized as addressing personal growth and healthy relationships and contributing to worthy social issues. Personal growth goals include issues such as physical health, psychological health, learning new things, pursuing self-understanding, attaining self-acceptance, as well as understanding and pursuing a meaningful life. Included in healthy relationships are goals such as consistently experiencing love, intimacy, friendship, commitment, and support. Contributing to worthy social issues is a broad category that includes altruistic behaviors, working for the betterment of others, contributing to society, and facilitating a greater good. In contrast, *extrinsic goals* are generally categorized as focusing upon possessions, fame, and beauty. Goals focusing upon possessions include wishing to be wealthy, having a consumer orientation, or wanting to accumulate power. Fame goals include wanting to be known or admired by many people, to be in the media often, and to be famous. Goals of beauty include achieving an image, hiding aging, and pursuing fashion. Accumulating power means wishing to control others, engaging in competition for its own sake, and wanting power without a vision of the greater good.

Proponents of Self Determination Theory assert that the ability to create well-being from intrinsic goals is explained by the goals addressing the fundamental psychological needs of people to thrive. That is, people grow and thrive when they experience autonomy, competence, and relatedness (Deci & Ryan, 2000). Goals are strongly influenced by culture (Nurmi, 1993; Oyserman & Fryberg, 2006), but the specific selection of goals is idiosyncratic (Carver & Scheier, 1990), as is the motive or reason a goal is pursued (Deci & Ryan, 2000). While specific goals are culturally and idiosyncratically influenced, the long-term importance of goals on well-being has been found to be associated with intrinsic or extrinsic goal contents

(Deci & Ryan, 2000; Dittmar, Bond, Hurst & Kasser, 2014; Kasser, 2002). More explicitly, when a goal contains intrinsic contents (i.e., personal growth, healthy relationships, or contributing to worthy social issues), then long-term well-being is more likely to occur regardless of the contents' origin.

Not every goal needs to be intrinsic. But if extrinsic goals take precedence over intrinsic goals, then studies reveal that problems are likely to occur. For example, individuals who primarily pursue extrinsic goals more often suffer lower psychological well-being and social adjustment, as well as increased psychological problems and substance abuse (see Dittman et al. [2014] for a more detailed review).

A client's intrinsic goal is a client strength, which reveals the client's values, culture, and wisdom. When asking a client to try out a specific behavior, the rationale for the therapeutic request should fit with the client's wisdom—that is, it should be framed within the client's intrinsic goal. Research results support the advantages of couching a behavioral directive in terms of a meaningful intrinsic goal for improving learning, performance, and persistence (Vansteenkiste, Simons, Lens, Sheldon, & Deci, 2004). For example, a client will learn more from performing a therapy homework assignment when stating that the assignment will facilitate future parenting skills (an intrinsic goal) rather than stating that it will save money in the future (an extrinsic goal).

Even when a client selects an intrinsic goal, spending time to be certain that the client experiences the goal as personally self-selected and advantageous, rather than being pushed into a goal, can be critical. Clients will want to please you, so careful attention to clients' personal desires and reactions are vital. The client's understanding that the goal includes self-development and autonomy of choice ensures heightened motivation. When personal values are clear and actions are based upon those personal values, intrinsic motivation as well as a sense of integrity occurs (Deci & Ryan, 2000). For example, a client will be more motivated to develop empathy when understanding its value in accomplishing the goal of developing close relationships (Kasser, 2002; Vansteenkiste, Neyrinck, et al., 2007; Vansteenkiste, Simons, et al., 2004). Additionally, the client's validation of the therapist's belief that relationships and empathy are client goals is critical. Multiple questions about the linking of the issues to the client's desires helps therapy stay client focused.

In conclusion, the selection of goals has great importance in GFPP. Helping a client orient toward what is desired in life, an approach goal, is important in giving direction and revealing values. Helping the client renew or establish significant life and therapy approach goals with intrinsically focused content captures the essence of the ideal goal selection. The client's energy, dedication, and persistence are enhanced through a well-chosen, meaningful goal that fits with the client's values.

CLIENT STRENGTHS

Focusing upon client strengths is central to GFPP. The positive psychology and humanistic psychology literature historically champions the importance of client strengths. Strengths are conceptualized in several ways in the literature. Strengths can be considered existing in a finite list, much like personality traits (e.g., Values in Action Classification of Character Strengths [Peterson & Seligman, 2004]; Personality Strengths Project [Linley, 2008]; and Gallup's Signature Themes of Talent [Hodges & Clifton, 2004]). But GFPP conceptualizes strengths as infinite and malleable (Biswas-Diener, Kashdan, & Minhas, 2011; Dweck, 2008). A client strength in GFPP includes anything that a client has done, believed, or felt (past, present, or future intention) that can facilitate the client's growth in a healthy way—a very inclusive definition! In our research and therapy we define strengths as a client revealing something:

a. The client did well or intends to do well;
b. Likable about the client;
c. Insightful or creative;
d. Revealing engagement in active coping (i.e., going after what is wanted, planning to act, and using appropriate patience or good judgment);
e. About an ability for or involvement in a healthy activity;
f. About an accomplishment that brings enjoyment and meaning, enhances a relationship, or contributes to others' well-being;
g. Regarding a good relationship or describing positive feelings toward someone;
h. Reflecting positive health, a healthy belief, a positive characteristic, or confidence (Conoley et al., 2015).

The broad definition of client characteristics facilitates finding as many strengths as possible within a client and honors each client's unique conglomeration of strengths.

The assertion that everyone has strengths is an assumption. Strengths are not characteristics that need to be comparatively better than other people or even better than other characteristics within the client. If the client experiences the strength as meaningful or can believe the strength is meaningful, then the strength is important.

Another assumption is that strengths are the fastest route toward a goal. Incrementally building toward a goal using strengths requires less change and creates positive emotions in the process (Wood, Linley, Maltby, Kashdan, & Hurling, 2011).

The final assumption about strengths is that clients are better off with a primary self-definition based upon strengths (and values) than failures, mistakes, or pathology. This is not to say that we do not have failures, mistakes, and pathology, but our assertion is that self-definitions based upon strengths and values lead to greater well-being. Experiencing high levels of well-being provides clients with a better ability to remedy or accept failures, mistakes, or pathology.

Strengths facilitate the psychotherapy process and outcome in a number of ways. First, your focus upon the client's strengths begins to orient the client's attention toward ability rather than disability. The attention to strengths leads to experiences of agency or competence (Chang, Huang, & Lin, 2015; Sheldon, Ryan, & Reis, 1996). Increased experiences of agency lead to increased hope and easier growth for the client. Agency is central in Hope Theory and Self Determination Theory. Hope Theory defines hope as believing that the person has pathways to reach a goal and the ability or agency to accomplish the goal (Snyder, 2002). Self Determination Theory asserts that when the psychological needs of competence, relatedness, and autonomy are high, a person experiences well-being and experiences easier growth (Ryan & Deci, 2000). Both theories have abundant research supporting the assertions that belief in ability is therapeutic.

Second, highlighting strengths reminds the client about the associated personal values that lead to a meaningful, purposeful life. The therapy process of highlighting simple personal strengths facilitates the client's self-recognition or self-understanding. Autonomy as a central psychological need in Self Determination Theory relies upon self-knowledge of values; that is, what is important in life to the client (Chirkov, Ryan, Kim, & Kaplan, 2003).

Third, highlighting strengths creates positive emotions and well-being (e.g., Wood, Linley, Maltby, Kashdan, & Hurling, 2011). Increasing the client's positive emotions and well-being is a central goal of GFPP. The increase of positive emotions stimulates the Broaden-and-Build growth cycle, leading to behavioral activation, which can be very important to people who feel stuck (Mazzucchelli, Kane, & Rees, 2009).

Finally, the focus on strengths contributes to the extoling of cultural or individual differences. As clients reveal their strengths, you can extol them by focusing upon them and helping clients to explore their value. Because of the inherent power differential between therapist and client, when you explore strengths, the client will be more empowered and affirmed than when you explore the client's pathology. The client's experience of the therapist's focus (on strengths vs. on inferior characteristics) is even more important when the therapist comes from a different, more privileged ethnic/racial, gender, economic, or educational group.

Focusing upon strengths can prevent the risk of further harming the powerless. Research reveals the harm of focusing upon the negative stereotypes associated with groups of people (Major & O'Brian, 2005). Research indicates that individuals who are reminded of their negatively stereotyped group behave in a manner more consistent with the negative stereotype. In the psychotherapy context, the concern is that focusing upon the pathology attributed to a person can bring out more of the pathological symptoms (Corrigan, Rafacz, & Ruesch, 2011). The iatrogenic effects of a diagnostic interview can lead to the client becoming more like the diagnosis. By recognizing and focusing upon strengths, the therapist can directly support people who have been negatively stereotyped, especially when they have been diagnosed with a mental health disorder as well as another identifier demeaned by society (Pedrotti & Edwards 2010).

Many of the therapeutic techniques in the next chapter focus upon uncovering or highlighting client strengths. Clients, and even people not under stress, often do not know their strengths (Biswas-Diener, 2012). Unfortunately distress makes it even more difficult for clients to identify their strengths because of ruminating about personal deficits (Nolen-Hoeksema, 2000). In GFPP, a therapist facilitates the client's discovery or rediscovery of strengths continuously throughout therapy. The therapist listens carefully to the client to identify as many strengths as possible.

Highlighting client strengths can achieve one of the most powerful client gifts to therapy, the client's collaboration, acceptance of treatment, and cooperation (Wampold & Budge, 2012). The client's contributions to positive outcomes in therapy may be the most important variable in any psychotherapy model (Lambert, 1992). Yet the client's contribution to psychotherapy success is the most neglected of the factors that are common to all therapy models (Bohart & Tallman, 2010). GFPP focuses upon the importance of the client. Clients must believe in and be committed to what is happening in therapy—if not initially, then increasingly through the therapy process, as illustrated in the case study in Chapter 1. A therapist does not have enough power, and an intervention cannot be sufficiently influential, to create client change without cooperation from and collaboration with the client. In GFPP we do not "apply" a treatment to a specific problem. Instead we become expert at attending to the client to shape a treatment approach congruent with the client's context. Many strengths arise from the client's context, which includes culture, family, interests, religion, and a host of other contributors. Focusing on client strengths increases client agency and autonomy. GFPP focuses upon and facilitates clients' abilities to contribute to their own successes.

Research findings indicate that therapists commonly use client strengths in therapy (Scheel, Klentz Davis, & Henderson, 2013). Using client strengths in interventions increases the treatment acceptability and intervention implementation by clients (Conoley, Padula, Payton, & Daniels, 1994; Scheel, Seamon, Roach, et al., 1999). Flückiger and Grosse Holtforth (2008) found that when the therapist is reminded of the client's strengths before each session, the therapy outcome is significantly enhanced. When using multiple intelligences as client strengths, Pearson, O'Brien, and Bulsara (2015) found strength focused therapy to be effective and to enhance the therapeutic alliance. In a review of the major studies examining strength-based interventions with persons having a serious mental illness diagnosis, Tse and colleagues (2016) concluded that the interventions were effective. Sin and Lyubomirsky (2009) performed a meta-analysis of strength-based interventions for clients diagnosed with depression. In the 25 studies, the treatment for decreasing the depressive symptomatology and increasing well-being was successful with a medium effect size (i.e., they worked well!). Research supporting the helpfulness of using client strengths appears from many therapy approaches and many definitions of client strengths. The wide support of using client strengths in therapy reveals that the use of any healthy client strength in therapy facilitates therapeutic progress.

Many researchers have searched for strengths in specific cultural groups. We provide a sampling of the literature to help broaden awareness of possible strengths. The research contributes to psychotherapy by suggesting strengths that may be missed if therapists are not culturally informed. While the strengths of one culture often appear in another, being sensitive to the probability of particular strengths may help the therapist to recognize them when they appear in the therapeutic conversation. The following is only a partial enumeration of strengths associated with several cultural groups:

- The literature suggests that African American clients may reveal strengths related to giving or receiving support as well as respect to family and community. Often African American clients find strength in their religious or spiritual beliefs. The historical as well as current experience of oppression has developed many forms of coping that provide resilience to psychological and physical harm. African Americans display a work and achievement orientation in the face of oppression (Bell-Tolliver, Burgess, & Brock, 2009; Hill, 1999). African American and White women who were highly successful in their careers were found to have an increased focus upon righting injustice associated with racism and sexism. The women had a "big picture" of societal issues, wished to share their success with others, and felt committed to their careers. The women's core strengths were described as persistence, connection, and passion (Richie, Fassinger, Linn, Johnson, Prosser, & Robinson, 1997).
- Research focusing upon people identifying as gay and lesbian has revealed strengths of creating supportive communities, serving as role models for others, and living authentically (Riggle & Rostosky, 2011). The communities included creating families of choice, forming strong connections with selected people who support their authenticity. Lesbian and gay persons expressed strengths in becoming involved in social justice and activism, demonstrating freedom from gender-specific roles, and exploring sexuality and relationships (Riggle, Whitman, Olson, Rostosky, & Strong, 2008). Coming out, or self-disclosure of a gay or lesbian identity to self or others, is a strength in achieving a positive identity when the disclosure includes assessing the safety of the environments (McCarn & Fassinger, 1996; Riggle, Whitman, Olson, Rostosky, & Strong, 2008).
- Studies into Latino culture reveal strengths of *familismo*, a strong familistic orientation that includes cooperation, support, and decision-making from a large extended family (Esquivel & Keitel, 1990; Hovey & King, 1996; Santiago-Rivera, Arredondo, & Gallardo-Cooper, 2002). Another strength lies in being bilingual and bicultural (Crawford, 1999; Cummins, 1994; Gopaul-McNicol & Thomas-Presswood, 1998). A study of Latino men explored the positive side of machismo, *caballerismo* (Glass & Owen, 2010). *Caballerismo* includes Latino men's strengths of dignity, honor, respect, familial responsibility, and a father's role as a provider (Arciniega et al., 2008; Falicov, 2010; Hernandez, 2002).
- The strengths of White men have been identified as a male relational style, male ways of caring, self-reliance, generative fathering, membership in fraternal service organizations, worker-provider tradition, courage, daring and risk taking, humor, and heroism (Kiselica & Englar-Carlson, 2010).

- An important traditional Hmong culture strength is forgiveness (Sandage et al., 2003). Traditional Chinese cultural strengths include education, morality, self-cultivation, and gentleness in men (Sung, 1987). Additionally, physical strength in men is denigrated in contrast to intellectual capacities, as captured by the Chinese saying "strong limbs, simple mind" (Qin, Way, & Mukherjee, 2008).
- Collectivism is a cultural strength often found in Asians, Pacific Islanders, and Indian and Latino peoples. Collectivism focuses upon prioritizing the group's needs and goals above the goals and desires of the individual (Hofstede, 1980) and describes a relational orientation in which the self is defined within the interdependence of others (Enriquez, 1993; Markus & Kitayama, 1991). The interdependence is healthy according to Self Determination Theory when the person chooses interdependence; then interdependence fits within the definition of autonomy (Chirkov, Ryan, Kim, & Kaplan, 2003). Behaving well in society and the family is a Chinese strength associated with filial piety arising from Confucian ancestry as the foundational virtue of civilization (Chao & Tseng, 2002; Hwang, 1999).

We hope this listing of strengths from several cultural contexts will help you to recognize client strengths. Strengths are also revealed in clients' hobbies, sports, relationships, schooling, work, and many other human endeavors. GFPP therapists intentionally attend to eliciting client strengths in order to facilitate the therapeutic alliance, the change process, and client and therapist hope; to enhance the client's self-definition and self-knowledge; and to use the strengths as tools to accomplish client goals. The techniques that elicit, enhance, and facilitate the use of a client's strengths are presented in Chapter 3.

HOPE IN THERAPY

Frank and Frank (1991), in their seminal work *Persuasion and Healing*, first emphasized client hope as an essential factor common to all types of therapy. They asserted that clients come to therapy demoralized, so the primary task of therapy is remoralization, which is the generation of hope. Frank and Frank believed that client hope grows through a collaborative relationship and a healing context. Additionally, the therapist must provide a compelling rationale to the client explaining how the treatment is effective and fits the client. Through this compelling rationale, the client comes to believe that the therapeutic approach could be beneficial, thus spawning hope. In GFPP, we recommend that therapists explain the reasoning behind focusing on positive processes using the client's worldview. Knowing something about the client's belief aids the therapist in presenting a rationale that fits with the client's belief structure. For some clients, the therapist might say something similar to the following at the end of the first session:

You may have noticed (or will discover) that I emphasize your strengths, and wish to help you clarify what you want to make your life more enjoyable and meaningful. I will be helping you learn to achieve your goals in a way that is kind to yourself and to build upon what is going well in your life. By making a little progress, problems get smaller and some go away altogether. At the very least, I believe that focusing and building on what is right about you and your life will help you to cope more effectively with the issues in your life that are troubling you.

The client's hope for a better life through therapy is crucial. Unfortunately, in a psychotherapist's zeal to identify problems, the importance of client hope may get lost. GFPP incorporates Hope Theory (Snyder, 2002) because of the model's clarity, simplicity, and strong research base. Snyder posited three components of hope: goals, pathways thinking, and agency. Goals are the target that defines therapeutic change. Agency is the client's belief in personal competence. However, without pathways (means of reaching goals), goals become unanchored whims. All three components must be in place or the client may be engaging in wishful thinking but not really believing that the goals are attainable. The therapist needs to supply believable reasons for why an intervention or therapeutic direction (i.e., pathways) will ultimately lead to change, and the focus on strength supports the client's agency. The therapist may initially need to actively support the client's commitment to a certain pathway for a desired goal. By achieving small successes (which the therapist underscores), the client incrementally experiences increased agency and increased confidence in the ability to achieve goals. Through this process, the low-hope client eventually becomes more hopeful.

Research evidence supports the contribution of hope to several essential process and contextual variables in therapy. Bartholomew, Scheel, and Cole (2015) developed the Hope for Change in Counseling Scale (HCCS) based on Snyder's Hope Theory. They found that clients who had higher hope for change in psychotherapy also had stronger working alliances with the therapist, lower levels of symptom severity and hopelessness, and higher levels of client well-being. Similarly, Snyder (2002) found that high-hope individuals are more resilient than low-hope individuals. Specifically, when high-hope clients were blocked in one pathway, they did not get discouraged, and instead moved on to alternative pathways. The therapist can also act to explore possible new pathways when initial change attempts are blocked in some way. Establishing hope in clients helps them to persevere through difficult life problems. When they have high hope, clients believe that the overall approach will eventually help, which contributes to perseverance along one pathway or another. Overall, in a meta-analysis of 96 studies, the results reveal that hope consistently predicts psychological and physical well-being (Alarcon, Bowling, & Khazon, 2013). GFPP increases client hope by focusing on client strengths, setting goals, and focusing on incremental growth rather than on client deficits.

IMPLICIT THEORY OF PERSONAL CHANGE

The implicit theory of personal change influences hope and ultimately progress toward goals through the client's belief in personal growth. Carol Dweck and her colleagues champion the implicit theories of incremental versus entity beliefs about growth that created a vast amount of research supporting the construct in many contexts (e.g., Molden & Dweck, 2006). The belief in an incremental theory of growth is also known as having a "growth mindset." An incrementalist, a person with a growth mindset, believes in the ability to slowly develop toward a different personality, intelligence level, social situation, or emotional state, among many other issues. The incrementalist has many advantages over the entitist, a person who believes in entity theory. In contrast to the incrementalist, the entitist has a "fixed mindset" and believes that the amount of an attribute is not subject to personal development. Unfortunately, clients usually enter therapy as entitists, believing that they are stuck in their present predicament. One function of therapy is to facilitate change, which is antithetical to entity theory. The therapist attempts to convert the client to a growth mindset because an incrementalist believes that change is possible, in small increments. An incrementalist responds better to failure, copes better with dysphoria, manages interpersonal conflicts better, and overcomes negative stereotypes better than the entitist (Molden & Dweck, 2006). Increasing incrementalism leads to diminished symptoms, increased coping strategies, and a preference for psychotherapy over medication for treatment (Schroder et al., 2015). Compared to an entitist, an incrementalist has increased persistence and creativity, but not dysfunctional perseverance (Karwowski, 2014). No concerns have been expressed in the literature for being an incrementalist.

The danger of implicit beliefs about personal change is that they are automatically invoked during times of failure without a person's awareness. Stress automatically activates the implicit theory, which invokes a set of beliefs, behaviors, and feelings that influences motivation, goals, activities, and self-definitions (Burnette et al., 2013). Also, a person's implicit theory about change depends on the situation (e.g., Molden & Dweck, 2006; Yeager, Trzesniewski, & Dweck, 2013; Yeager, Trzesniewski, Tirri, Nokelainen, & Dweck, 2011). That is, implicit theories are not necessarily logical or consistent. A person can adhere to the incrementalist belief that persistence will lead to small steps toward becoming more successful in learning Spanish while also adhering to the entitist belief that mathematical ability is unchangeable and fixed, so nothing can be done to become "smarter" in mathematics.

The belief that "personality cannot change" can have far-reaching consequences for an individual. For example, people with more of an entity theory of personality (i.e., believing that personal characteristics are unchangeable) show more negative reactions to social adversities such as exclusion (Yeager & Dweck, 2012) and feel worse about themselves when perceiving social slights (Yeager et al., 2011). Self-blaming attributions increase in those with an entity theory of personality. People tend to believe they deserve exclusion (Erdley, Cain, Loomis, Dumas-Hines, & Dweck, 1997).

A client's implicit theory of change influences change in more than the obvious ways. In a meta-analysis including over 28,000 participants and 113 studies, Burnette and colleagues (2013) used a three-stage self-regulation or self-control model to examine the research on implicit theory. Incremental theory was superior to entity theory in each of the three processes: goal setting, goal-accomplishing behaviors, and goal monitoring. The initial advantage of an incrementalist is the use of approach goals; the incrementalist chooses a goal toward a desired state. During the goal operating or action phase, the incrementalist enlists active coping. Active involvement in accomplishing a goal is superior to reacting helplessly. And finally, during goal monitoring or the stage of evaluating success, the incrementalist experiences less negative emotion and increased optimism. Negative emotion during evaluation of success contributes to avoidance and furthers self-criticism, both of which can inhibit the desire to monitor goal attainment as well as to engage actively in goal attainment. Optimism increases a client's willingness to engage in goal-oriented activity.

Unfortunately, clients entering therapy usually are experiencing stress or failure. Their implicit theory of change is fully engaged and they are probably feeling stuck and helpless—that is, experiencing the influences of entity theory. Researchers have examined a person's ability to learn incremental theory for specific issues. In a brief intervention that directly taught an incremental theory of personality (i.e., that people can change their personality), researchers found that the intervention reduced negative reactions to social adversity, including shame and aggressive retaliation (Yeager, Miu, Powers, & Dweck, 2013; Yeager et al., 2011). In a separate study Yeager, Trzesniewski, and Dweck (2013) taught adolescents incremental theory for six weekly sessions. In the 3-month follow-up, the incremental group behaved more pro-socially and less aggressively than both the social skills groups and the no-treatment control group. In a more ambitious intervention study, Yeager and colleagues (2014) found that teaching an incremental theory of personality to adolescents resulted in less negative reactions to social adversity, and 8 months later the treatment group had lower overall stress and physical illness.

One approach that can be used to convince clients about the worth of incremental theory of change or a growth mindset is the research on brain plasticity. Brain plasticity or neuroplasticity is a neuroscience term that describes the brain's ability to change at any age. Research reveals that the child and adult brain has a significant degree of plasticity, allowing the brain to change in response to life experiences (Kelly & Garavan, 2005). Learning changes the organization of the cerebral cortex at multiple levels of the central nervous system (Karni et al., 1998; Kolb & Wishaw, 1998).

Positron emission tomography (PET) and fMRI reveal the brain's ability to alter its structure in response to physical and mental activity (May & Gaser, 2006). Experiencing negative emotions immediately produces changes in the brain region consistent with pain and suffering. Similarly, verbally reported feelings of kindness, warmth, and concern create non-overlapping brain changes in positive affect and reward areas (Klimecki, Leiberg, Ricard, & Singer, 2014). Changes in the brain structure can last beyond the moments marking the experience. For example, after thinking through complex routes over years, London taxi drivers develop parts of the brain that deal with spatial information to a greater extent than London bus drivers, who follow a specified route (Maguire, Woollett, & Spiers, 2006). Research revealed that people who are bilingual have a larger left inferior parietal cortex than monolinguals (Mechelli et al., 2004; Ressel et al., 2012), and the brains of musicians had larger gray matter (cortex) volume compared to non-musicians (Gaser & Schlaug, 2003). Not only does the brain change structure in the moment, but repetition creates lasting changes and speeds up processing, if not creating automatic processing (Thomas & Baker, 2013).

Belief in the plasticity of the brain offers hope to clients. Knowing that repeated involvement in healthy thoughts can change the brain provides motivation for clients to persevere. Believing that change is possible relates back to hope. There are many examples of brain plasticity leading to lasting benefits for clients. An 8-week experience in mindfulness meditation changed the brain structure in the areas of positive affect as compared to a control group (Davidson et al., 2003). Additionally, brain plasticity means that clients can change what we have historically called personality. The unfortunate, emotionally reactive "nature" that clients struggle with can change through psychotherapy—that is, through learning, experience, and mindfulness meditation (Davidson, 2000; Davidson et al. 2003). People can become incrementally calmer and happier with effort.

The more an area of the brain is used, the faster the neural reaction and the more effortless the firing becomes—that is, "neurons that fire together wire together" (Keysers & Perrett, 2004, p. 504). The studies focus primarily on gray matter shrinking or thickening, as well as neural connections being forged and refined, or weakened and severed. The changes observed in behaviors match changes in the physical brain.

An interesting addition to the literature has been the research on exercise. Exercise or activity during learning benefits the brain by stimulating the production of new neurons, which has not been found when learning occurs without activity (Kempermann et al., 2010). Creating a new neuron is very exciting. Several studies support the brain study results. For example, a Swedish military study of over 1.22 million soldiers found that cardiovascular fitness was predictive of intelligence measures while muscular strength was not in 18-year-old men. Therefore, clients may enhance their ability to change by adding cardiovascular exercises to their psychotherapy regimen.

Interventions that directly or indirectly address the implicit theory of change are discussed in Chapter 3 (e.g., scaling, best-possible-self, success-finding, and miracle question). Also, simply teaching about brain plasticity, the growth mindset, and incremental theory helps. Often the issue bringing the client in for services has activated the implicit theory of entity thinking—that is, the stress of the problem brings forth the client's hopeless beliefs about not being able to change. The client feels stuck and avoids action because of the belief that "there's no use in trying." Therefore, introducing the implicit theory of change early in therapy may raise the client's level of hope and facilitate greater engagement in therapy.

SELF DETERMINATION THEORY AND HOPE

Feeling competent and experiencing agency are central to both hope (Snyder, 2002) and motivation (Ryan & Deci, 2000). Ryan and Deci's Self Determination Theory focuses upon competence, relatedness, and autonomy as the three determinants of motivation and the fundamental psychological needs. GFPP focuses upon developing a strong relationship with the client (relatedness) and facilitates the client's choice of goals (autonomy), which facilitates motivation for therapy. As the therapist, you will suggest focus and direction, or educate the client about the benefits of a particular approach, but the route must be self-advantageous and desired when the client reflects upon the suggestion. According to de Shazer (1988), you can enhance therapy success by using the same language the client uses to describe the reasons for seeking therapy. The wise therapist incorporates the client's language and accompanying cultural nuances when communicating with the client about therapy. Communicating your understanding to the client accurately from the client's perspective will enhance the working alliance and the client's motivation for therapy. By communicating an understanding of the client's world in both explicit and subtle ways, you can emphasize strategies the client finds fitting and helpful. Fostering an approach that capitalizes on the client's worldview, strengths, cultural perspective, and overall subjective well-being allows the client to freely choose to participate in therapy, thus fostering client autonomy.

In summary, hope is a central concept in GFPP for several reasons:

1. Hope can be defined as a positive emotion that fuels the Broaden-and-Build change process.
2. Hope functions as motivation for therapy.
3. Hope is a major client contribution to successful psychotherapy.
4. Hope directly counters the demoralized state.

CONCLUSION

Chapter 2 presents GFPP theory and the major contributing constructs. The four hallmarks of GFPP—positive emotions, goals, strengths, and hope—are defined and supported with research. The Broaden-and-Build Theory of change is fueled by brief positive emotions (Fredrickson, 1998). The momentary positive emotions that are produced within the session when an intrinsic approach goal, strengths, or hope occurs can contribute to lasting change.

A standard goal in the process and outcome of GFPP is more frequent, brief experiences of positive emotions; however, other client-generated goals are essential as well. Goals are central to the GFPP model because they provide direction and information about the client's values. The client's definition of a meaningful life is revealed through goals. The client is encouraged to frame goals in an approach orientation—that is, what is wanted rather than what is to be avoided. Clients are encouraged to form intrinsic goals. Intrinsic goals focus upon (1) growing intellectually, emotionally, or physically; (2) building healthy relationships; and (3) contributing to worthy social issues.

Capitalizing upon client strengths is central to GFPP and a hallmark of positive psychology in general. In GFPP, strengths are conceptualized as infinite and malleable. A strength includes anything that a client has done, believed, or felt that can facilitate the client's growth in a healthy way. The definition and process of uncovering a client strength fit with the client's culture and worldview. Eliciting client strengths facilitates the therapeutic alliance, the change process, client and therapist hope, and the use of strengths as tools for accomplishing goals.

The client's hope for a better life is the final central construct of GFPP. Hope Theory (Snyder, 2002) posits three components: goals, pathways thinking, and agency. The client's experience of competence is focused on in GFPP, which fits with the centrality of competence in Hope Theory (Snyder, 2002) and motivation in Self Determination Theory (Ryan & Deci, 2000). Hope contributes to the therapeutic process by fueling the Broaden-and-Build change process, and motivating the client's involvement. Positive emotions, goals, strengths, and hope interact to strengthen each other. As the four constructs are focused upon in therapy, the client experiences enhanced motivation to participate fully in therapy. Chapter 3 presents interventions to accomplish the lofty purposes outlined in this chapter. Theory should be evolving, and we look forward to further clarity, refinement, and improvements in the theory. However, as you apply GFPP, we ask you to keep the GFPP theory as a whole. We invite interventions other than those described in the next chapter that accomplish the theoretical purposes of GFPP.

Major Techniques
and Interventions

The techniques and interventions described in Chapter 3 will bring greater clarity to the enactment of Goal Focused Positive Psychotherapy (GFPP) sessions. Many of the psychotherapy process goals are common to all psychotherapy approaches (e.g., building trust, openness, therapeutic alliance), yet we part company with most theories by prioritizing the identification of client strengths; the promotion of positive emotions and experiences; and the illumination of the client's healthy desired states, which become approach goals. If you have taken a beginning psychotherapy class, many of the techniques in Chapter 3 will be familiar to you, but the use of the techniques will display subtle yet fundamental differences from a problem- or pathology-based psychotherapy theory.

Each psychotherapy theory describes the purpose of using the techniques associated with that theory. Psychotherapy process research examining therapist in-session behaviors at the technique level has not yielded productive information (Hill, 1992; Malan, 1973; Strupp, 1973). That is, neither the discrete measure of skill in performing a technique, nor the number of techniques deployed at a specific time in therapy, appear to be correlated with therapy outcomes. However, a productive area of process research emerges when examining the therapist's *intentions* for performing a set of techniques. The intersection of technique and therapeutic attitude was initially developed in researching the facilitative conditions championed by Carl Rogers (1957). Clara Hill (1992) furthered the understanding of therapy process by underscoring the intentions of the therapist when using a technique in therapy. Examining therapist intentions provided a much clearer understanding of the ability of the therapist (Kivlighan, 1989), and a more robust predictor of success in therapy (Hill, 1992), than examining therapy at the level of technique. Therefore, we provide information about both the technique and therapeutic intent from the GFPP perspective. During therapy, the client quickly recognizes the therapist's intent (Fuller & Hill, 1985), and therefore the clear and consistent use of GFPP to highlight strengths, facilitate positive emotions, and encourage approach goals is promoted. This chapter reveals the multiple ways that therapeutic facilitation occurs through the techniques and larger interventions.

The therapeutic intent to encourage the client's hope and agency is supported by psychotherapy research. Lambert (1992) estimated the contributions to therapy outcome. His analysis found that the greatest amount of influence toward psychotherapy outcome (40%) was from the client and the client's context (i.e., the client factor), with the second largest influence (30%) from common factors,[1] particularly the therapeutic relationship. Tied for third place was the influence of placebo effects and treatment effects (15%). Knowledge resulting from decades of aggregated research has prompted largely ignored recommendations that psychotherapy prioritize facilitating the client's motivation and agency.

GFPP prioritizes the client "factor" through focusing upon client strengths, beliefs, and hope. Many researchers advocate for moving away from the view of psychotherapy as a set of potent treatments that change the client (i.e., the physical science metaphor, as discussed in Chapter 1). Instead, psychotherapists should view clients as intelligent, resourceful people who fit the therapist's information into their own frame of reference if the therapist can make sense of the material to the client (Bohart & Tallman, 2010). The therapist then is viewed as a facilitator of client strengths, motivation, hope, and goals.

Additionally, GFPP focuses upon the importance of the therapeutic alliance, the factor identified as the second largest influence upon psychotherapy outcome after client factors. The therapeutic alliance begins with the first conversation between client and therapist. As therapy begins, the techniques provide the means for listening to the client's initial presentation—a story that is often about pain and suffering. All too often, the client has not felt heard or understood before meeting with the therapist. However, feeling validated does not usually create change. In GFPP, as soon as is comfortable for the client, the therapy process transitions to focusing upon client strengths, forming approach goals, and facilitating positive emotions to promote openness for change.

Focusing on strengths, forming approach goals, and promoting positive emotions may be the reason that clients rated the therapeutic alliance significantly higher in GFPP than in cognitive-behavioral therapy and short-term psychodynamic therapy in the study described in Chapter 1 and 6. The therapeutic alliance is the central collaboration between the client and therapist and consists of developing a relationship bond, as well as agreeing upon the therapeutic goals and tasks (Hatcher & Barends, 2006; Horvath & Bedi, 2002). A higher therapeutic alliance predicts client success (Del Re, Flückiger, Horvath, Symonds, & Wampold, 2012) and reduced client dropout (Sharf, Primavera, & Diener, 2010). Therefore, the therapeutic alliance is considered a central psychotherapy process for all treatments and client contexts (Hatcher & Barends, 2006; Horvath & Greenberg, 1994; Horvath & Luborsky, 1993). Comparing the therapeutic alliance across treatment models is important because research results indicate that the therapist contributes more to the success of a good alliance than does the client (Del Re, Flückiger, Horvath, Symonds, & Wampold, 2012). The therapeutic alliance may be central to examining the issues of clients who drop out or generally benefit less from psychotherapy. For example, clients with lower educational levels tend to report a lower therapeutic alliance (Sharf, Primavera, & Diener, 2010). We anticipate that future research will reveal that GFPP can help therapists facilitate a therapeutic alliance for many underserved populations.

Again, to promote the therapeutic alliance, your initial intention as the therapist is to listen to the client's presenting concern or initial story so that the client feels heard and respected. As soon as the client is able, you then shift to the primary intention of GFPP of uncovering and celebrating client strengths and value-driven goals. When the client feels listened to and respected via the uncovering of strengths and goals, the therapeutic alliance is facilitated. The movement is often nonlinear: the client may from time to time in therapy feel compelled to tell another story of pain and deficits. Again, the intent of the GFPP therapist is to listen and validate the client's story. Then, as soon as the client can shift, your intent is to discover the strengths and hidden desires (i.e., approach goals) embedded in the story and the client's context.

An important intention for the therapist includes providing a compelling rationale to the client that a healthier and more fulfilling life creates stronger and more plentiful resources for facing inevitable challenges. Indeed, learning to self-motivate via positive emotions is the best way to live life generally. While no one can exclusively self-motivate with only positive emotions, as the proportion of motivation via self-shaming or self-flagellation decreases, the better life becomes. Well-being increases if the client can create motivation by visualizing achieving success in an important approach goal (Gable, 2006). For example, the preferred self-motivating strategy is to visualize being with potential friends at an enjoyable outing instead of using threatening visualizations that motivate through the fear of being alone and depressed if the outing is avoided.

In GFPP, the therapist's affirmation of the client's strengths and values that are embedded in approach goals builds the client's positive emotions and hope. The therapist's belief in the client's strengths and desired states is central to therapeutic success, and the therapist's intention is for the process of therapy to become the client's way to self-affirm, self-motivate, and live life. Clients can eventually believe that they deserve and can attain a good life. In short, the process of experiencing GFPP should be an enjoyable and meaningful experience that broadens the client to consider new life possibilities (i.e., increased hope) and encourages building toward life goals.

THE CASE OF WILL

The case example of Will exemplifies the way in which a strong and trusting therapeutic relationship can be forged with GFPP.

Will was a 14-year-old freshman in high school who was referred because of his severe symptoms of social anxiety, sporadic school attendance, chronic hopelessness, and persistent thoughts of suicide. Will reported extreme discomfort in classrooms, the lunchroom, and the school hallway—anywhere that other students congregated. He reported constant fear of being embarrassed by the other students. He coped with these fears through avoidance, which he described as "trying not to be noticed." At home, his mother was a neglectful parent with her own problems related to alcohol and drugs. Will had two older brothers who were constantly high on drugs and repeatedly beat Will. He had only one friend, his girlfriend, who also had frequent suicidal thoughts and skipped school regularly. Will's appearance was marked by hair that he combed over his face, hiding his eyes. He seldom made eye contact in therapy and spoke mostly in monotones and short phrases. When the therapist probed for information, Will would often reply, "I don't know" or "It doesn't matter, nothing will change." Will came to therapy very hopeless about his present status and his future. He was extremely unhappy.

The therapist met with Will once each week at school. Her initial goal was to get to know Will beyond his appearance and behaviors—especially his internal processes related to his social anxiety, suicidal ideation, and skipping school—in order to elicit his story. As the therapist probed for this information, she also continually listened intently for strengths and positive experiences and emotions—the desired states to build on in therapy. GFPP therapists assume that all clients have strengths and the capacity to experience positive emotions. In this case, uncovering strengths and positive emotions was challenging. To this end, the therapist introduced the concept of self-compassion and mindfulness activities in sessions,[2] asked about Will's interests and strengths, and encouraged Will by promoting social connections with his peers and teachers. The therapist also conveyed a genuinely caring attitude toward Will. Caring, in this case, was conveyed through constant monitoring of Will's suicidal thoughts and by cultivating hope for the future. The therapist used a best-possible-self activity to help Will envision a more hopeful future and to identify approach goals. Activities and interests that Will enjoyed were identified, such as playing the guitar. Consequently, the therapist was able to get Will enrolled in a beginning guitar class at school with a compassionate and patient instructor. Will also completed the Values in Action (Park, Peterson, & Seligman, 2004) questionnaire, identifying his five top character strengths. Will's strengths were also explored through the therapeutic process, and he was encouraged to use the strengths in his interactions with others at various times both at school and home.

All these activities, interventions, and techniques helped in building an alliance between the therapist and Will. The foundation of the alliance was based on a genuine caring that the therapist developed toward Will and authentically conveyed to him. The therapist also constantly demonstrated empathy and positive empathy in her work with Will. Slowly, Will became more relaxed and talkative with his therapist. The approach goal of feeling more connected to specific people was developed. The therapist pointed out to Will what he had done to build a trusting and more comfortable relationship with the therapist. She encouraged Will to try to duplicate the relationship with a few teachers and peers at school who were identified as potentially trustworthy. Progressively, Will reported fewer instances of suicidal thoughts, and his school attendance steadily increased.

Will's case demonstrates the benefit of the therapeutic relationship as it fosters a client's strength to access positive emotions as a result of feeling cared about and valuable. The rest of this chapter presents many of the therapeutic techniques and interventions used in GFPP.

THERAPEUTIC TECHNIQUES

Nonverbal Skills

Nonverbal skills are essential for clear communication. Communication that occurs between people without words includes posture, gestures, tone of voice, facial expression, personal space, pace of speech, clothing, and office decor. Research supports the importance of a welcoming office and persona, as well as therapist nonverbal communication that is consistent with the therapeutic verbal message. The office furnishings and the therapist's attire should match the cultural expectations of the clientele (Devlin et al., 2013; Hubble & Gelso, 1978). For example, Native Americans tend to value the wisdom of older adults, so therapists dressed in styles that were favored by older people and not fashionable with youth increased their trust in the therapist's skills (Littrell & Littrell, 1983). Benton and Overtree (2012) provide guidelines for designing a multiculturally friendly psychotherapy office. These ideas can be used to create a multiculturally friendly website as well. The website and office are often the first opportunities a client has to form an impression of the therapist.

The most important research finding regarding nonverbal communication highlights the significance of a high degree of consistency between verbal and nonverbal communication (Graves & Robinson, 1976; Haase & Tepper, 1972; Hill, Siegelman, Gronsky, Sturniolo, & Fretz, 1981). When the therapist's body language, facial expressions, or voice quality does not fit with the verbal message, the client doubts the authenticity of the verbal message. For example, if the therapist has closed eyes when speaking to a client, the therapist might be thinking deeply about the issue. However, the client may interpret closed eyes as avoiding being truthful. *The important issue is how the client interprets the nonverbal communication, not what the therapist believes the behavior means.* Cultural expectations and beliefs add to the complexity of the client's interpretation. For example, formality of dress (Hubble & Gelso, 1978), *personalismo* (Kanter et al., 2010), interpersonal distance, and touching (Collett, 1971) have all been found to influence the client's perception of feeling respected by and being able to trust the therapist. The client constructs the meaning of both the nonverbal and verbal communication of the therapist based upon the client's past experience. Therapists should seek feedback from people familiar with the culture and life circumstances of the client to help build their nonverbal communication skills.

Mirroring

Mirroring is the therapist's matching of the client's nonverbal behavior so that the client feels understood. Especially important in the initial reactions, mirroring builds therapeutic alliance and predicts outcome (Ramseyer & Tschacher, 2014). If the client speaks slowly and softly, the therapist can mirror that pace and volume, which communicates understanding. If the client leans forward, then the therapist connects by leaning forward as well. Mirroring the client's emotional arousal communicated by the voice is correlated with ratings of empathy (e.g., high frequencies could be excited, angry, or nervous; low frequencies could be bored, calm, or content). After the connection occurs, the therapist can then lead the client's emotions through nonverbal behavior such as becoming calmer in tone and pace in order to help the client become calmer (Bernieri, 1988; Bernieri, Davis, Rosenthal, & Knee, 1994). The experience of mirroring is not typically within awareness of the client (Ireland & Pennebaker, 2010).

Open and Closed Questions

Asking questions gathers important information from the client and simultaneously communicates to the client the beliefs of what is important to the therapist. *Closed questions* are focused probes that inquire about issues and often have a one-word response. An example is "How old are you?" Closed questions are a very efficient means of gaining specific information. Also, the client may enjoy answering a closed question if it is easy to answer correctly and the information is client enhancing. The disadvantages, however, are important to remember. When too many closed questions are asked, the client may expect that the process of therapy will proceed similarly. The client may expect that the therapist will shoulder the greatest amount of time talking and working in therapy. Big mistake: the client should do at least as much talking as the therapist! An additional problem occurs when the questions focus upon issues that the client does not wish to answer; the client can feel cornered (Conoley et al., 2016). As a rule, ask as few closed questions as possible. And when you do, use caution while inquiring about potentially embarrassing issues.

Open questions are probes that explore or reveal experiences, thoughts, or feelings in a manner that encourages the client to answer with complex responses. The question allows the client more latitude in response. A benefit of an open question resides in the implicit communication that therapy requires effort and self-disclosure on the part of the client. The client's understanding of therapy as effortful, engaged in self-disclosure, and furthering self-understanding is an accurate portrayal of the process of successful therapy.

We often suggest asking about the feelings, thoughts, and events around an important issue. Clients often discover more about their experiences, feelings, or beliefs due to circling through these questions. When initially talking about an issue, clients reveal a style of understanding their world. The issue may be described using philosophical thoughts, immediate feelings, or vague stories. Open questions asking for information from other perspectives (i.e., feelings, thoughts, and events) can help the client to go deeper into understanding issues.

We recommend including questions that communicate high expectations and success. Most often the client expects questions about problem areas and personal failures. A question that communicates high expectation is, "In 10 years, when you look back on this, what do you hope you will have gained?" The question presupposes success and asks for an approach goal. The question reinforces the implicit message that the intended outcome of therapy is increased well-being.

Using the case of Will from earlier in this chapter, the therapist might ask questions in the initial session about what he enjoys doing now or what he enjoyed doing in the past. Typically questions about hobbies are easy for clients to answer. The answers are valuable in that they typically reveal client strengths and produce positive emotions. Questions about client strengths communicate the therapist's belief that the client is more than a diagnostic category or personal failure. For example:

> Therapist: What do you like to do for fun after school, Will? (Open question)
> Will: I don't know. I don't do much of anything. Just go home.
> Therapist: Anything at home enjoyable for you? (Open question)
> Will: Well, I like to play my guitar.
> Therapist: Is it a six-string? (Closed question)
> Will: Yeah.

Paraphrase and Reflection

When the therapist uses the client's own statement of experience or feeling to present back to the client what was just stated, the therapist is performing the technique of paraphrasing or reflection, respectively. *Paraphrasing*, in which the therapist repeats a selected portion of the client's statement, presents the client with a focus of what to consider and further discuss. The information contained in the therapist's paraphrase focuses the client to think and reveal more deeply about the specific topic. Therefore, the therapist should select the portion of the client statement that could lead to therapeutic movement according to the theory, in our case GFPP. The response of the client should provide new information for the therapist and perhaps even the client. Restatement differs from empathy because restatement uses only the information given by the client, not the information the therapist feels or believes (i.e., intuits) exists because of the client's statement.

A danger of restatement is that the client can interpret the restatement as therapist agreement with the restated issue (Conoley et al., 2016). As the therapist, you may wish only to be certain that the client meant what was said or fully understood the statement. Therefore, use caution when using a restatement with content that you find problematic for the client's progress. For example, restatement of paranoid thoughts could be viewed as agreeing with the client's misinterpretation of events, thereby reinforcing problematic beliefs. Also, the restatement of problematic issues can be viewed as agreement that the client is problematic. However, restatement of client strength can be viewed as agreeing with the strength as well as asking for greater clarification.

Reflection of feeling occurs when the therapist states the client's feelings as the client stated them. The restatement of the client's feelings focuses the client and implicitly asks for more information. Therefore your selection of a reflection should be purposeful in promoting the client's progress. If you have concerns that the client may not accept that the reflection is an accurate characterization of the stated feelings, temper your reflection. Stating the feelings in a less intense form than the client did can enhance the client's willingness to claim ownership of the feeling. Similar to restatement, the therapeutic technique of reflection of feelings is different from empathy because reflection of feelings uses only the information given by the client, not the information that the therapist feels or believes exists. For example:

> *Will: I have been worried about the kids laughing at me.*
> *Therapist: You are feeling worried. (Reflection)*
> *Will: Yeah, I don't like it at all. I want to run away. I want to leave school and
>   never come back.*
> *Therapist: You want to run away. (Paraphrase)*
> *Will: I do want to run. But I don't. I just sit there.*
> *Therapist: Wow. How do you get yourself to come back to school after that?*
>   *(Open question that might reveal a strength)*

Challenge

At times the client reveals contradictions that could be helpful to point out. A *challenge* diplomatically (and typically gently) confronts the client with contradictions in beliefs, feelings, or actions that the client has revealed. Stating the discrepancies allows the client to consider the issues more deeply and attain greater self-understanding. Before using challenges, you should take care to ensure that the therapeutic alliance is sufficiently strong. Avoid this technique in the first session, and do not use it often. Here is an example related to Will:

> *Therapist: You say now that you cannot think of a reason to keep on living. Yet
> earlier in the session you told me about wanting to get better at the guitar, and
> get a job this summer so that in three years you can buy a car. You also said
> you enjoyed spending time with your girlfriend. Last session you talked about
> eventually having your own apartment. How do those fit together?*

Summarizing

An important technique that should be used frequently is *summarizing*. Summaries are similar to paraphrases but are lengthier, occur less frequently, and can include client feelings. The summary pulls together the logic or significant parts of the therapeutic conversation, allowing the client and therapist an opportunity for mutual understanding and correction if necessary. The client's perception is always accepted as correct! A summary may list the highlights of the client's response to a series of questions, or provide a structure for understanding therapy. An example of a summary that aids the understanding of GFPP could contain the logical link between the client's initial concerns, the approach goal being addressed, and the pathways to accomplishing the goal. While the logic connecting these three issues may seem obvious to you, the client may not understand or even agree with the logic. The summary provides an important function in presenting the therapist's perspective of the conversation. For example:

> *Therapist: OK, let's pause for a minute to be sure I understand. You said that you were very upset about your mom calling you names and cussing at you. And you thought as long as she was on drugs she would never change. We talked about you having the goal of having friends. Friends are important to you because you would have people to enjoy doing things with and people who are nice to you. In some ways friends might balance some of your mom's negativity. That would be good for you. Is that right?*

Empathy

Empathy is perhaps the most important therapist skill and therapeutic technique. Going beyond the client's statements, empathy involves both sensing the client's experience and sharing with the client what the therapist senses (Elliott, Bohart, Watson, & Greenberg, 2011). The client can feel deeply understood. Empathy is a major contributor in establishing a therapeutic alliance and creating beneficial outcomes (Elliott et al., 2011; Greenberg, Watson, Elliott, & Bohart, 2001; Wynn & Wynn, 2006). Traditional empathy is an accepted and effective therapist practice that is integral to most therapies. In his work on the American Psychological Association Division 29 Task Force charged with reviewing therapist behaviors that contribute positively to relationship formation, Norcross (2010) classified empathy as the only therapist behavior that is *demonstrably effective* when considering research findings of empathy and therapy outcome.

Rogers (1957, p. 98) defined empathy as "the therapist's sensitive ability and willingness to understand clients' thoughts, feelings, and struggles from their point of view." Broadly, traditional empathy is defined as sensing the client's inner world and conveying an understanding of that world to the client. *Traditional empathy* typically focuses upon negative, difficult, and problematic client states. This focus on the negative differentiates traditional empathy from positive empathy. An empathic statement communicates to the client a deeper meaning of the client's original statement (Bohart & Greenberg, 1997; Carkhuff, 1969; Rogers, 1961). The therapist decides which deeper meaning to focus upon depending on the purpose of the empathic statement. Historically the client's discouragement, pain, or fear has been privileged (Rogers, 1961). Typically the therapist focuses on the affective domain, using feeling statements such as "It seems you are deeply saddened and hurt by your partner's betrayal." An aim of empathy is to dig deep to understand and communicate the essence of the client's experience.

In comparison, *positive empathy* is sensing and communicating the unspoken message of the client for a better life that is hidden behind the client statement of distress or dissatisfaction (Conoley & Conoley, 2009). Positive empathy is a foundational process and intervention of GFPP. Effective use of positive empathy leads to the formation of approach goals, strengths, and positive emotions (Conoley et al., 2015). As the therapist, you shift the focus from the negative and problematic to the positive and solution-oriented. Positive empathy provides a hopeful message to the client by tapping into the unstated desire for happiness. To do so, the therapist identifies and conveys positive states and positive emotions that are opposite to the pain, problem, or detrimental state the client overtly expresses. For instance, a client may say, "I just feel lousy. I feel defeated. I am at a loss for how to get over this. I am just drowning, feeling there is no hope for getting through this. I never used to be this way." The therapist would listen for the unspoken desired state embedded within the client's statement. Using positive empathy, the therapist might say, "You are really struggling right now, feeling lost and directionless. It seems you desperately want to find a way out, to feel more in charge of who you are and what you are feeling. Your past experiences have informed you that your life should be more enjoyable. It seems you would like to find a way back to being that hopeful and optimistic person you used to be." As you might have observed, the positive empathy statement included an approach goal for the client feeling in charge of life and being hopeful.

Positive empathy is a powerful tool for moving the process of GFPP toward approach goals, positive emotions, and identification of strengths. In two analogue studies, Conoley and colleagues (2015) compared traditional empathy with positive empathy. In the first study, positive empathy produced more approach goals than traditional empathy; in the second study, positive empathy was more successful than traditional empathy in generating positive emotions and identifying client strengths. Positive empathy can move the client forward in focusing on three of the four hallmarks of GFPP: approach goals, positive emotions, and strengths. Clients may be more hopeful as a result of positive empathy when approach goals are paired with pathways that provide specific methods of attaining the goals.

As noted earlier in this book, clients tend to come into therapy with avoidance goals. They want the troubling condition they have sought therapy for to improve, their problems to be solved, and their emotional pain and distress to be alleviated. The GFPP therapist becomes skilled in changing avoidance goals to approach goals by uncovering the client's unstated desire for a better life. For instance, a client may say, "I just let my boyfriend treat me terribly. It makes me feel cheap and worthless." The GFPP therapist would listen carefully for the hidden desire. The hidden desire serves as the beginning of an approach goal. Thus, the therapist might say in response, "You want to be treated with respect, to feel good about yourself in all your interactions, not only with your boyfriend, but in any relationship in your life. When others treat you well by treating you as a worthwhile person, you regard yourself more positively too."

The recommended sequence in using positive empathy is as follows:

1. Paraphrase the client's statement.
2. Typically acknowledge the client's pain before focusing upon the hidden desire.
3. Tentatively state the unexpressed healthy desire hidden in the client's statement (i.e., positive empathy). Clarify the client's strength that is associated with the hidden desire.
4. Be ready to paraphrase the client's response to the statement of positive empathy and perhaps ask a follow-up question that focuses on the uncovered approach goal (the hidden desire).
5. Be tentative in presentation, allowing the client to modify or reject your empathic statement. Even if you are certain that the empathic statement is correct, the client is always right! Follow the client's response.

For example, consider an exchange with a client who is worried about being lonely and alone over the weekend:

Client: *I'm tired of being alone with nothing to do over the weekend. I get depressed and lonely. I sit and eat and watch TV. (Problem statement)*
Therapist: *You believe that being alone with nothing to do during the weekend is not good for you. (Paraphrase of client statement)*
Client: *That is right. I'm likely to start into a downward spiral that doesn't end until I pry myself out of bed on Monday for work . . . and I'm likely to be late! (More information about problem)*
Therapist: *So on the weekend it sounds like what you really want is an activity, perhaps an activity that involves a person you could enjoy being with. Is that what you want? (Positive empathy)*
Client: *Yes, that's right. If I get out to a movie with a friend my whole weekend is different. I'm likely to do some artwork or writing—something productive! (Approach goal—movie with friend; Positive emotion—enjoying the memory of a good weekend; Strengths—artwork and writing that are meaningful activities)*
Therapist: *Wow! So tell me more about this productive weekend.*

Interpretation

Interpretation is another therapeutic technique that goes beyond the client's statements by taking disparate information the client has revealed and weaving the information together to present the client with a new understanding about important issues. An interpretation offers the client new insight into experiences, thoughts, or feelings in concert with the client goals. For example:

*Therapist: You said last week that learning new skills at work is something
   that makes you happy—perhaps the best thing about work. However, today
   you have been stating that you don't think you would enjoy going to a
   workshop out of town that could offer you many new skills. (Confrontation)*

-or-

*Therapist: I wonder if you are not giving yourself the opportunity to discover
   something else you might enjoy because you want certainty before you try it
   out? (Interpretation)*

Self-Disclosure

While the client should be the focus of therapy, at times the therapist may state
non-obvious personal revelations that are historical in nature (i.e., the therapist is
not experiencing at present). Initial therapist *self-disclosures* are often about professional status or therapeutic beliefs. However, therapists may bond with a client
when similarities are revealed in a "me too" manner. The therapist must be certain
that the focus stays upon the client when using a self-disclosure (Pipes, 2016).
A self-disclosure may achieve bonding through the client feeling greater comfort
or trust, but the focus needs to remain on the client.

The client may ask for information about the therapist's personal experiences,
which is a request for therapist self-disclosure. As the therapist, your goal in
response to the client's request would be to process the issue that is queried about
more deeply with the client. If an issue is asked about, the issue has relevance to
the client. However, in processing the issue, do not self-disclose if the information
disclosed might harm the therapy process (Pipes, 2016).

In cross-cultural counseling, if you self-disclose something that focuses on a
cultural advantage that you may have over your client, the self-disclosure may be
particularly risky. For example, stating a cultural advantage that you have over
the client may upset the client: "I had it easier leaving home to go to college.
My family expected me to go far away." Such a self-disclosure from a European
American therapist engendered anger in a Mexican American client (Conoley
et al., 2016). Perhaps traditional empathy regarding the client's difficulty leaving
home for college would have facilitated the bond as opposed to the problems created by self-disclosure.

An example of self-disclosure that could be helpful is as follows:

*Therapist: After my mother died, I wished that I had asked a lot of questions
   before she died. I wonder if there are things you would like to know before
   your mom dies? (Self-disclosure followed by open-ended question)*

Notice that the self-disclosure acknowledges that the question is based upon the
therapist's history. The self-disclosure provides a rationale for the therapist to ask
a question that might otherwise feel confusing to the client.

Immediacy

The therapist at times reveals a feeling or experience that is occurring with the client in the present moment. The therapist may trust the therapeutic impulse in the moment or the feeling may have occurred before and the therapist is awaiting another opportunity to disclose the feeling or experience. The difference between therapist self-disclosure and immediacy is that in *immediacy* the experience is in the present moment, not historical.

Cross-cultural counseling research reveals that immediacy is one of the most favorable therapeutic techniques (Conoley et al., 2016). However, the therapists in the study did not use immediacy often. Immediacy directly reveals the therapist to the client. The client is often eager to know the therapist's "true feelings." However, therapists may feel vulnerable and concerned about immediacy because of the uncertainty regarding when and how to use the technique.

> *Therapist: I feel like you are waiting for me to tell you what to do. I am hoping that if we slow down and think, you will have an idea about what you want to do.*

-or-

> *Therapist: I sense that you don't want to talk about your relationship today.*

-or-

> *Therapist: I believe that you are acting very confident and pleased today!*

Information Giving

At times, as an expert or as simply another person, the therapist provides the client with knowledge or information. The information can be verbal or written. Research, assessment results, and opinions are all forms of information that the therapist might provide. As the therapist, you often have specialized knowledge that can benefit the client. However, information giving can be problematic. A critical psychotherapy tenet is that the client must focus inward for discovery of personal meaning and values rather than depend upon answers coming from an expert. Information giving should facilitate client self-understanding and skills, but not teach values.

> *Therapist: I am glad that you are willing to try out this exercise. There is research that supports its effectiveness when it is done every day for two weeks. I'll be interested in knowing what you think of it after you practice it every day for two weeks.*

Direct Guidance

As the director of the process, you may at times ask or advise the client to do something. These directives, suggestions, or advice can tell the client something to do in the session or can be an assignment for outside of the session. *Direct guidance* facilitates the client's understanding of your expectations. However, the danger of this technique is that the client may become reliant upon the therapist rather than developing self-reliance. Examples of direct guidance include asking clients to do an intervention such as the formula-first-session-task or gratitude interventions described below.

INTERVENTIONS

Capitalization

In positive psychology, *capitalization* describes the benefits a client gains from disclosing a positive personal event (Langston, 1994). The success of capitalization lies in the therapist's reaction to the client's disclosure. Upon hearing the client's disclosure of a positive personal event, the therapist needs to celebrate the occurrence with an enthusiastic, positive response. The disclosure and celebration occurring in capitalization help the client in three ways: the client values the disclosed deed to a greater extent, enjoys an increase in positive emotions, and experiences the relationship with the therapist more positively (Gable, Reis, Impett, & Asher, 2004). The key is for the therapist to listen carefully for client successes and then actively celebrate.

Capitalization also benefits the therapist who celebrates. By listening and celebrating, you will experience increased positive emotions and compassion toward the client when you celebrate in a genuine manner and the support is well received by the client (Conoley, Vasquez, Bello, Oromendia, & Jeske, 2015).

You can use capitalization frequently from the beginning of therapy. You can state the desire to understand the client more broadly and ask about non-problematic issues. For example, you can ask, "What are your hobbies? What do you do for fun? What is a favorite memory?" The open questions reveal strengths or successes that can be celebrated. The process enhances the therapeutic relationship and increases the value of the strength to the client, and the client experiences a positive emotion (Gable et al., 2004).

Capitalization can be assigned to the client to use as homework in addition to the therapist using it during session. Asking the client to listen for positive disclosures and then celebrate the disclosure benefits the discloser, the client, and the relationship between them. The disclosure and the subsequent celebration increase the trust and the relationship satisfaction and reduce conflicts in relationships (Gable et al., 2004). Additionally, capitalization accrues benefits with people who are at varying levels of closeness, from strangers to romantic partners (Ilies, Keeney, & Scott, 2011; Reis et al., 2010). A homework assignment of capitalization requires the client to focus upon what the other person is saying. That helps the client feel less self-conscious and focuses the client on what the other person is saying that is uplifting. The homework assignment is an approach goal that focuses upon growth of relationships and relating to others in a supportive manner.

Self-Affirmation

Self-affirmation interventions consist of the client reflecting upon important, self-relevant values that support the client's self-definition as efficacious as well as good and moral. Self-affirmation buffers the client from harmful threats and enhances the client's ability to face threats more bravely (Cohen & Sherman, 2014). The research of self-affirmation reveals many contexts in which the harmful effects of perceived threat are decreased. For example, self-affirmation can do the following:

a. Improve the relational security of insecure individuals who are at risk for social rejection (Stinson, Logel, Shepherd, & Zanna, 2011);
b. Facilitate viewing physical threats as less frightening (Harber et al., 2011);
c. Reduce stereotype threat in minority students in elementary school, thereby facilitating better grades (Cook et al., 2012);
d. Buffer ruminations about past failure in college students, thereby facilitating better grades (Koole et al., 1999); and
e. Facilitate the recognition of threatening issues so they are less likely to be denied or avoided (Cohen et al., 2007; Koole et al., 1999; Sherman et al., 2000; Taylor & Walton, 2011).

The ability to face difficulties more bravely helps clients because ignoring or trivializing problems can delay learning from or dealing with the problems. Finally, self-affirmation increases the likelihood that clients will recognize difficulties with less anxiety (Aronson, Cohen, & Nail, 1999; Sherman & Cohen, 2006; Steele, 1988).

Helping clients talk about or discover their values is an example of self-affirmation. Another example is facilitating clients' exploration of the activities that give their life meaning. The valued activities might include work, friendships, hobbies, or interests. Activities reveal values. The discussions need to reveal issues that the client feels good about, that are sources of pride. The values or activities may be more helpful when they are not associated with the challenging issue (Cohen, Aronson, & Steele, 2000). The self-affirmation intervention typically occurs when the client's strengths are discussed. In self-affirmation, the client needs to state the affirmation rather than hear the therapist state the positive aspects. When self-affirmation occurs, the client benefits via increased ability to face difficulty and by experiencing positive emotions associated with the affirmation. Psychotherapy is facilitated by the increased bravery of the client in being open to confronting threats, setting higher approach goals, and being willing to pursue goals (for a review, see Cohen & Sherman, 2014; Sherman & Cohen, 2006).

Formula-First-Session-Task

As the name implies, you can assign the *formula-first-session-task* (FFST) as homework for most clients at the end of the first session. To assign this exercise, ask your clients to attend to any occurrence during the week that they enjoyed and wish to continue (de Shazer, 1988). The assignment orients the clients' attention toward something going right in their life instead of focusing upon what is going wrong. The following therapist statement is an example of an FFST homework assignment:

> Between now and the next time we meet, I would like you to observe, so that you can describe it next time, what happens in [your life] that you want to continue to have happen. (de Shazer, 1988, p. 137)

The FFST intervention research results indicated that clients exhibited higher compliance with treatment and clarity of treatment goals compared to other homework interventions focusing upon the client's problems (Adams, Piercy, & Jurich, 1991). Additionally, clients reported improvement in their initial problem concern and were more hopeful about achieving their goals when compared to a problem identification homework assignment (Jordan & Quinn, 1994). FFST fits well with other research in positive psychology indicating that well-being is facilitated by the process of focusing on good things that occur daily (Emmons & McCullough, 2003). Additionally, time spent savoring the good things in their life (e.g., what clients are grateful for) generates positive emotions that facilitate broadening and building (Fredrickson, 2001). FFST is an easy intervention that can provide an early success for the client–therapist collaboration while contributing to the client's sense of agency and hope.

Reframing

Therapeutic *reframing* introduces a new perspective to the client that results in viewing a problem or context differently so that therapeutic progress occurs (Watzlawick, Weakland, & Fisch, 1974). The new frame fits the data as well as or better than the old frame and has the advantage of creating greater hope, opportunity for growth, or a solution. Therefore reframing asks the client to understand an experience in an equally believable manner, but one that has more benefits for the client. Reframing does not mean asking the client to disown or deny an experience, but to understand the experience differently. A perfect reframe makes so much sense to the client that the previous perspective becomes superfluous. A common example is being unable to find an extension cord that will reach the ironing board; then someone suggests moving the ironing board closer to the outlet. The new perspective provides a solution to ironing a shirt without an extension cord. The new perspective creates an understanding that does not allow one to see this issue in the same old manner.

A therapy example that has been successful for the authors may be helpful:

> *A divorced mother expresses hurt and anger when revealing that her son saves money to buy his inattentive, distant father a birthday gift but never remembers*

her birthday. The mother knows that her daily work, caring, and sacrifice on her son's behalf is not noticed. She feels unappreciated and unloved by her son. A reframe would not challenge the mother's observation of what her son does, but it could suggest a different meaning for the son's behavior. Perhaps the son takes his mother for granted because he is certain of her love and devotion to him. Perhaps her son works hard to please his father because he feels uncertain of his father's love and feels threatened that his father might simply forget about him. The therapist cannot be certain how the boy feels and why he behaves as he does. However, the new explanation can fit the data as well as the mother's original explanation. If the mother's goal is to further develop her relationship with her son, then feeling validated in providing the stable parental bond, and feeling compassion rather than anger for her son, creates a therapeutic perspective toward building an even better relationship with her son. Also, the mother has greater hope to build upon the foundation of her more secure relationship with her son. (Eventually she can teach him how to express gratitude as well!)

Reframing is one of the most common interventions associated with therapist reports of facilitating client's strengths (Scheel, Klentz Davis, & Henderson, 2013). Reframing has been used successfully with depressed clients (Beck & Strong, 1982; Conoley & Garber, 1985). For example, in a therapeutic reframing intervention, lonely, depressed college students were told, "A nice part of being lonely now is that it allows you to develop and discover more about yourself at a time when others may be so wrapped up in a relationship that they end up spending their time trying to be what someone else wants them to be" or "Your development and personal growth is being experienced as loneliness at this time. As you are moving away from dependence on your family through this period of self-discovery, you are learning new ways to express your own uniqueness" (Conoley & Garber, 1985, p. 140).

The behavioral and cognitive-behavioral therapy literature has equated reappraisal with reframing (e.g., Beltzer, Nock, Peters, & Jamieson, 2014; Ranney, Bruehlman-Senecal, & Ayduk, 2016). In a cursory review of the literature, about half of the examples of reappraisal interventions did not meet the criteria for reframing using our definition. An example of reappraisal that did not fit was to tell a person to become more detached from an event. The reappraisal was described as a researcher displaying "a picture of a sick man lying in a hospital bed and instructed participants to 'view the sick person from the detached, clinical perspective of one not personally connected in any way to the pictured individual'" (Willroth & Hilimire, 2016, p. 469). From our perspective the intervention seems to ask the person to deny the meaning of the experience—that is, to pretend that the event has less relevance to you. In summary, when reading the research about reappraisal, be careful in equating the intervention to reframing.

However, other examples in the reappraisal literature ask the subjects in the research to consider a perception as having a different meaning than initially considered, which could be considered as an instance of reframing. For example, a research project investigated the helpfulness of reinterpreting the experience of anxiety as adaptive rather than problematic, when experiencing stress from giving a speech. The subjects were told:

> In stressful situations, like public speaking, our bodies react in very specific ways. The increase in arousal you may feel during stress is not harmful. Instead, these responses evolved to help our ancestors survive by delivering oxygen to where it is needed in the body. We encourage you to reinterpret your bodily signals during the upcoming public speaking task as beneficial. (Beltzer, Nock, Peters, & Jamieson, 2014, p. 763)

Reframing is not an easy intervention to master, but it is well worth the effort to learn and apply. Offering another perspective or interpretation of an experience can provide clients with hope and solutions.

Success-Finding

Success-finding is an intervention that identifies a client's strengths for the purpose of accomplishing an approach goal. The strengths are uncovered by asking about past success or partial successes in achieving the approach goal. Solution Focused Therapy uses a similar process named exception finding (De Jong & Berg, 2008; de Shazer et al., 2007). In exception-finding, the client describes the last time the problem did not occur. We prefer the term *success-finding* to facilitate our focus on approach goals. A typical intervention might sound like this: "Tell us about the last time (the approach goal) occurred, or some part of it occurred." The description of the context and interactions surrounding the success or partial success reveals the existing strengths that can be built upon to achieve the approach goal. Melidonis and Bry (1995) found that exception-finding increased a client's positive appraisal of difficulties and enhanced relationship interactions as well as reducing the focus upon problems in family therapy. The clients focused more on what they liked about each other and what could be done to make family life better.

Asking detailed questions about the circumstances leading to partial successes leads clients to identify strengths that lead to growth. Introducing the growth mindset of believing that incremental growth leads to large change is important for facilitating hope that change is possible (Dweck, 2006). Positive emotions like pride and hope are also kindled by highlighting abilities and past successes. For example:

> *Therapist: When was the last time you felt good about going to work? Start from when you woke up in the morning.*
> *Client: Well, that is hard. It seems so long ago. I guess I remember my last job. I used to wake up early. Work out on my stationary bike while I watched the news, have breakfast, and even get to work early. But back then I wasn't depressed and I believed I could eventually become a professional artist.*

Therapist: Wow, this is really great that you can remember the way you used to build toward feeling good at work. What a great routine. Did you have to go to bed early so that you had all that energy in the morning?

Client: I think I go to bed about the same time now. I used to work on my art most evenings before bed . . . and I didn't drink as much every night.

Therapist: Oh, so you think it would help you feel more energetic, hopeful, and enjoy work more if you worked on art in the evening and drank less? Tell me more. How does that all fit together?

The therapist would ask the client to explain how each strength makes the next strength easier to express. The client should be asked to explain the chain of thoughts, feelings, and behaviors that lead to accomplishing the approach goals that counter the avoidance goals. Finally, the therapist asks which part of the chain can be the easiest starting point.

Encouragement

Encouragement stimulates broadening in clients and balances the client's attention regarding problems and deficits with positive statements about abilities, successes, potentials, and intentions. Wong (2015, p. 180) defines encouragement as "the expression of affirmation through language or other symbolic representations to instill courage, perseverance, confidence, inspiration, or hope in a person(s) within the context of addressing a challenging situation or realizing a potential." The origin of the use of encouragement in therapy can be traced to a number of sources. Adlerian therapists see encouragement as an antidote for client discouragement; discouragement is the absence of hope. The installation of hope, one of the four hallmarks of GFPP, was seen by Frank and Frank (1991) in their Contextual Model as the primary purpose of therapy. Bandura (1997) viewed encouragement as verbal persuasion and a method that promotes self-efficacy. Kratz, Wong, and Vaughan (2013) identified encouragement as a means of social support. Finally, in a qualitative study investigating the phenomenon by using client strengths in therapy, experienced therapists who represented a variety of theoretical orientations recognized encouragement as a method they regularly use to identify, amplify, and promote client strengths (Scheel, Klentz Davis, & Henderson, 2013). Thus, encouragement as a therapeutic process is used commonly in therapy to promote hope, identify strengths, communicate social support, and increase self-efficacy. In GFPP, we see encouragement as an important broadening process that influences each of the four primary functions of GFPP.

Encouragement is effective only when the client perceives the therapist as trustworthy and the message as credible and realistic, in which case encouragement instills confidence (Wong, 2015). Encouragement can be challenge-focused: "You have been so resilient and it helps me believe that you can overcome this current hardship." Or encouragement can be potential-focused: "Have you ever considered going back to school? I think you would do very well." And encouragement should be concentrated on positive aspects of the client: "You have excellent interpersonal skills."

As a therapeutic process, encouragement probably fuels positive emotions for broadening and building. In Wong's (2006) Strength Centered Therapy model, encouragement is used to make client strengths more explicit, to envision means of using strengths, to empower clients to use their strengths, and to point out how client strengths have evolved. Therapists in the study by Scheel and colleagues (2013) described the use of encouragement as a means of amplifying client strengths by pointing out client growth, affirming client successes, or recognizing client efforts to move in positive directions. Therapists saw encouragement as a way to insert a positive voice advocating for the client and balancing out client expressions of low self-esteem and negative self-messages.

Misuse of encouragement can also occur. Encouragement should be used only in a trusting context and authentically. Encouragement should not be used to urge the client to ignore an experience or problem: "It isn't that bad!" or "Come on. Don't even think about that." We do not recommend using these statements! Encouragement should be authentic—that is, based in reality—and should be both believed by the therapist and believable to the client. If you heap praise and encouragement on your clients without having a basis for these positive statements, then of course encouragement will be ineffective.

A properly timed and formed encouraging statement from a therapist may be one of the few times a client receives such a message from another person. The encouraging statement can broaden the client's self-perception, thereby building a new self-definition that embraces a happier and more hopeful future.

Visualizing Success

A client can increase the probability of success by *visualizing* the accomplishment of a new behavior or therapy homework assignment. Research reveals that visualizing successful accomplishments increases positive affect, reduces negative affect, facilitates social engagement, and enhances problem-solving (Taylor, Pham, Rivkin, & Amor, 1998). Motivation increases when visualizing an occurrence because the client's belief that the event could happen increases (Pham & Taylor, 1999). Ultimately, visualization increases the likelihood that the behavior will occur (Taylor, Pham, Rivkin, & Armor, 1998). For example, visualization can increase study time (Pham & Taylor, 1999), commitment to exercise programs (Ten Eyck, Gresky, & Lord, 2008), sports performance (Weinberg, 2008), and therapy attendance (Buckner et al., 2009). Feelings of optimism were increased for clients who wrote down and then visualized their "best-possible-self" for five minutes a day over two weeks (Meevissen, Peters, & Alberts, 2011).

The most helpful visualization includes three steps. The antecedent step includes the occurrences, feelings, and thoughts that happen leading up to the sought-after goal. The visualization of the enactment of the goal behavior includes the thoughts, feelings, and occurrences surrounding successful accomplishment.

The final step is visualizing the experience of success and savoring the emotions (Pham & Taylor, 1999; Ratcliff et al., 1999). Making the visualization easy to imagine enhances the believability of eventual accomplishment. Visualization becomes easier by using concrete descriptions of actions (Hansen & Wänke, 2010) that match the client's affective state (Johnson & Tversky, 1983; Risen & Critcher, 2011). For example, a client will experience difficulty visualizing being social when feeling resentment and anger. Facilitating the client's mood toward memories of feeling cared about or enjoying laughter with friends would better accomplish visualizing social success. Then outlining a step-by-step process of social interaction makes visualization easier. Visualizing an enjoyable social encounter is critical to believability. Additionally, the client may report roadblocks that the therapist did not anticipate. Enactment visualization is often embedded in the next intervention, the Miracle Question.

Miracle Questions

Made famous by Solution Focused Therapy (de Shazer et al., 2007), the *miracle question* adds an air of playfulness in forming approach goals and anticipating the incremental steps toward reaching a goal by asking the client to visualize life without the problem. The problem miraculously disappears without explanation; a miracle has occurred! You should deliver this intervention in a way that subtly suggests that the miracle may eventually become a reality while also communicating a playful lightheartedness that sets the mood for the visualization of a better life. This mixture makes the client's task easier and more believable.

An important contribution of the miracle question occurs as the client considers what life would be like without the problem: "Once your depression has lifted, what is the first thing you will do in the morning?" "What will you notice?" "What will you do next?" The first step-by-step sequence of events may feel disjointed. Asking about and then summarizing the events, as well as the client behaviors, thoughts, and feelings in detail, will help the visualization. Reacting in a curious and impressed manner can facilitate the client's positive emotions that fuel change. Remember that creating a lively and excited interaction style provides the visceral fit for the positive affect associated with the therapeutic process of goal achievement—Broaden-and-Build.

Asking many concrete questions about what life will be like without the problem is a crucial part of the process. Becoming very curious about how behaviors, emotions and thoughts that the client describes leads toward the client's approach goal (and further away from the problem). In discussing the aftermath of the miracle, help the client recognize how each of the client's personal contributions led to accomplishing the new miracle life. Underscore the client's personal competence or strength that is uncovered in the process. Each incremental, effortful step should be underscored. A successful miracle question can lead to hope, motivation, positive emotions, and goal direction.

You can implement the miracle question as soon as the client knows that you have deeply understood the pain and the problem the client is communicating. Interventions moving away from pain too soon can create difficulties. Additionally, the miracle cannot be the denial of reality. At times, clients would predictably want the miracle to be something impossible that would turn back time. Sample unworkable miracles include: to have more time before death, to have my partner love me again, and to have my child alive again. If these kinds of desires are likely to be the focus of the miracle, then do not employ the miracle question. The miracle could be acceptance of these terrible occurrences. The miracle question could help uncover what the miracle of acceptance would mean for the client.

When the client seems ready to follow your directives and the time is right to develop an approach goal, the miracle question intervention can help. It can even be used in the first session. The client's ability to create details during the miracle question leads to a visualization of the goal and its constituent parts. During the description, many client strengths are likely to appear as well. Prolonging the discussion helps uncover many useful details about the client. Be very curious.

The following is an example of the miracle question. The client has an initial goal of getting rid of her depression. Since getting rid of depression is an avoidant goal, one of the purposes of the miracle question intervention is to uncover what the client would like to achieve as an approach goal. Additionally, strengths and positive emotions typically emerge when the timing of the miracle question intervention fits with the client's receptiveness. The following example represents a successful intervention.

Therapist: (Changing voice volume and tone to signal mysterious and mischievous fun.) I'm about to do something very odd. OK? Yes, this is very odd. Do you believe in miracles?

Client: I am not sure . . .

Therapist: Well, get ready, because a miracle is about to happen! OK, let's say this miracle is going to happen tonight!! (Snapping fingers loudly) Just like that! Your problem is gone. Tonight while you sleep it disappears! Wow! A wonderful miracle, huh? Is that OK with you? Now you wake up in the morning. What is the first sign that the miracle happened? How do you know that your depression is gone?

Client: Well . . . I guess I would wake up when the alarm clock goes off and feel like I want to go to work.

Therapist: Wow, great! You would reach over to turn off the alarm clock and what would you be thinking?

Client: I don't know . . . I would think, I'm going to go to work and concentrate and finish the report that I'm behind on.

Therapist: Good! So you're going to turn off your alarm clock, feel like you want to go to work because you're going to get the report finished! Is that right? So you wake up thinking about the good feelings you will have upon *concentrating and finishing the report at work? Then what will you do next that continues to let you know that your depression has disappeared?*

Client: Well, I would text my friend to see if she wanted to go out for dinner.

Therapist: OK! Great! So you'd wake up thinking, I'm going to get this report done. Then you think you would like to have dinner with your friend and you text her. Right? Great! What do you do next?

Client: Well, let me think . . . I guess I would get up and exercise with my neighbors who are always bugging me to join them for their walk around the neighborhood.

Therapist: Oh, my! That sounds very healthy! Wow! (Capitalization)

OK! So let me see if I have this right. So you wake up; turn off your alarm clock; feel like you want to go to work because you're going to get the report finished; text your friend to arrange supper; and now you are heading out the door to exercise? Is that right? Great! Who do you think is the first person who notices that your depression is gone?

Client: I don't know . . . I guess my neighbors when I show up to walk with them.

Therapist: What will they notice about you that is different in addition to you being with them?

Client: I am not sure . . . I guess I'll be more talkative, more friendly. I have been very quiet with my depression.(When clients begin to describe the problem, the therapist interrupts and refocuses upon the goal description.)

Therapist: Oh, so you'll be more talkative. I bet people do enjoy your friendliness. Especially when you talk! That is good to know. (Paraphrasing, Encouragement)

So after your walk who will notice?

The intervention can explore the entire day to gather information about the client's ideal pattern. Notice several things about the miracle question:

- First, the miracle is presented as hypothetical initially, but quickly the language presumes that the client will be behaving, thinking, and feeling in the manner described by the client. This is called *pre-suppositional language*.
- Second, relational factors are highlighted by asking who will notice and what the client will be doing differently to be noticed. Relationships are important for the highest level of well-being (i.e., thriving). When relationships can be improved upon, the client benefits.
- Third, the therapist summarizes almost continuously as the non-depressed day unfolds. The continuous summarization helps the client remember the ideal day so that when the information is used to form approach goals, the client experiences ownership of the goals.
- Finally, the therapist celebrates the healthy changes the client describes as often as possible in a way that is believable to the client. The capitalization of the client's disclosures of a happier self accomplishes three process goals:
  - The client values the small (i.e., incremental) approach goal mentioned, such as thinking about accomplishing a work task.

- The client feels a brief positive emotion, creating a broadening effect and possibly building.
- The client increasingly values and trusts the relationship with the therapist.

The therapist creates repetition; asks about the client's thoughts, actions, and feelings with the successful day; and actively responds to the client's ideas. After the completion of the miracle question, the therapist asks a success-finding question, "When was the last time this miracle or part of the miracle happened?" Then the therapist can ask, "Will this miracle happen tomorrow? How many times will it happen this week?" To ensure success, the miracle or part of the miracle could be assigned as a homework assignment to occur about half the number of times the client suggested. Many of the accomplishments revealed in the miracle question can become approach goals.

Scaling Questions

A *scaling question* asks the client to rate the experience of an issue along a continuum from 0 to 10. The scaling question can address an infinite number of issues and has at least two purposes. The first purpose allows clients to communicate complex issues in a simple, direct manner (Berg, 1994; Berg & Miller, 1992, 1998; de Shazer et al., 2007). For example, a client can rate motivation to work toward a goal, confidence that the goal will be achieved, or when termination from therapy should occur (De Jong & Berg, 2008).

Another purpose of the scaling question is to communicate clearly what having a growth mindset or incremental growth means when accomplishing a goal. After the client provides a number corresponding to the present attainment level of an approach goal, the therapist asks what the next step would be: What is the smallest perceptible movement that could occur this week that could be viewed as moving in the right direction? The question clearly communicates that change occurs incrementally. Goal attainment should be viewed as a series of stepping-stones. Too often the only goal the client can describe is the ultimate goal or failure. Carefully developing small approach goals is important to developing a growth mindset, and having incremental goals allows for many celebrations along the way. Viewing large approach goals as lifelong aspirations can help. A client may never have enough close friends, skills at work, or success with hobbies, but lifelong aspirational approach goals provide guidance and meaning through life. The following is an example of a client with an approach goal of having friends:

Therapist: *Let's say that a zero means you are totally friendless and no one knows you. And a 10 is that you have so many friends you can't keep up with them all! What number represents where you are right now?*
Client: *I think I'm at a 2. I have a couple of friends, but they are married and they don't really have time for me.*

Therapist: So you rate your situation as a 2 now. That is great that you're not starting at zero, but clearly it is not where you want to be. What number along the friendship ruler do you need to achieve to be satisfied with the "friendship domain" of your life? Remember, 10 is having more friends than you could possibly keep up with! I guess a lifelong dream! What is the number you'd be happy with?

Client: Oh, I think I'd be happy with a 6.

Therapist: Great! What would a 6 be like for you?

Client: I'd have three or four friends that could do something with me about three days a week . . . and definitely be available on nearly every weekend.

Therapist: Great. That really helps. So you are not doing much with friends now. What is the smallest movement toward your ultimate goal that could happen this week that would be just noticeable? Something that would indicate that you are doing something that may result in gaining more friends? Moving a little toward 10, like a 3 or a 2.5? What would you need to do to move a little?

Client: Well, I guess I could go to dance class and maybe meet someone there. My married friends have been asking me to go and I used to like dance classes.

Therapist: Wow! That is a big step. Do you think you could really take such a big step? Going to a dance class this week? How would you go about doing that?

The scaling process communicates the importance of making progress in manageable steps. The small increments increase the client's confidence and allow for celebration along the way.

The scaling questions about approach goals can only be used after goals are formed. Scaling issues examining motivation, hope for change, and willingness to expend effort can occur early in therapy. The questions communicate that the client will have to contribute to the success of therapy. Scaling questions provide a rich context for presenting incremental change, as well as hope and change occurring with positive emotions.

Best-Possible-Self

The *best-possible-self* intervention asks the client to write an ideal future. The instructions ask the client to envision a future where everything has gone as well as it possibly could. The instructions should specify a time frame, and a more distant time frame may be easier for the client. The purpose of the intervention is to clarify values and goals, and help guide current decisions (Sheldon & Lyubomirsky, 2006). In addition to revealing important life values and approach goals, the best-possible-self intervention research shows increases in hope (Winter Plumb, Hawley, & Conoley, 2015), optimism (Meevissen, Peters, & Alberts, 2011), life satisfaction (Peters, Meevissen, & Hanssen 2013), and positive affect (Renner,

Schwarz, Peters, & Huibers 2014). In an initial study, Winter Plumb and colleagues (2015) found that the best-possible-self intervention benefited the Latina/o and White/European American ethnic groups more than Asian/Asian-American/ Pacific Islanders.

The following is a sample set of instructions used by Winter Plumb and colleagues (2015). The instructions may be best written out and reviewed orally:

> This week I would like you to think about your best-possible-self. Please imagine yourself in the future, after everything has gone as well as it possibly could. You have worked hard and succeeded at accomplishing your life goals. Think of this as the realization of your life dreams. You might think of this as reaching your full potential, hitting an important milestone, or realizing one of your life dreams: a time when you are expressing your best-possible-self strongly. The point is not to think of unrealistic fantasies, rather things that are positive and attainable within reason. Be sure to visualize your best-possible-self in a way that is very pleasing to you and that you are interested in. After five minutes of imagining your best-possible-self, please write for approximately ten minutes about the details of what you imagined. Writing down your best-possible-self helps to create a logical structure for the future and can help you move from the realm of foggy ideas and fragmented thoughts to concrete, real possibilities.

In reviewing the assignment, ask the client what it felt like to do the assignment. Ask about any long-term goals that appeared. Also, ask about what is happening in the client's life now to help move incrementally toward the goals. Ask how the life journey can be made enjoyable. Clients can be asked to visualize the best-possible-self for five minutes a day over two weeks to increase their positive emotions (Meevissen, Peters, & Alberts, 2011).

Count-Your-Blessings

The *count-your-blessings* intervention increases gratitude, which garners the many evidence-based benefits associated with gratitude. Gratitude is defined as the feeling of wonder, thankfulness, and appreciation of life gifts contributed to you (Emmons & Shelton, 2002). Gratitude is viewed as virtuous in all cultures and societies (Watkins et al., 2009). The feeling of gratitude, a positive emotion, occurs when appreciating life in the present moment (Lyubomirsky, 2007).

The benefits of gratitude are psychological, physiological, and interpersonal. Psychologically, clients benefit by experiencing increased positive affect and more energy, enthusiasm, and attentiveness (Emmons & McCullough, 2003). Furthermore, gratitude helps by increasing the savoring of positive experiences, bolstering self-worth, and enhancing coping with stress and trauma in a manner that may be related to benefit-finding (Frederickson, Tugade, Waugh, & Larkin, 2003; Watkins, Grimm, & Kolts, 2004). Gratitude also encourages moral behavior, builds social bonds, and inhibits envy and many other negative emotions (Lyubomirsky, 2007; Watkins, Van Gelder, & Frias, 2009). Physiologically, gratitude contributes to better sleep and fewer illnesses (Emmons & McCullough, 2003).

The count-your-blessings intervention is a homework assignment designed to promote gratitude. Two or three times a week at night before bedtime, ask the client to write down three things occurring during the day for which the client is grateful. The client could be grateful for something or someone. Examples of things to be grateful for include a friend, a meal, a flower, or a book. The client should savor or think about the benefit for a few minutes before going to sleep. Review the list with the client at the next session and ask in detail about the experience in order to increase the positive emotions. Many clients report that they begin to think about blessings more often during the day after implementing this intervention.

Self-Compassion

Self-compassion describes the experience of feeling caring and understanding toward oneself, especially when confronted with failure or personal inadequacies. An early advocate of the construct, Kristen Neff (2003), defines self-compassion as consisting of three components: self-kindness, common humanity, and mindfulness. Self-kindness is being caring and supporting of oneself, the opposite of negative self-judgment. Common humanity refers to recognizing that all humans have problems and shortcomings, thereby not becoming isolated from others because of faults. Finally, mindfulness is the state of not feeling overly identified or excessively entangled with difficulties and negative feelings.[3] Self-compassion fosters resilience (Neff, 2009) and correlates with higher levels of well-being (Zessin, Dickhäuser, & Garbade, 2015); feelings of competence, autonomy, and relatedness (Gerber, Tolmacz, & Doron, 2015); and lower levels of stress and psychopathology (MacBeth & Gumley, 2012). Generally, self-compassion does not appear to influence positive emotions as much as mindfulness meditation (Soysa & Wilcomb, 2015).

Self-compassion can be taught as an independent intervention to increase life satisfaction and decrease depression (Diedrich, Grant, Hofmann, Hiller, & Berking, 2014; Shapira & Mongrain, 2010). Alternately, self-compassion can be used in a similar manner as self-affirmation to prime the client's receptiveness to an intervention. For example, asking clients to use self-kindness before a cognitive reappraisal intervention increases the effectiveness of reappraisal in reducing depression (Diedrich, Hofmann, Cuijpers, & Berking, 2016).

Self-compassion is supported as beneficial in many cultures. A relationship between self-compassion and well-being has been found among individuals from Latin America, Thailand, Turkey, Taiwan, and China (Birkett, 2014; Edwards, Adams, Waldo, Hadfield, & Biegel, 2014; Neff, Pisitsungkagarn, & Hsieh, 2008; Yang, 2016).

Conceptually, self-compassion can be thought of as a good replacement for self-esteem. Increasing self-esteem frequently requires feeling better than others, but in comparison to self-esteem, self-compassion correlates more highly with resilience, accurate self-concept, and caring behavior, and less with narcissism as well as reactive anger (Neff, 2011). Self-compassion carries no requirements of being better than anyone else. Unfortunately, self-esteem can be associated with needing to be a winner to feel good. *A Prairie Home Companion* closed with the words, "Well, that's the news from Lake Wobegon, where all the women are strong, all the men are good-looking, and all the children are above average" (American Public Media, 2016). The tongue-in-cheek tease yields insight into the need to have comparatively more of an important quality in order to feel valuable—to have high self-esteem. We urge the replacement of self-esteem with self-compassion as our human benchmark of success. Self-compassion means doing the best we can, as often as we can, and feeling really good about our effort and accomplishments. Additionally, self-compassion means forgiving ourselves and accepting that we cannot always function at 100%, nor can we always feel good. Self-compassion defines a more reasonable, humanistic goal for improving self-regard.

The following is an example of standardized directions from an experimental study of self-compassion that significantly reduced depression:

Try to experience very clearly which feelings have been activated by these statements. Try to see yourself from an outsider's point of view, from the perspective of a compassionate, friendly observer, to actually visualize in your mind how you look, sitting here in front of the computer. Maybe you can notice from the outside which feeling upsets you at the moment. Try to perceive now how the negative feelings are reflected in your posture and facial expression. Then, try to let the warm and strong feeling of compassion towards yourself arise within yourself; this warm and strong feeling of compassion, that goes along with the desire to help yourself. If you sense this feeling, you can start approaching yourself in your imagination, enter the visualized scene and tell yourself that you are there to help. Maybe you can say to yourself: "It is understandable that you feel that way. You are facing a challenging situation. You experience a natural response to depressing thoughts. But I am with you. I am going to help you. You are not alone." In the next step you can start encouraging yourself internally: "Come on, you can do this. You can pull yourself out of this mood again. You have already accomplished so much; you will also be able to deal with this." If you want, you can also visualize putting your hand on your shoulder or hugging yourself to soothe and comfort yourself. Then, try to cheer yourself up by internally giving yourself a friendly smile. While smiling in a friendly manner at yourself, you can check if there are other things you want to tell yourself; things that would energize and encourage you to cheer yourself up. Take your time to think of some sentences and tell them to yourself. At the proper moment, you can start saying goodbye to yourself. Remind yourself that this will not be a farewell forever but that you can come back to yourself every time you want. Perhaps there is still something you want to tell yourself for farewell. If so, do this now before you come back from this exercise to the here and now, slowly, in your own way. (Diedrich, Grant, Hofmann, Hiller, & Berking, 2014, p. 46)

A typical client, however, needs more intensive work with self-compassion than one paragraph presented one time, as in the aforementioned exercise. Consider reading Kristin Neff's books on the topic, or review the many internet sites expanding on her work. These resources can be used to learn more and guide clients' independent exploration of self-compassion.

Mindfulness

In Western psychology, the most accepted description of mindfulness is "paying attention in a particular way, on purpose, in the present moment, and non-judgmentally" (Kabat-Zinn, 1994, p. 4). *Mindfulness* is the ability to dispassionately attend to the immediate experience that is traditionally developed through meditation training. The ability to experience thoughts, perceptions, and emotions with non-reactivity contributes to positive emotions and well-being (Geschwind, Peeters, Drukker, vas Os, & Wichers, 2011; Henderson et al., 2012; Nyklicek & Kuijpers, 2008; Orzech, Shapiro, Brown, & McKay, 2009). Mindfulness meditation has long been described in Eastern literature, especially Buddhism (Hanh, 1998). A simplification or reduction frequently arises in the translation of mindfulness into Western psychotherapeutic applications. Regrettably, we too follow in this tradition of oversimplifying mindfulness as part of GFPP. We hope that soon a scholar in the field will differentiate the constructs to avoid the risk of trivializing mindfulness. The psychotherapy application of mindfulness approximates only a small portion of mindfulness meditation. In GFPP, the intervention of mindfulness increases positive emotions, sensitivity to immediate experience, an ability to reduce reactivity to painful emotions and thoughts, and an ability to think more clearly in the moment.

The following is a research example that illustrates a small portion of our concern by demonstrating what psychotherapy models leave out of mindfulness. Cheisa and colleagues (2013) cleverly attempted to understand mindfulness by examining the process occurring within short-term practitioners (i.e., typical psychotherapeutic use of mindfulness) and long-term practitioners (i.e., one year or more). The researchers examined what they termed a top-down versus a bottom-up hypothesis of mindfulness's functioning between short- and long-term users. Top-down processing described mindfulness as noticing what is within awareness, then deciding what will be done with the thoughts or feelings, instead of reacting to the experiences without thought. Bottom-up processing described mindfulness as a state that allows a person to be aware of experiences but to have no active processing of the events, and rather to simply observe their passing. Top-down processing fits with traditional psychology in that mindfulness is a construct having to do with thinking, while bottom-up processing describes a process that does not involve prefrontal cortex functioning. The physiological measures indicate that short-term users of mindfulness function with top-down processing and long-term users function with bottom-up processing. The manner in which mindfulness functions changes with greater use, and perhaps also with gains in user "understanding." The research indicates that becoming an expert in mindfulness offers a great deal beyond what is described in psychotherapy; however, the short-term use provides valuable benefits as well.

A great deal of research supports that short-term mindfulness training can help a client observe disturbing thoughts and feelings in a manner that is less upsetting than the typical client's initial response to negative internal experiences. Mindfulness is beneficial for increasing self-compassion (Neff, 2003) and well-being (Carmody, Baer, Lykins, & Olendzki, 2009). Additionally, mindfulness has proven effective in the treatment of depression (Williams & Kuyken, 2012), anxiety (Evans, Ferrando, Findler, Stowell, Smart, & Haglin, 2008), eating disorders (Baer, Fischer, & Huss, 2005), and personality disorders (Neacsiu, Rizvi, & Linehan, 2010). In a meta-analysis of 209 studies, mindfulness was found to be effective with a host of psychological problems (Khoury et al. 2013).

Self-monitoring and self-knowledge are increased through mindfulness meditation (Kabat-Zinn, 1982). A client can have greater self-knowledge and become more self-accepting. The increased awareness facilitates eating a healthy amount (Kristeller & Hallett, 1999), recovering from addictions (Marlatt, 2003), and noticing negative emotions earlier in order to facilitate prevention and avoid relapse (Teasdale et al., 2000). Additionally, having greater sensitivity and openness to examining experiences allows individuals to have better judgment in relationships (Dimidjian & Linehan, 2003). Acceptance increases via mindfulness meditation by enhancing the ability to experience what is occurring more fully without backing away (Hayes, Follette, & Linehan, 2004). Additionally, mindfulness meditation is relaxing, which helps with many stress-related issues (Jain et al., 2007).

Mindfulness can be a highly efficient intervention. Therapists should practice mindfulness as well in order to be knowledgeable of the intervention. However, be cautious because the client might have initial negative reactions to becoming more self-aware, which is a common experience for beginning mindfulness practitioners. The initial self-awareness meditation practice should be with the therapist. The following example introduces mindfulness with a rationale for its use that matches the client's goals:

Therapist: I would like to explore the idea of you learning mindfulness. Can I tell you about it?

Client: Yes . . .

Therapist: What do you know about it?

Client: Not much. Sounds a little weird. I guess I've heard about it but really don't know much.

Therapist: OK. I'll tell you about it because I think it would be really beneficial for you. A lot of research has found mindfulness to be very helpful. I think it can help you be nicer to yourself and be more patient with your partner.

Client: Well, I really want to be more patient . . .

Therapist: Great. Yes, and mindfulness helps many other parts of our life, like enjoying life more. Can't beat that! There is a catch . . .

Client: Uh-oh . . .

Therapist: Yes, the catch is that it requires effort on your part.

Client: Oh, no . . .

Therapist: Yes, it will require 10 minutes a day. People typically see results within two weeks. though, and those who keep using it report that there are many more benefits down the line: eating and drinking only a healthy amount, sleeping better, worrying less, having more energy, being nicer to others, being nicer to themselves, physically healthier . . . Great stuff!

Client: Sounds too good to be true . . .

Therapist: Well, you get to find out! Are you still interested?

Client: OK.

Therapist: Mindfulness is something that has to be learned in small steps, but even as you learn, good things can begin to happen. The first part is learn- ing to focus better—learning to focus where you want to focus and learning to bring your attention back to your focus point. Focus is really the key to the first stage. Can we start out with a five-minute introduction to focusing?

Client: OK.

Therapist: This exercise helps us focus on the present moment. Practicing focusing on one thing, right now. This builds an ability that will feel difficult at first, if you are like most people. Research indicates that practicing focus- ing on one thing for 10 minutes a day will change your brain for the better! And focusing gets easier with practice . . . which is great for many life skills.

Notice how much time was spent in developing a rationale for mindfulness and presenting mindfulness in such a way that motivates the client by matching the client's goals and life circumstances. The homework at the end of the session could be to use a workbook such as Stahl and Goldstein's (2010) *Mindfulness- Based Stress Reduction Workbook,* or to use an online audio mindfulness session. A highly motivated client could begin with a community class in mindfulness or yoga, which saves therapy time and also involves the client in social outings.

In GFPP, the short-term goal for clients using mindfulness meditation is to accomplish the top-down skills of learning to observe perceptions, thoughts, and feelings purposefully and with reduced emotional reactivity. The process should be pursued in ways that fit the client's goals.

CONCLUSION

Chapter 3 presented the major techniques and interventions often used in GFPP. The techniques and interventions—while common to many psychotherapy models—differ in GFPP by the intent of their use. The GFPP therapist's intentions prioritize the identification of client strengths, the promotion of positive emotions and experiences, and the illumination of the client's desired states (which then become approach goals). The techniques initially provide the means for understanding and forming a relationship with the client by listening to the client's story while highlighting strengths. However, as soon as is therapeutically advisable, the GFPP therapist moves from a problem-centered, avoidance goal stance to a strength-based, approach goal focus. The working alliance is carefully nurtured in GFPP by closely following what the client desires and the strengths that the client expresses. The therapist takes time to understand the client and carefully weaves how the client's desires fit with the goals and interventions. Therapy proceeds by enlisting the client's motivation via highlighting strengths, tying goals and interventions to the client's original problem, and fostering hope through the GFPP processes.

The techniques and interventions included in the chapter are not an exhaustive list of all interventions that can be used by GFPP therapists. We urge the practitioner to use GFPP's theoretical model to guide the intentions that direct therapy and to use any techniques and interventions that fit with the client and the GFPP model.

4

Training Therapists in GFPP
and Building GFPP Skills

Training therapists in Goal Focused Positive Psychotherapy (GFPP) not only includes skill building corresponding to the GFPP approach but also requires therapists to shift their thinking and orientation (i.e., mindset) concerning how human change occurs in psychotherapy. With many traditional approaches—such as cognitive-behavioral or psychodynamic therapies—change efforts are primarily driven by problem definition and implementation of treatment as dictated by the nature of the problem and its symptoms. Correspondingly, meta-analyses of psychotherapy reveal that successful therapy is indicated by alleviation of distress and diminishment of symptoms associated with identified problems (e.g., Benish, Imel, & Wampold, 2008). Conceptualizations of treatment often focus narrowly on client complaints, causes of the problem, and associated symptoms of the problem. The focus epitomizes the physical science change metaphor as applied to the psychological experience of human beings. The physical science view assumes that understanding the origin of the problem leads to the solution of the problem. This perspective works well with machines: if we know why the car won't start (e.g., dead battery), then we know how to fix it (e.g., a charged battery).

However, as discussed in previous chapters, we do not believe the physical science approach is the most helpful perspective for dealing with psychological issues. Many times the cause of the problem—if it is even knowable—does not lead to the one corresponding correct solution. Also, most clients are more active in the therapy process than a car! Instead, we believe that a psychological metaphor of well-being creates the requisite mindset for a GFPP clinician. The resulting paradigmatic shift frees the therapist from seeking a single solution and facilitates exploration of multiple ways that a client might achieve increased meaningful happiness whether or not the current problem can disappear. The client builds resources to sustain well-being and to effectively address the inevitable problems of life when these arise.

This chapter focuses upon the training and education of GFPP therapists. Therapists trained in traditional psychotherapy models typically require a shift in mindset. GFPP therapists cannot fake believing in the theory: they must have an authentic commitment to increasing the client's well-being. A GFPP therapist focuses on supporting the client's competence, relatedness, and autonomy; these are the basic human needs targeted through Self-Determination Theory (SDT) that foster motivation and well-being (Deci & Ryan, 2008). When faced with the problems that clients bring into therapy, the GFPP therapist must believe that increasing the client's well-being will lead to decreased suffering. Such is the mindset or orientation necessary for successful implementation of GFPP.

GFPP-oriented therapists believe in helping clients create happier and healthier lives as the goals of a successful therapeutic change process. Clients with meaningful, engaged, and pleasurable lives have greater resources to solve or accept psychological problems and reduce distress. GFPP therapists are committed to increasing the size of the well-being circle introduced in Chapter 1. When the well-being circle is experienced as larger than the problem circle, the client is better equipped to overcome or accept the inevitable problems that life presents. The GFPP orientation is challenging to realize and maintain, especially when clients initially expect an exclusive focus on their deficits and presenting complaints. The therapist must be prepared to provide "a compelling rationale," as Frank and Frank (1991) suggest in their seminal work *Persuasion and Healing*. The basic rationale for GFPP is that by concentrating on strengths, as well as harnessing positive emotions to broaden thought-action repertoires, clients open up to new possibilities of increased well-being in their lives. The increased well-being enables clients to more effectively change what is changeable and accept what cannot be changed. Life is met from a position of psychological strength. The rationale should be presented in a manner that best fits with the client's worldview so that the client understands and engages fully (Conoley et al., 1991, 1994; Scheel et al., 1998, 1999).

To summarize, the therapist's mindset shifts from a physical science metaphor of psychotherapy to a psychological metaphor of human change. The GFPP therapist views change as a broadening process with no one best solution; rather, there are many avenues to happier and healthier lives. The shift in mindset represents several layers (Fig. 4-1). Among these are the following:

a. Moving from being problem-focused to strength-focused;
b. Moving from attending to extrinsic goals (i.e., external indicators of worth) to attending to intrinsic goals oriented toward personal values that foster autonomy, competence, and relatedness;
c. Moving from focusing on avoidant goals (i.e., avoiding the problem, avoiding symptoms of the problem) to focusing on approach goals (i.e., gaining desired states that lead to happiness);
d. Moving from fearing problems and negative emotions to feeling confident about experiencing negative emotions due to more easily accessible positive emotions;
e. Moving from experiencing infrequent positive emotions to purposefully pursuing frequent experiences of positive emotions; and

From a *physical* metaphor of human change mindset	→	To a *psychological* metaphor of human change mindset
Physical science change model	→	Psychological science change model
Problem focus	→	Strengths focus
Therapy goals of client problem symptom alleviation	→	Therapy goals of promoting happier and healthier client lives
Attention to extrinsically oriented client goals	→	Attention to intrinsically oriented client goals
Forming avoidance goals	→	Forming approach goals
Identifying causes of client problems	→	Identifying client desired states
Fearing problems and negative emotions	→	Feeling confident about experiencing both negative and positive emotions
Random experiences of infrequent positive emotions	→	Purposeful pursuit of frequent experiences of positive emotions
A self that is defined by pathology	→	A self that is defined by personal strengths
Therapist hopelessness from feeling controlled by the client's problem	→	Hope for the client and hope for therapy
Therapy process defined by the problem	→	Therapy process defined by client values

Figure 4-1 Shifts in mindset required of GFPP-committed therapists.

    f. Moving from a self-definition largely comprising a pathological view to a perspective of self that is based on personal strengths.

FOCUSING ON CLIENT STRENGTHS

Human history and the current presiding political and social systems (e.g., the American Psychiatric Association's *Diagnostic and Statistical Manual of Mental Disorders* [DSM-5]; managed care) conspire to make it difficult for therapists to adopt a psychological change model. Insurance reimbursement is tied to client problem definitions and problem-focused treatments. DSM-5 (2013) and managed care entities are predominately problem-focused. Managed care infrequently rewards healthy behavior and building strengths, nor does it recognize the value of promoting prevention. In a few notable exceptions occurring now, businesses reward employees for healthy lifestyles such as regular exercise and not smoking. These companies recognize that problems can be prevented or decreased by encouraging healthy practices; this also reduces costs to the companies. If the health movement created a revolution in healthcare, individuals would be encouraged by their schools, employers, and insurance companies to pursue a wide range of practices that foster well-being. In the more perfect world, individuals would be supported to practice strength-engendering activities such as gratitude, self-compassion, forgiveness, acts of kindness, savoring positive experiences, fostering social connections, experiencing flow, and similar activities that facilitate well-being and happiness. A society oriented toward strengths and fostering frequent positive emotions would surely reduce the occurrence and severity of human problems. Insurance companies and individuals would both benefit from encouraging the identification of human strengths and experiencing positive emotions.

In the context of psychotherapy, GFPP offers this kind of revolutionary way of preventing problems, or at least lessening their effects! In this revolution, GFPP therapists have a commitment to focus therapy on client strengths and positive emotions. Most importantly, they are committed to helping clients in their journey toward a happier life, the good life! Training methods promoting belief and commitment to the psychological metaphor for human change are presented in this chapter.

Use of Client Strengths by Therapists

Even though positive psychology is an important movement with many advocates within the field of psychology, some therapists are hesitant to explicitly adopt a psychotherapy model in which strengths, positive emotions, hope, and approach goals dominate. However, research findings demonstrate that many if not most therapists use client strengths in therapy no matter what theoretical orientation they implement (Harbin, Gelso, & Rojas, 2014; Scheel, Davis, & Henderson, 2013).

The use of client strengths was examined in a qualitative study of therapists from a variety of therapeutic approaches (i.e., psychodynamic, person-centered, cognitive-behavioral, eclectic, interpersonal, feminist, and multicultural; Scheel et al., 2013). Five themes representing positive therapist processes emerged from the interviews: (a) amplification of strengths, (b) strength-oriented processes, (c) strength-oriented goals, (d) positive meaning-making, and (e) contextual framing of problems (Table 4-1). The strengths *amplification* theme included the techniques of highlighting strengths that emerge naturally in therapy, using exception-finding, and encouraging clients to experience positive emotions. The strength-oriented *processes* theme included interventions that explore and identify strengths, the client–therapist relationship being used as a client strength, therapist self-disclosures about perceived client strengths, and identification of enhanced client self-awareness. The strength-oriented *outcomes* theme included forming approach goals and pathways to goals, as well as instilling hope, motivation, and empowerment. The positive *meaning-making* theme included the use of positive metaphors, positive reframing, interpreting client resilience in the face of problems, and encouraging generalization of strengths to broader contexts. The final theme, *context framing* of problems, described the therapist seeing the occurrence of problems as a natural consequence of the context in which

Table 4-1 THEMES, MEANING UNITS, AND INVARIANT CONSTITUENTS OF THE USE
OF CLIENT STRENGTHS IN PSYCHOTHERAPY

Theme	Invariant Constituents
Amplification of strengths	
	Exception-finding
	Encouragement
	Therapist highlights client strengths
Strength-oriented processes	
	Explore and identification process
	Therapeutic relationship as a strength-oriented process
	Therapist self-disclosure of client strengths
	Client self-awareness identified as a strength
Strength-oriented outcomes	
	Approach goals and pathways
	Hope, motivation, and empowerment
Positive meaning-making	
	Use of metaphor to access strengths
	Resiliency as strength
	Generalization of strengths
	Positive reframing
Contextual considerations	
	Barriers to the use of client strengths
	Understanding the problem is related to a context
	Matching strengths with problems

Note. Themes from the Scheel et al. (2013) study, *Therapist Use of Client Strengths: A Qualitative Study of Positive Processes.*

they reside (e.g., immediate attention to the problem during a crisis; problems occurring due to cultural incongruence). The study by Scheel and associates also demonstrated that the therapists participating in the study attempted to balance a problem focus with a strength focus, no matter what approach they were using with the clients.

The study results may indicate that the shift to the psychological change metaphor could be less challenging than originally thought. Perhaps the acceptance of using client strengths in therapy could facilitate the acceptance of the other hallmarks of GFPP—that is, the use of positive emotions, approach goals, and hope. A roadblock in fully adopting GFPP may be the lack of knowledge about positive psychology interventions (Magyar-Moe, Owens, & Scheel, 2015) and perhaps a misinterpretation of the aims and processes that GFPP promotes. As authors, we hope to remedy the lack of knowledge and the misunderstanding of positive psychology through GFPP.

Balancing Problems with Strengths

GFPP requires attending to a balanced view of the client's deficits and strengths, negative and positive emotions, and problems and solutions. In Chapter 5, four case studies will demonstrate that when using GFPP, client problems are not ignored or abandoned. The case examples illustrate how GFPP helps clients by acknowledging problematic concerns and broadening through positive emotions. Even with the most severe problem situations, such as threat of suicide, broadening through promotion of positive emotions and identifying client strengths can still occur. Broadening and building client processes and resources can potentially lead to the alleviation of client suffering and the solving of client problems in many circumstances. Positive emotions can counter anger, guilt, and shame in clients suffering from posttraumatic stress disorder, as well as decrease depression among clients diagnosed with a major depressive disorder (Garland, Fredrickson, Kring, Johnson, Meyer, & Penn, 2010).

GFPP therapists use the problems a client identifies as references for constructing approach goals that describe the client's desired states, which consequently lead to greater well-being. The experiences of problems and distress can be reframed so that the client views problems as indicators of what is personally most important. Desired states are translated into approach goals, and client strengths can provide pathways to achieving the goals. For instance, if a client suffers from loneliness and isolation, the therapist shows empathy for the client's distress, and then explores whether the suffering means that the client wants to gain social connectedness and improved relationships. If the client is open to the reasoning that building social connections is an approach goal that will mitigate the suffering, then more attention can be focused upon fostering strengths and positive experiences to achieve the goal. The approach goals do not always obviate the problem. At times the client is asked to be willing to feel and function better first, and then, if the concern is still present, to focus on the problem. With all of the strengths of the client functioning better (the bigger well-being circle from Chapter 1), the problem can be dealt with or accepted with greater ease. Clients have often reported solving the issues independently after successfully cultivating greater well-being!

The therapist change efforts are concentrated on helping the client create a happier life, rather than on problem reduction. Thus, the GFPP therapist intently listens for client strengths and assets in order to move clients toward desired states defined by what the client wants. Client desires may or may not be directly related to problem alleviation. We believe that client well-being can and should be promoted despite extant problems. This is not an either/or situation: clients can move toward happier lives while experiencing problems. Fredrickson (2001) posits that negative emotions are associated with narrowed attention that focuses on the negative occurrence. Sometimes, *not focusing* on the problem is a very important change event known as broadening!

FACILITATING A GFPP ORIENTATION

Gaining therapist allegiance toward viewing psychotherapy as a process to help clients lead happier lives can require more than intellectual persuasion. Based on the reports of trainees, a potent means of developing a GFPP orientation occurs through personal experience. Personally experiencing the benefits of autonomously choosing to build assets and strengths in the trainees' own lives through positive emotions is powerfully persuasive. One of this book's authors teaches a graduate course entitled Positive Psychotherapy. He includes positive psychology assignments as experiential learning opportunities in the course: students practice gratitude, self-compassion, loving-kindness meditations, savoring, capitalization, and mindfulness, among other interventions. Personally benefitting from the activities predictably earns the trainee's allegiance. The graduate students in the Positive Psychotherapy course directly and personally experience the Broaden-and-Build phenomena, the attitudinal changes when focusing upon strengths, and the benefits of focusing upon meaning, in addition to a variety of other psychosocial gains.

After taking the Positive Psychotherapy course, trainees tend to commit to a strength-oriented therapy process and to continue the personal growth activities that produced increased well-being and meaning in their own lives. In practicum classes where therapy is learned, trainees use supervision to focus on their therapy successes, not just deficiencies. Generalization of the knowledge gained from the Positive Psychotherapy class spread to the practicum. Student therapists exhibit a growing understanding of the helpfulness in supervision of discussing strengths, being less self-critical, being mindfully present with the client, and using positive emotions. Overall, the personal involvement of trainees benefitting from positive psychology facilitates their adoption of GFPP's model of psychological change.

POSITIVE SUPERVISION AS A GFPP TRAINING METHOD

We encourage the use of a positive supervision approach when training students to promote their growth and efficacy. The positive supervision model parallels the GFPP model in that positive supervision consists of (a) identifying supervisee strengths, (b) forming approach goals oriented toward supervisee growth, (c) capitalizing on supervisee successes in supervision and in therapy, and (d) encouraging hopefulness in supervisees for both their growth and the growth of their clients. As in GFPP with clients, positive supervision does not ignore negative experiences, but they are not the focus.

An example from a supervision case can illustrate positive supervision and the movement from a more traditional understanding of therapy to a GFPP orientation. This case example demonstrates the transition of a supervisee who was initially dedicated to a therapy model that focused upon the client's pain but eventually changed her treatment model to GFPP.

The supervisee's client was exhibiting symptoms of depressed mood, lethargy, hopelessness, and passive suicidal ideation. The supervisee was committed initially to the application of a shame resilience method of therapy. The shame resilience approach was a four-step process of (1) recognizing the presence of shame, (2) recognizing the client's reactions to experiencing shame, (3) suggesting the client make meaningful empathetic and compassionate connections with others, and (4) encouraging the client to share the shame by talking about it. Treatment focused on the experience of the negative emotion of shame, and the alleviation of shame. Progress was monitored through supervision, weekly verbal client reports, and weekly client ratings of the Outcome Rating Scale (ORS) and Session Rating Scale (SRS; Miller et al. 2005). The client's shame was explored each therapy session by asking the client to become more mindful of feelings and thoughts related to experiences of shame, and to talk about shame experiences in therapy. Each week the client reported worsening symptoms that included increased frequency and intensity of suicidal thoughts. Client reports and observations by the supervisor, in addition to the ORS and SRS scores each week, confirmed that therapy was on a descending trajectory. The concern became sufficient for a safety plan to be formed and implemented with the client (Stanley et al., 2008). The client's mood continued to worsen as the therapist followed through with the shame resilience treatment plan. In summary, week after week the client's symptoms increased as the supervisee increased the focus even more intensely on the negative emotion of shame.

One of the authors supervised this case using positive supervision that supported the therapist's approach and focused on the supervisee's strengths. The supervisor identified the supervisee's courage and resilience in working with the client, the conscientiousness with which she cared for her client and worked to keep her safe, and the therapist's capacity for empathy toward the client. The supervisee reported feeling like a failure in helping the client because of the client's downward trajectory. She also revealed how helpful it was to feel supported in supervision even though client progress was not being made. The supervisor revealed the positive supervision process of identifying strengths and focusing upon approach goals in supervision. The discussion about strength-finding helped the supervisee to become aware of benefitting from strength identification in supervision that broadened her ability to be present with her client in therapy and reduce the supervisee's self-doubt. The supervisor suggested that the strength-oriented process used in supervision could be used by the therapist in focusing upon the client's strengths. The techniques of positive empathy and forming approach goals as interventions were suggested and practiced in supervision.

The client's report of well-being changed almost immediately as the therapist concentrated on identifying client strengths and emphasizing the client's desired states. The supervision process paralleled the therapy process. The client liked self-compassion as a desired state or approach goal to counteract the experiences of shame. The supervisee practiced self-compassion to counteract the difficulties of being a therapist as well. The therapist positively reframed the client's response to her struggles as resilience. The supervisor framed the therapist's willingness to face the initial failure of her helpfulness as courage, resilience, and conscientiousness. The therapist celebrated the client's statements (i.e., capitalization) that revealed strengths and progress, as the supervisor celebrated the supervisee's capitalization. The client practiced using self-compassion in the session and at home, just as the supervisee practiced self-compassion in supervision and at home.

The similarity of the processes in therapy and supervision helped the therapist understand the benefits of GFPP and provided modeling on the application of the techniques as they fit the client and supervisee. The supervisee often experienced negative emotions and self-criticism as she worked with a client who consistently felt hopeless to climb out of depression. The support of supervision offered the supervisee insights into how GFPP works, and kept the supervisee from withdrawing or being less open in supervision in the face of difficulties or even failure.

The client's SRS and ORS scores continued in a positive direction, paralleling the shift to the strength-oriented treatment. As the semester supervision ended, the client reported only brief moments of suicidal ideation, with no intent to act on those thoughts, and reported hope for her future. She disclosed plans for an enjoyable summer. The relationship between client and therapist was viewed as a strength that the client could generalize to other relationships in her life. In parallel fashion, the supervisor pointed to the supervisory alliance as a strength that the supervision dyad had relied on as well. By the end of supervision, the supervisee was committed to purposefully integrating a strength focus in her work with all her clients. Supervision included education and training about additional aspects of GFPP.

This supervision case provides an example of how supervision can support and even introduce the practice of GFPP. Some supervisees will not have the advantage of an experiential course in positive psychology to provide an orientation. However, the case illustrates how the experience of supervision can provide a supervisee insight into the helpfulness of GFPP. This case also provides an example of the use of a psychological change model in supervision. Depression and suicidal thoughts require concern in supervision and therapy sessions. However, just as depression symptoms can absorb a client's life and leave no room for approach goals, depression symptoms can absorb the attention in a therapy and supervision session. Even though the supervisor was aware that therapy was not going well, he resisted the temptation to focus exclusively on what seemed wrong. Instead, the supervisor promoted the supervisee's strengths and effectively helped her to see how a strength focus might be more helpful with her client. When the therapist changed focus with the client, self-compassion became the approach goal that replaced the approach goal of examining shame, and the avoidance goal of decreasing depressive thoughts and feelings.

The promotion of autonomy and relatedness was also a part of this successful supervision case. The supervisor did not dictate how the supervisee should work with her client, and the supervisory relationship was a supervisee strength that supported the therapy work with her client. The supervisee became conscious of her desire to emulate a strong supportive relationship with the client.

GOAL FOCUSED POSITIVE SUPERVISION

The GFPP supervision model benefits from the wisdom of three extant supervision models: the Integrated Developmental Model (IDM; Stoltenberg & McNeill, 2010), the Events-Based Model (Ladany, Friedlander, & Nelson, 2005), and the Strength-Based Supervision Model (Wade & Jones, 2015). IDM is a developmental model of supervision that provides suggestions based upon the trainee's stage of growth. The Events-Based Model is a process-oriented supervision model that focuses on training events that occur during psychotherapy supervision (Bernard & Goodyear, 2014). Wade and Jones's (2015) Strength-Based Supervision Model adds a focus upon the supervisee's strengths. First each supervision model is presented, and then the Goal Focused Positive Supervision (GFPS) model that builds upon the three models is discussed.

Stoltenberg and McNeill (2010) developed and continue to improve upon IDM, which is probably the best-known and most widely used supervision model. IDM describes trainee progress across time and suggests interventions to support the trainee's growth at each stage of development. IDM consists of four stages of development, and within each stage are three dimensions: self-other awareness, motivation, and autonomy. For example, in the first stage of development and the first dimension of motivation, supervisees are oriented more toward themselves and their performance as therapists than attending to their clients. The second dimension of motivation describes early trainees as highly motivated but anxious. The third dimension predicts low autonomy—that is, supervisees are highly dependent on their supervisor for guidance and support. The three dimensions evolve with each stage. The end stage characterizes experienced therapists who exhibit a mindful balance between self and client, are highly motivated without anxiety about their performance in therapy, and are autonomous in utilizing intrinsically oriented values in their treatment choices. An interesting connection appears between the three dimensions of IDM and the three basic human needs described in SDT (Deci & Ryan, 2008) required to achieve intrinsically oriented motivation (Fig. 4-2). Stoltenberg and McNeill view their three dimensions of self-other awareness, motivation, and autonomy as dimensions of supervisee development. Ryan and Deci hold that autonomy, relatedness, and competence must be present for an individual to be self-regulated and possess a strong sense of well-being.

Self-other orientation (from IDM) and relatedness (from SDT) are similar in highlighting the importance of relationships. IDM describes supervisees in their early training, who tend to focus on their performance as a therapist, and may neglect attending to the client and the relationship formation. Thus,

IDM Dimensions of Therapist Growth		SDT Human Needs in Achieving Self-Regulation
Self-other orientation (*self-preoccupation, awareness of the client's world, enlightened self-awareness; anxiety*)	--------------	Relatedness (*sense of belonging; supported*)
Motivation (*interest, investment, and effort*)	-------------- (autonomy/ dependency)	Competence (*self-efficacious, confidence about skills*)
Autonomy (*demonstrated independence*)	--------------	Autonomy (*volition, purposefulness, explicit attention*)

Note. IDM = Integrated Developmental Model of Supervision developed by Stoltenberg & McNeill, 2010. SDT = Self Determination Theory of Motivation developed by Ryan & Deci, 2000

Figure 4-2 Drawing connections between IDM and SDT.

the supervisor supports the therapeutic relationships by helping the supervisee understand and focus on the client. The effective supervisor also promotes a sense of confidence in the supervisee through encouragement. As the supervisee becomes more confident, the focus becomes more oriented toward others such as the client and supervisor.

Turning to the second paired dimension illustrated in Figure 4-2, competence (from SDT) and motivation (from IDM) are also related concepts, but autonomy also plays a part in their relationship. In general, people who feel competent about a skill, whether it be basketball, playing music, social relationships, or psychotherapy, will be motivated to continue to work on more development of the skill. The basketball player who feels competent tends to enjoy playing basketball and seeks challenging situations to become even more skilled. Thus, the basketball player is motivated to be even better through training. Psychotherapy is another skill in which competence can build motivation: the supervisee who feels competent is motivated to do more psychotherapy and to become even better. However, predicting the level of motivation when a supervisee lacks a sense of competence can be difficult. Often an individual who feels less competent, no matter what skill is being learned, might become discouraged and disengaged, resulting in low motivation. Individuals lacking competence in statistics may even reject a career in research, believing they do not have the talent for such an activity. Similarly in psychotherapy, the less competent individual may become discouraged and lack motivation to continue. This is where autonomy/dependence comes in. Supervisees who feel less competent may depend on the supervisor to help them continue to have hope that they can eventually become better therapists. Thus, less competent therapists are also less autonomous and more dependent on supervision. Perhaps if less competent students of statistics had teachers they could rely on to help in more vulnerable times, even statistically challenged students would persevere through their feelings of lack of competence.

The third dimension, autonomy, is highlighted in both IDM and SDT. Therapists exercise volition by making choices about directions to take in therapy without relying on the supervisor to guide them in a dependent way. Autonomy does not mean that the therapist ignores supervision and supervisor suggestions. The supervisee and the supervisor may appear to be collaborative, on equal ground, when the supervisee possesses a sense of autonomy in the skills of therapy.

The Events-Based Model (Ladany, Friedlander, & Nelson, 2005) is a process model of supervision in which specific events in supervision are noted and interaction sequences are examined. The supervision events include remediation of a skill deficit; fostering greater multicultural awareness; negotiating role conflicts; working through countertransference; repairing gender-related misunderstandings; and addressing problematic thoughts, feelings, and behaviors such as vicarious traumatization, crises of confidence, or impairment. Tasks that the supervisee and supervisor should accomplish when an event is discussed include exploring feelings, focusing on the supervisory alliance, normalizing the experience, and exploring countertransference. The overall aim of the Events-Based Model is resolution of conflicts, impairments, and deficits.

GFPS expands and highlights the focus of supervision by including positive events associated with supervisee strengths and successes. GFPS shines a light on positive events that are potentially growth-producing and many times independent of supervisee deficits. Events may include exploration of sequences of interactions when therapy is going well and progress is being made. Beyond exploring the barriers occurring in therapy, GFPS also includes examining the uses of positive transference and countertransference in therapy and in supervision. Countertransference is defined by Gelso, Nutt Williams, and Fretz (2014, p. 233) as "an internal experience of the counselor," and positive countertransference would be positive feelings the counselor has toward the client. The supervisor may also experience positive countertransference toward the supervisee. Such feelings can be helpful in both therapy and supervision if understood and managed appropriately. In a GFPS model that incorporates an Events-Based focus, positive emotions and successes are attended to and celebrated (i.e., capitalization).

Wade and Jones's Strength-Based Supervision Model (2015) describes supervisee growth using Broaden-and-Build Theory. As such, positive emotions and experiences are seen as facilitating growth. In their strength-oriented model, approach goals are formed concerning the supervisee's growth, as well as goals for the supervisee's work with the client. Additionally, skill development is facilitated. In the Strength-Based Supervision Model, if the supervisor focuses exclusively upon negative emotions and deficits of the supervisee, the focus is viewed as expressing avoidance and attacking behavior. Thus, Strength-Based Supervision is oriented toward identifying and improving the strengths of the supervisee. Approach goals are formed to cultivate self-efficacy, resilience, optimism, and hope in the supervisee. Successes and achievements are celebrated. Supervisees are encouraged to develop identity and coherence as therapists. Mindfulness is promoted in the supervisee's work with clients. A strong supervisory alliance is seen as the basis for supervisee development. Supervisee strengths and limitations are equally identified and explored. Narrative techniques are used to formulate questions to be explored in supervision such as the following:

"How can you remind yourself of your competence when you are faced with a difficult situation?"
"Given this goal, what new skills or resources do you need?"
"When you look back at this year's work, what are you most satisfied with?"
(Wade & Jones, 2015, p. 38)

GFPS is an amalgam of the three models of supervision reviewed above. It seeks to (a) balance focus on supervisee deficits and strengths; (b) examine and focus on supervisee successes and positive emotions; and (c) form approach goals and encourage growth toward the goals. We conceptualize trainee growth using the theory of Broaden-and-Build. We strive to help our supervisees gain resources through repeated experiences of momentary positive emotions and celebrating successes so that the supervisee can use past success to constructively address the problems and struggles that inevitably arise in the process of therapist development. In supervision, we also emphasize strength identification. Such experiences can be generalized to the client–therapist context.

GFPS incorporates the IDM developmental insights. Supervisees are encouraged to practice mindfulness at each stage of training to diminish anxiety, self-preoccupation, and dependence. Mindfulness helps trainees identify areas of strength and enables increased capitalization on successes that build self-efficacy and competence in the trainee. Approach goals are formed and updated throughout the GFPS process. For example, the supervisee may desire to achieve congruence between self-identity and the therapeutic approach. Or a supervisee may identify the approach goal of maintaining an authentic and hopeful stance toward the client or portraying a strength orientation by noticing and appreciating positive contributions made in therapy. Each goal could be accompanied by discussions of multiple pathways made up of approach behaviors to accomplish approach goals. Examples of possible pathways include supervisees working to be more fully present (i.e., mindful) in supervision and therapy; savoring and capitalizing on successes when viewing recordings of therapy sessions; practicing self-compassion in supervision and encouraging self-compassion with the client; and fostering trust, openness, and the use of self in the supervisory relationship.

THERAPIST HOPE/CLIENT HOPE

The promotion of client hope is one of the four hallmarks of the GFPP therapeutic approach. In focusing on training therapists in GFPP, this chapter began by explaining that skills are not enough: the therapist must also possess attitudes and beliefs that the psychological change model promoted through GFPP can be effective. In other words, therapists must have hope for success when using GFPP. Several client factors challenge therapists' hope for their clients, such as clients who (a) describe challenging and complex problems; (b) demonstrate very severe problem symptoms; (c) exhibit lack of readiness to understand or change their current position; (d) profess a desire to change yet are unable to act; and (e) seem to lack the necessary human resources to change due to external factors and contexts. Basically, clients may appear so demoralized that happiness seems beyond hope. The extent of this demoralization might convince the therapist to lose hope for the client and for GFPP.

Snyder (2002, p. 249) defined hope as "the perceived capability to derive pathways to desired goals, and motivate oneself via agency thinking to use those pathways." Snyder asserted that the "hope motive" is "the desire to seek goals" (p. 249). Following this definition, a therapist's hope for a client's well-being consists of having therapy goals, therapy methods to reach the goals (i.e., pathways), and a personal ability to use the therapy methods to reach the goals (i.e., agency).

Client hope and therapist hope co-occur. Coppock and colleagues (2010) found a correlation of .46 between therapist hope and client hope in the first sessions and again in the last sessions of therapy. It may be that hope is as contagious as happiness (Fowler & Christakis, 2008)! When the therapist has hope that the client can achieve a happier life, then perhaps the client becomes hopeful as well. Contagion could be bidirectional. Therapist hope for the client should influence the clients to have hope (Parkinson, 2011). Conversely, a demoralized client may convey such a sense of hopelessness that the therapist finds it difficult to envision a better life for the client. For example, some supervisees with whom we have worked have disclosed experiencing difficulty in having hope for their clients from the correctional system who convey hopelessness. When clients foresee only failure and more prison time as possible futures, hope can be difficult. The client's hopeless attitude can influence the therapist to feel it is fruitless to pursue anything better for the client.

A beneficial aspect of GFPP is that it provides hope through a process not tied to the client's current problem state. Hope is derived through understanding that every individual is capable of positive emotions and experiences that broaden him or her to adopt new perspectives and more creative ways of thinking.

Some problems cannot be solved, no matter how creative, brilliant, and dedicated a client is. Does that mean well-being cannot be increased? A GFPP assumption is that well-being can be increased. Victor Frankl's life and writing provides an expression of the belief that well-being can be increased through meaningful values even with the horrors of being imprisoned in a Nazi death camp (Frankl, 1984). Frankl provides an example of hope and inspiration: his value of love

Client problem presentation ➜

Problem validation and demonstrated empathy for client suffering ➜

Identifying and amplifying client strengths ➜

Facilitating and using positive emotions ➜

Identifying and pursuing client desired states ➜

Broadening

Figure 4-3 Therapist hope: paths to the goal of broadening.

provided him with meaning, while his ability to focus on love offered him trea-sured moments of well-being, and—as he stated—bliss.

Attending to the client's problems and well-being through the lens of Broaden-and-Build informs the training of GFPP therapists by providing new avenues to prevent feeling stuck because of a problem description. *Stuckness* here means hitting a wall and feeling powerless to get around it. Sometimes in therapy the therapist hits this wall while trying to identify the problem and find effective treatments for it. GFPP offers a different path marked by strength identification, positive emotions, and approach goals (Fig. 4-3). This path counteracts stuckness and fosters both therapist hope and client hope. Therapist hope can be infectious in its influence on the client (Parkinson, 2011). Hope is important in building therapeutic alliances with clients. Bartholomew, Scheel, and Cole (2015) found that the therapeutic alliance and client hope were significantly and strongly cor-related ($r = .82, p < .001$). Client hope was also significantly negatively correlated with hopelessness ($r = -.58, p < .001$) and client problem symptoms ($r = -.66, p < .001$). It was significantly positively correlated with six dimensions of well-being measured through the Ryff Well-Being Scale (1995) ($r = .44$ to .66). Creating and maintaining hope in therapy not only predicts the therapist–client alliance and client well-being but also exhibits a strong negative relationship to client problems and symptoms.

BUILDING SKILLS

We started this chapter by explaining that training in GFPP requires more than just acquiring skills; effective training necessitates embracing and trusting the GFPP orientation toward change. This section presents the essential skills for GFPP therapists. A detailed explanation of GFPP interventions is provided in Chapter 3 so repetition will be minimized here. The selected skills presented in this section are those that facilitate the therapeutic goal of lessening the focus on the feelings, thoughts, and behaviors that the client wishes to avoid, while increas-ing the focus on the client's values, strengths, and desired experiences (i.e., feel-ings, thoughts, and behaviors). The enhanced therapeutic focus on these assets and aspirations should lead to increased frequency of positive emotions, intrinsic approach goals, pathways (i.e., increased hope), and well-being. The skills section begins with positive empathy.

Positive Empathy

At the top of the list of essential skills is the use of positive empathy. *Positive empathy* is sensing and communicating the client's unspoken message of desire for a better life that is hidden behind the client statement of distress or dissatisfaction (Conoley & Conoley, 2009). The positive empathy process links the client's problem to an approach goal that is based upon what the client wants instead of the problem. Then the client explores possible pathways to the goal, thereby fostering hope. Thus the skill of positive empathy uses the client's problem statement to understand the client. Then, through the empathic connection, the therapist can tentatively communicate the client's desired state and ask about pathways for reaching that state.

The client often accesses three hallmarks of GFPP as a result of the positive empathy process: the client reveals strengths, identifies approach goals, and experiences positive emotions (Conoley et al., 2015). In addition, hope *for* the client can appear through the use of positive empathy. For example, a client might communicate, "I let my boyfriend treat me so badly. It makes me feel cheap and unworthy." The GFPP therapist first uses traditional empathy to communicate understanding of the client's experience: "You are really struggling in your relationship. You feel like you are allowing your boyfriend to make you feel less than you are." Traditional empathy is followed by the therapist's expression of positive empathy based on the client's healthy hidden desire, which the therapist empathically experiences as explained below. Successful positive empathy results in the client's view of the same experience changing from signaling a problem to communicating a desire. Positive empathy reframes the perspective of the same experience from an entirely negative experience to an experience revealing the client's positive desires (see Chapter 3 for more on reframing). The client's change from a problematic experience to a desired state can also be described as *flipping*. The therapist could flip or turn around the client's stated experience of "feeling cheap and unworthy" to see what the statement might mean that the client desires. When the client states feeling "cheap and unworthy," what does the client really want but has not expressed or perhaps not even clearly considered? Is the client's statement indicating that she wants respect? Or does she want to feel good about herself in interactions with others? Perhaps she wants to stand up for herself in relationships? The therapist's statement of positive empathy might communicate any of these thoughts, all of which convey a healthy client desired state that fits the client's context. The therapist's tentative delivery of the positive empathy statement allows the client to accept or reject the therapist's empathic interpretation. If the client rejects the therapist's statement of what the client might desire, then the therapist asks for clarification from the client so that the therapist can understand better. The best approach is to accept the client's rejection even if the therapist feels certain that the client should accept the positive empathy statement!

If the client accepts the positive empathy statement, then asking follow-up questions helps concretize the approach goals suggested in the conversation, such as, "So that is what you want. You want to feel respected. That is your goal." State several times what the client revealed as desirous: the approach goal. Then, if the client is agreeable, celebrate the client's accomplishment. The client has made an important step! Support the growing hope by emphasizing that setting an approach goal is significant progress. Linking the approach goal back to the problem or to an important client value can help communicate the significance of the accomplishment. Asking the client to make the connection between the goal and the problem or values allows the client to experience competence in accomplishing progress and to integrate enhanced self-understanding. For example, the therapist might say, "Great! So how will feeling respected help you to feel less cheap?" While the answer may be completely clear to the therapist, when in the middle of negative emotions, thinking clearly is difficult. Asking the client to sort through the connection can support the client's reclamation of strengths.

If the approach goal is very broad and perhaps vague, like the goal of wanting to feel respected, then the broad goal should be delineated into more specific sub-goals. In order to construct clear sub-goals, the therapist could ask the client to explore all the ways in which feeling respected might happen. Enhanced clarity of the approach goal can also occur by asking about pathways to the goal that can increase hope. For example: "How can feeling respected happen more often for you?" The answer can reveal the client's personal and specific meanings of feeling respected.

An additional response is to engage in success-finding, as detailed in Chapter 3. The therapist might ask the client, "Tell me about the last time you felt respected, or a little respected." The description of the context and interactions surrounding the success or partial success will reveal the existing strengths that can be built upon to achieve the approach goal of respect.

In summary, the meta-goal of GFPP is for clients to have happier lives. A meta-position for a positive empathy scenario would be that clients come to therapy identifying elements of unhappiness in their lives. A simplified map of therapeutic progression could be that the GFPP therapist demonstrates empathy for the client's statement of unhappiness, identifies the unstated desire for happiness, develops approach goals from the client's newly explicit desire, and explores pathways to achieve the approach goals on which the therapist and client have collaboratively agreed.

Highlighting Client Values

Another essential skill of GFPP lies in *highlighting the client's values*, which are often embedded within the client's goals. Values typically come from the client's family, culture, and society, but are ultimately interpreted and influenced by the individual. SDT describes a process in which societal and cultural values become transformed into personally endorsed values for an individual. However, this transformation does not always occur (Deci & Ryan, 2008), so do not assume that a client fully embraces a goal that fits with societal or cultural values unless the client has accepted the value personally.

Chapter 2 described the ways in which intrinsic goal contents contribute more to well-being over a longer period of time than extrinsic goal contents (Kasser & Ryan, 1996). Intrinsic goals address personal growth, healthy relationships, and contributing to worthy social issues. However, clients may identify healthy approach goals with intrinsic goal content that is problematic because the goal is not freely chosen (i.e., not autonomous). The value represented in the goal is not really the client's value, but rather an imposed value. The client may have been lured toward, or felt coerced in, selecting the goal. For example, goals that are not autonomously chosen can be achieving approval, gaining rewards, or avoiding punishment. Goals with unendorsed, not freely accepted, values embedded in them have much less chance of success because the person's motivation is comparatively low and, if accomplished, the experience of well-being is brief (Deci & Ryan, 2008).

Non-autonomously selected goals occur often with younger clients. In a high school dropout prevention program, that incorporates GFPP concepts directed by one of the authors, ninth-grade clients often identify non-autonomously selected goals with unendorsed values. For example, a ninth-grade client with a history of school failure and uncooperativeness identified an approach goal of getting all A's at the beginning of a new year. While achieving perfect grades is a desirable approach goal that fits societal and cultural norms, the values represented in the goal probably were not the client's values but an imposed value from the school, parents, and teachers. The GFPP therapist searches for the endorsed value that the young student may have for doing better in school so that the goal can be transformed into one that is autonomously selected. SDT (Deci & Ryan, 2008) suggests that relatedness, competence, and autonomy are basic psychological needs worth exploring with clients. An endorsed value might be the client's desire to feel more competent or more accepted at school (i.e., relatedness). Exploring these values as the basis for motivation to support clients can increase the client's chances for success. A client acquiescing to pressures such as rewards, punishments, seeking approval, avoiding shame, or feeding ego-driven quests for self-esteem will likely experience diminished motivation. Frequently acquiescing to external pressures over a long period of time can make it difficult for clients to recognize and articulate their own personally important, autonomously endorsed values. The challenge for the GFPP therapist is to help the client find the endorsed values that will motivate goal-directed action and support long-term well-being.

Often, endorsed values appear when identifying client strengths. For instance, a young adolescent client may choose to do better in school after discovering a personal strength. Students in the Building Bridges program routinely complete the Values In Action assessment (VIA; Park, Peterson, & Seligman, 2004) to assist them in identifying their strengths. Many of the VIA strengths—such as zest, creativity, love of learning, honesty, or some other of the 24 character strengths—fit well with school-related goals. Discussing the VIA-identified strengths with the student uncovers associated values. The student's sense of autonomy increases when using an endorsed value that is freely chosen rather than coerced, and knowing the endorsed values makes them more influential during client decision-making processes. Thus, in GFPP we work with the client to develop approach goals that are tied to the client's endorsed values in order to enhance motivation (Deci & Ryan, 2008) and hope. The GFPP therapist works to form autonomously chosen approach goals that fit with the client's endorsed values and strengths.

Identifying Client Strengths

The formal and informal identification of client strengths is also an essential skill in training GFPP therapists. Structured identification of strengths comes from an assessment tool such as the VIA (Park, Peterson, & Seligman, 2004). Interpersonal identification occurs when the therapist vigilantly and purposefully listens for client strengths during therapy. GFPP therapists are continually alert to client strengths that emerge throughout therapy. A fundamental GFPP assumption is that all clients possess strengths. Some clients are less privileged in life than others, often making their strengths comparatively less apparent than their deficits. Therapists can use several approaches to facilitate the client's revelation of strengths. Perhaps the most obvious is simply asking clients what strengths they see in themselves or what a friend might say about the client's strengths. Strength identification starts during the intake and continues throughout therapy. Typically, intake interviews concentrate on the client's presenting problems and the history of all the client's problems and symptoms. During the intake interview, GFPP therapists balance asking the client about problems and deficits with asking about personal strengths and strengths accessible in the immediate environment.

Opportunities to identify client strengths occur continuously throughout therapy based upon the seemingly infinite source of client strengths. The strengths inherent in the client's racial, ethnic, and cultural identities are often helpful to explore. Resilience and courage in the midst of the client's struggles are emphasized, becoming a source of pride—which is a positive emotion—rather than shame. Pursuing therapy is a courageous act, a means of taking back control, and a strength. One frequently emphasized strength is the client's willingness to trust the therapist—an unknown person—to form a therapeutic relationship. The client–therapist relationship provides a fertile context for building upon the client strengths of interpersonal bravery and insights, which can then generalize to other relationships in the client's life. Areas that are going well for the client are celebrated through capitalization and viewed as strengths. The technique of positive reframing is used to identify strengths embedded within problem contexts (e.g., the anxiety of a traumatized client is viewed as a means of protection from re-traumatization). Past successes are viewed as strengths to be remembered and developed. The client's awareness of self and others is highlighted as a strength that is applicable across multiple contexts. The abilities that a client uses to make gains inside and outside of therapy are strengths to be replicated and built on. As you see, there are many opportunities for therapists to identify and amplify client strengths if the therapist is attuned to those strengths and committed to making them explicit in therapy.

Developing the habit of noticing strengths automatically is important. The skill of noticing strengths could begin by examining people's self-disclosures of troubles on self-help websites. Underlining the strengths revealed by the self-statements is helpful practice. Also, practicing by noticing the strengths revealed in conversations with friends and family helps. Paraphrasing strengths and celebrating statements revealing success in conversations is excellent practice as well as a way to create wonderful relational side effects!

Promoting Positive Emotions

Another essential element of GFPP training is *promoting positive emotions*. Many tools are available to the therapist to facilitate the client's use of positive emotions. Before enumerating some of the ways to facilitate clients' access to their positive emotions, we will address several unhelpful myths about positive emotions:

1. The client will not be able to experience positive emotions because of the problems and pain.
2. Highlighting and encouraging positive emotions when a client is suffering minimizes or denies the client's lived experience.
3. As the therapist, you must be a comedian; the only useful positive emotion is joy.
4. Negative emotions are denigrated when focusing upon positive emotions.

These myths are—from our perspective—critical misunderstandings and will be discussed in the next paragraphs.

Fortunately, orienting toward positive emotions and experiences is not a complicated therapy process. More complicated is the timing and balance of focusing upon negative and positive emotions. Initially and also throughout therapy, a client will desire to share upsetting experiences. The GFPP therapist respects the client's need to be heard. The client typically needs an upsetting experience to be validated. The GFPP therapist listens and responds with respect for the client's suffering: "That must have been very painful." When the time is right, the therapist inquires, "How do you deal with that?" The question reminds the client that the painful experience is being dealt with and can potentially be a source of positive emotions for the client: pride perhaps. The client probably wishes to have another way to deal with the problem, which can lead to an approach goal. In respecting or validating the client's negative emotions, the GFPP therapist does not necessarily deepen the conversation by asking questions or paraphrasing the statements about the pain. The complicated shifting of the conversation between the painful and positive emotions occurs cyclically through the therapy sessions. The client does not all at once become focused entirely upon only positive emotions. Indeed, an exclusive focus upon only positive or negative is not healthy. As negative issues surface, several paths exist to avoid minimizing the pain or shame: the chosen path toward positive emotions depends on the client's readiness. The positive emotion may be momentary and bookended by negative emotions. Remember, only a momentary positive emotion is required for Broaden-and-Build.

The technique of positive empathy attends to the client's experience of both the negative and the positive emotions. The therapist focuses upon the experience that the client expresses in the moment and attempts to help the client understand the experience at a deeper level. Initially, the therapist attends to the expressed problem by paraphrasing (i.e., repeating back the spoken content) the client's problem or pain, until the therapist senses that the client is ready to hear the client's hidden desire that may reside behind the spoken content. If the client accepts the empathic insight of the therapist about the hidden desire, the client often experiences a positive emotion, while also identifying an approach goal and revealing strengths (Conoley et al., 2015).

Fortunately, most clients *want* to experience positive emotions, and this is a wonderful advantage for GFPP over many other therapy models! Typically clients seek therapy because they are unhappy and desire to be happier. The GFPP theory of change, Broaden-and-Build, focuses upon the importance of positive emotions. Brief positive emotions support problem-solving, engaging, exploring, experimenting, playing, and creative thinking (Fredrickson, 2001). The broadening function of positive emotions opens the individual up to consider a larger repertoire of possibilities. The client is assisted in increasing the frequency of positive emotions rather than the magnitude of the emotional intensity (Diener, Sandvik, & Pavot, 1991). Understandably, the client often wants to experience a very large dose of positive emotions immediately (as do we all), but long-term happiness occurs in small, frequent doses of positive emotions.[1] Therefore, clients are encouraged to find ways to engage in experiences that create positive emotions while simultaneously supporting the client's values and goals. For example, helping a client engage in gratitude interventions not only sets the stage for Broaden-and-Build but also supports the value of gratitude. Performing tasks that support values can contribute to the client experiencing a meaningful life (Baumeister, Vohs, Aaker, & Garbinsky, 2013)!

Chapter 3 presented many therapeutic techniques and interventions available to a GFPP therapist. While reviewing these resources, be sure to remember that the most important skill of all is *to be responsive to the client*. For instance, if a client is experiencing shame, the therapist assesses the client's readiness for change and the client's trust in the therapeutic relationship. Is the client ready to join with the therapist in a time-consuming, effortful intervention? In describing an intervention, the therapist must understand the client's worldview to present an acceptable rationale for how the intervention will help (Conoley et al., 1991, 1994; Scheel et al., 1998, 1999). When the client is ready, then the client might learn self-compassion, or only selected components of the complex intervention. Self-compassion contains acts of self-kindness, attending to what is right in the client's life, learning mindfulness to reduce the pain of ruminations as well as to increase feelings of positive emotions, and realizing that the client's negative experiences are similar to everyone's (i.e., common humanity; Neff, 2003). We routinely encourage clients to practice at least some components of self-compassion, loving-kindness meditation, or gratitude interventions. We often use encouragement to build hope and to help clients attend to the positive occurrences in their lives. When clients reveal successes, GFPP therapists celebrate these revelations to maximize the benefits of capitalization. GFPP therapists also want clients to savor positive emotions. Clients are also encouraged to regularly plan pleasurable times in their days—to engage in activities giving them enjoyment. Many opportunities exist for helping clients experience more frequent positive emotions. Positive emotions are even more valuable when experienced in the context of values and goals because the resulting well-being that is often produced can be more enduring.

Mindfulness

The last essential skill we note of GFPP therapists is *mindfulness*. Mindfulness is probably an essential skill for all therapists, no matter what their psychotherapy model. Mindfulness meditation by therapists has been found to promote self-compassion (Shapiro, Astin, Bishop, & Cordova, 2005; Shapiro, Brown, & Biegel, 2007) and more empathy for the client (Aiken, 2006; Shapiro, Schwartz, & Bonner, 1998; Wang, 2007). With mindfulness training, trainees become more attuned with themselves and their clients, more comfortable with silence, less reactive, more reflective, and more attentive during therapy (Davis & Hayes, 2011). Overall, the integration of mindfulness practices in therapist training is associated with improvements in the skills of the trainees (Newsome, Christopher, Dahlen, & Christopher, 2006; Schure, Christopher, & Christopher, 2008). We see mindfulness meditation by therapists as particularly helpful in GFPP, helping therapists to model mindfulness for their clients, to have more moment-to-moment presence, to notice client strengths and positive emotions when these occur, and to develop a stronger therapeutic alliance with their clients. Without mindfulness, a therapist can become too focused on what to do next in therapy or on performing a technique perfectly. Empathy toward the client and relationship formation suffer from a lack of therapist mindfulness.

Mindfulness meditation can be an integral part of a GFPP therapist's training. Experiencing mindfulness helps therapists gain greater awareness of their own positivity, experienced in the form of emotions, strengths, and approach goals. Through the therapist's experience of mindfulness, the client can be understood more richly, and the client's experience of learning mindfulness meditation can be facilitated.

ASSESSMENT

Supporting the training and practice of GFPP is the client's assessment of the therapy session and the client's experience of well-being during the week. The Partners for Change Outcome Management System[2] (PCOMS), a two-minute paper-and-pencil assessment, is an effective client feedback system that gives the client a clear voice in therapy about whether progress is being made and the quality of the therapy session (Duncan & Reese, 2015). The therapist can compare the client's level of well-being across the weeks to see if the client is improving (as described in the case example at the beginning of this chapter). Similarly, examining the client's opinions of the sessions can be graphed over time so that the therapist can know whether the current session was better or worse from the client's perspective. Based upon the scores, the therapist can ask the client follow-up questions to learn from the client how to be as helpful as possible.

The Outcome Rating Scale (ORS) and the Session Rating Scale (SRS) are part of PCOMS (Miller & Duncan, 2004). At the beginning of each session, the client answers the four-item ORS (Miller & Duncan, 2000), which indicates the client's perception of the past week's well-being. The questions ask clients to rate their functioning individually (i.e., personal well-being), interpersonally (i.e., family, close relationships), socially (i.e., work, school, friends), and finally overall (i.e., general sense of well-being). The ORS informs the therapist immediately of concerns, and graphing the results over time reveals whether the client is progressing. If the client does not progress, then the therapist can rethink how to proceed in therapy.

At the end of the therapy session, the client completes the four-item SRS (Miller, Duncan, & Johnson, 2000), which measures the client's opinion of the just-completed therapy session. The SRS asks the client about the therapeutic relationship (i.e., feeling heard, understood, and respected), the goals and topics covered in the session (i.e., working on and talking about what was important), the approach or method used in therapy (i.e., the approach used in the session was a good fit), and the session overall (i.e., the session was right today). The SRS is based upon the therapeutic alliance (Bordin, 1979), which is highly predictive of psychotherapy success (e.g., Martin, Garske, & Davis, 2000).

Detailed information in the use of the measures can be found in the PCOMS manual (Miller & Duncan, 2004). The use of the ORS and SRS in the PCOMS system has been found to improve the therapy outcome regardless of the psychotherapy approach used (Miller et al., 2003; Miller, Duncan, Sorrell, & Brown, 2005; Reese, Norsworthy, & Rowlands, 2009). The use of the ORS and SRS in training GFPP therapists allows the client to have a clear voice in communicating the success of therapy and the value of a particular session.

CONCLUSION

This chapter described both attitudinal and skill components necessary for training GFPP therapists. GFPS was introduced as the training model that we recommend to assist therapists in becoming adept and effective as GFPP therapists. We emphasized that GFPP therapists must be committed to a GFPP orientation for human change (i.e., the psychological science metaphor) in contrast to a physical science metaphor. This means the therapist must do the following:

- Have a strengths-based focus;
- Be committed to well-being as the primary goal of therapy;
- Use client-endorsed values to orient therapy;
- Form approach goals based on client-desired states (rather than avoidance goals);
- Have confidence in the benefits of expressing both positive and negative emotions;
- Be resolute in the pursuit of positive emotional experiences;
- Help clients form an identity based on their strengths; and
- Genuinely demonstrate hope for clients and for GFPP therapy.

We also emphasized the importance of the reciprocal and contagious qualities of therapist hope and client hope. We offered arguments for why GFPP therapists can take the lead in being hopeful, and we explained hope as the foundation of the therapeutic process and the change phenomenon of broadening. Skills of GFPP that we view as essential include (a) positive empathy, (b) finding the client's personal value of a goal, (c) identifying client strengths, (d) promoting positive emotions, and (e) mindfulness meditation.

In Chapter 5, we offer four case studies demonstrating the application of GFPP.

5

Goal Focused Positive Psychotherapy Case Examples

CASE AUTHORS IN ORDER OF APPEARANCE:
EVELYN WINTER PLUMB, ROBERT BYROM,
THEODORE T. BARTHOLOMEW, AND KATE HAWLEY ■

This chapter presents four case examples, written by therapists trained in the Goal Focused Positive Psychotherapy (GFPP) approach. Each therapist was asked to write a summary description of using GFPP with a client. The case examples illustrate the use of key GFPP principles. As you read through each case, notice how each therapist pays attention to client problems, promotes client motivation, and provides a balanced approach between attending to client strengths and concerns. These applications of GFPP depict an approach that is not mechanistic or linear in delivery. The therapist forms a relationship with the client based upon the client's concerns, attitudes, trust, and aspirations. Strengths are identified in the midst of the client revealing significant problems. The techniques of identifying approach goals and eliciting positive emotions are utilized based on client readiness for these important aspects of GFPP. The therapist's approach fits the client's concerns and strengths. The client's initial concerns form the foundation for the strength-oriented work that the therapist builds with the client. Each therapist uses techniques such as positive empathy to identify the client's desires. Client desires are understood to be in juxtaposition with client difficulties. GFPP is used within the context that each individual client presents. Client contexts can be conceptualized as comprising client problems, complaints, and difficulties, along with client strengths, assets, and cultures.

A therapist mindset of belief in and commitment to the GFPP psychological model of human change toward well-being appears in each of the case examples. Each case demonstrates a therapist in tune with the client and the client's needs. Each case also depicts a turning point in which the client becomes more motivated and committed to the therapeutic process. In two of the cases, client safety is a particularly salient issue that is emphasized with plans to ensure client harm will not occur. Each case exemplifies a different way that a client can express reluctance to participate fully in therapy. In every case, the therapist responds by focusing on client strengths and desired states to promote client motivation. Additionally, the therapists gather clear descriptions of client problems and complaints. The change efforts, however, center on strength identification, approach goals, and promotion of positive emotions. The theory of Broaden-and-Build works well in each case as a framework to conceptualize client change.

A brief analysis follows each case presentation. The end of the chapter contains a qualitative analysis of the cases highlighting the common threads and distinctive features of the four cases.

CASE #1: THE RELUCTANT CLIENT, BY EVELYN WINTER PLUMB

Case Presentation

Peter—a heterosexual, cisgender Caucasian male in his late 30s—came to counseling at the behest of his partner, Wendy. Following Peter's disclosure of a brief incident of infidelity, Wendy gave the ultimatum that in order to "salvage" their relationship, he needed to attend counseling to "figure out who he is and why he does the things he does," and also to help him find a steady job after several years of sporadic underemployment. Accordingly, Peter's recalcitrance during his first session was reminiscent of the defiance of a mandated client: he seemed to be attending "under orders" as a way to placate his partner rather than out of a sincere desire for change. In outlining his expectations for therapy, he described treatment as "mandatory saying-my-feelings-out-loud time," and in response to my initial inquiries about his hopes and goals for treatment, he stated, "I'm just along for the ride." Consequently, the first step in treatment was an effort to engage him on his own terms, drawing on his strengths and values to cultivate motivation and meaningful goals for treatment. A fitting challenge for GFPP!

Much as one might do with a mandated client, I began by acknowledging that treatment was not Peter's idea, but that while he was "serving his time," we might as well see what we might do about enhancing a life that he described as "just fine the way it is." His stated goals during the first session included vague avoidant themes of "getting a job so I can stop stressing about money" and "proving to Wendy that I'm not going to cheat on her again." With my facilitation, Peter identified several meaningful personal strengths, including his affinity for teaching (he had previously served in a variety of temporary tutoring/mentoring positions and described "inspiring the students and connecting with them on a personal level" as a source of satisfaction in previous positions); his appreciation of nature; his creativity and artistic talents as a recreational musician; and a supportive family of which he felt "very lucky" to be a member.

The first several sessions focused on identifying and amplifying sources of motivation in order to instill hope, increase flexibility, and galvanize commitment to treatment. A major theme that emerged during this phase was Peter's emphatic aversion to a constellation of factors that patently narrowed his options for employment, including bureaucracy, paperwork, authority, corporate institutions, structure, and generally planning for the future. He spent much time in his initial sessions opining on the difficulty of finding a job at his level of qualification that would not rob him of his identity. In describing such jobs, Peter used expressions such as "alienation of labor," "soul-sucking routines with no creativity," and "colluding with 'The Man.'" His detailed and poetic musings on this series of topics earned him the nickname "Peter Pan" from the supervisorial staff and established an ongoing therapeutic motif in which he became notably intractable in response to directive or otherwise structured approaches to treatment. He additionally noted that his "plan for the future has always felt like just a backup plan" and that "planning ahead doesn't really work out well anyway." An auxiliary challenge to securing employment was Peter's resistance to using technology as part of his job search: he expressed a loathing for computers in general and the internet in particular, and he vehemently asserted that "online job postings are my absolute last choice." The abundance of avoidance goals featured in this litany presented a clear starting point for enhancing positive affect, hope, and motivation.

Thus, an early task was to establish client-congruent vocational approach goals, which I initially facilitated by using positive empathy and success-finding to identify qualities of previous jobs that had inspired Peter to feel invested in and inspired by his work. The best-possible-self exercise was then introduced to consolidate the themes evident in his "Dream Job," which Peter identified as "running an organic homesteading farm where I could teach people how to grow and make their own food and supplies." Through this process, Peter was able to establish that he felt more motivated, hopeful, and willing to persist through job-search challenges when he sought positions that were "creative, outdoorsy, independent, non-traditional, healthy, flexible" and "involved teaching or mentoring others in important skills." He expressed a sense of satisfaction upon discovering that these qualities aligned felicitously with the personal strengths that he and I had explored during earlier sessions.

The week after this session, Peter arrived to treatment with several job applications in hand (several of which he had located online!) that he identified as fitting these criteria, including positions at a natural history museum, a native plant nursery, and a local health food co-op. This was the first time that Peter had proactively brought clear goals and successes into treatment, and he introduced these materials by exclaiming, "I've been looking forward to showing these to you."

Peter and I practiced capitalization by celebrating his job-hunting progress, which led to an exploration of the ways in which he shared important news with Wendy. Up until this point, Peter had been reticent about discussing his feelings about his partner, but in the wake of his excitement over gaining momentum in his job-search process, he disclosed freely for the first time about his fears concerning the relationship, including their lack of communication. After exploring the values and virtues that undergirded these fears, Peter reoriented his original avoidance goal of "proving that I'm not going to cheat on her again" to "building trust" and "recapturing some of the fun and playfulness from when we first started dating." He agreed that one incremental step toward these goals would be to purposefully practice capitalization with Wendy, both by sharing his good news and by expressively savoring her good news.

As treatment progressed, Peter continued to open up about subjects on which he had previously proven tight-lipped, including his concerns about his future with Wendy and his apprehensions about communicating his feelings to her, and also his sense of sorrow and loss concerning the deaths of several beloved friends and family members. In a session in which he brought in the lyrics to several songs that he had written (a tactic that predictably elicited considerable positive affect as he proudly shared several of his "favorite pieces" with me), Peter was able to identify the ways in which the love he felt for the deceased inspired him to "create heartfelt music" and lead "a more real, raw, life." After a brief exploration of posttraumatic growth and an exercise in which he envisioned what he hoped to accomplish before his own passing, he was able to independently tie these sentiments to his increasingly clear goals concerning both his ideal job and his plans to cultivate a warm, trusting, and open relationship with Wendy. In sharing these hopes, he spontaneously pointed out that his aversion to planning for the future "kind of gets in the way sometimes" of working toward these types of long-term goals, and expressed openness to "maybe committing to a few things—the important things," in order to reach his vision of a meaningful life.

In his penultimate session, Peter brought in the lyrics to a song that he had written for Wendy, in which he expressed his appreciation for her and communicated his hopes for their future together. He subsequently reported that this creation was "quite a hit" with Wendy.

In his final session, Peter reflected on his growth during treatment. He noted that while the job that he had secured was "definitely not the Dream Job," he was now satisfied to work in a position that fit "the most important criteria" in order to incrementally approach his other goals of contributing financially to his relationship, having enough money to "go on last-minute adventures," acquiring skills and experience valuable for future enterprises, and saving money in order to build toward the bona fide Dream Job. He laughed while stating, "I guess [treatment] was more useful than I thought it was going to be," and expressed disappointment that his new work schedule would prevent further sessions with me. Before leaving, Peter assured me that I would be welcome any time at his homesteading farm to learn how to make hard apple cider, "once I get that Dream Job up and running."

Analysis of Case #1

Peter's change in motivation was dramatic over the course of 12 sessions, from a defiant and sarcastic presentation to an enthusiastic, active, autonomously oriented participant in a process of self-exploration. To counter the client's reluctance, therapy was adapted to meet his readiness to use therapy. Strength identification helped the client begin an internal examination. In highlighting the client's strengths, the therapist also increased the client's motivation for exploring goals, the future, and his relationships. The therapist adopted Peter's position that therapy was not his idea, but also introduced the concept that the client could gain something from the experience anyway. Following the GFPP model, the therapist had no need to identify a problem or focus on possible feelings of guilt or shame that Peter may have secretly experienced. Thus, the therapist did not directly address the client's transgressions in his relationship because in the GFPP model, focusing on the problem does not lead to what the client wants—especially when the client does not want to focus on the problem! Attempting to extract an admission of guilt would most likely lead to defensiveness, defiance, and leaving therapy. Fortunately, GFPP is an excellent approach for mandated clients or, in Peter's case, clients who come to therapy at someone else's request.

Consequently, the therapist immediately moved toward strength identification, and the client was open to and perhaps needed the support. The therapist followed the client's lead in identifying a problem on his terms: that of finding an appropriate job that met his values and preferences. This focus led to a series of avoidance goals by Peter: jobs and occupational constraints that Peter wanted to stay away from. The avoidance goals provided the therapist with a starting point to employ positive empathy, success-finding, and the best-possible-self intervention to discover Peter's desired states and to identify approach goals. Peter's initial desired state took the form of his ideal job.

Settling on Peter's approach goal of finding an ideal job cemented the alliance and promoted Peter's autonomy in using his values, thereby facilitating his motivation. Each cooperative move was viewed as a strength of Peter's and celebrated (i.e., capitalization). Capitalization provides an opportunity to savor success and experience positive emotions. Positive emotions trigger broadening that can lead to building, and this was the case for Peter. Peter's broadening allowed him to talk about his relationship difficulties and become more flexible in his job pursuit. Peter accepted a not-ideal job and applied in a less-than-ideal manner, via the internet. At the same time, the therapist helped Peter to use incremental steps to improve his relationship and perhaps win back Wendy's trust. Peter demonstrated his trust of the therapist and therapy as he used capitalization with his partner. Perhaps because of the successful relationship with the therapist, Peter opened up more and more to Wendy about his feelings toward her. The client's sharing of his songs, an activity chosen by him, was particularly helpful in producing positive emotions. Perhaps Peter's courage to become more deeply intimate in his relationship with Wendy was supported by his increased well-being. His song of love for Wendy was his own strategy for solving his problem.

Peter came into therapy as a reluctant client unmotivated to work on the problems of his relationship. His demeanor, motivation, and focus transformed as a relationship grew, built upon finding his strengths, moving toward approach goals, and experiencing positive emotions. The therapist followed Peter's lead in the directions therapy took but stayed in control of the process of highlighting strengths and promoting positive emotions. Peter autonomously chose to discuss improving his relationship and obtaining a job as the processes of GFPP and the therapeutic relationship developed.

CASE #2: MUCH TOO MUCH FOR MUCH TOO LONG, BY ROBERT BYROM

Case Presentation

Maggie was an undergraduate junior who identified as a White bisexual woman and sought counseling to help her handle a variety of life stressors. From her perspective, the main goal for therapy was finding motivation to complete anything, whether that meant academically or socially. She reported receiving a number of diagnoses in the past. She was taking multiple prescription medications to ameliorate the symptoms of the diagnoses with limited success. Re-entering into therapy, she discussed wanting to resolve her motivation difficulties and her suicidal ideation. She reported that her suicidal ideation had been a part of her life "for as long as I can remember." She described several previous suicide attempts, explaining that the thought of killing herself was perpetually on her mind. Using the technique of success-finding helped identify times she did not experience these suicidal thoughts. The times she remembered being free of suicidal thoughts were when she smoked marijuana or used other substances. During our intake session, Maggie said that the one thing she wanted more than anything else was "to not feel this way anymore."

Despite what felt like an overwhelming inability to find motivation to handle life tasks (e.g., completing course assignments, studying, participating in social activities), Maggie demonstrated a considerable number of strengths in therapy. One salient strength identified early in our work together was her persistence, evidenced by how she consistently attended counseling sessions. This consistency allowed us to distinguish between feeling "not this way" (an avoidance goal) and wanting to actually feel centered, autonomous, and self-caring (an approach goal). Contrasting her stated lack of interest in many other life roles, in session Maggie was respectful, thoughtful, and engaged. Maggie seemed comfortable guiding the pace and direction of the therapy hour. She initially credited her consistent effort in therapy to wanting to achieve her future goal of becoming a counselor in order to help others with similar problems. Later she attributed her effort in therapy to the comfort she felt in the sessions caused by the focus on her successes rather than her failures. The comfort helped her begin to challenge previous thought patterns.

Even though she engaged meaningfully in therapy, the number of concerns she faced created initial doubt in me about whether our work could significantly help her. Our first few sessions were dominated by reports of the previous week's difficulties, which included decreasing grades, loss of medical support equating to facing (for the first time in many years) her emotional difficulties without familiar assistance, and the eventual loss of a romantic relationship that amounted to much of her support system. In short, Maggie felt like her life was in perpetual crisis, and we mutually agreed that our work together felt at times more like damage control than anything else. Maggie had come to expect much of her life to be one crisis after another. During the first part of the session, when supporting her pain from the problems of the week, we began to discuss a pattern of how Maggie applied her strengths (e.g., kindness, love, creativity) toward others and rarely to herself. Once the damage-control portion of the session had been addressed, we explored what it would be like for her to express concern for herself (i.e., be kind to herself) in the same way that she would for her loved ones (i.e., self-compassion). A major topic of the later sessions focused on applying her strengths of creativity and love toward herself. A surprising chain of events led to her finally being able to apply these strengths to her own life.

A critical moment in our work occurred when concerns about a possible repeat suicide attempt became apparent and the police were called to intervene in order to perform a safety check. In a session prior to this crisis, Maggie described her feelings of anger and frustration for someone calling the police "on her." However, the following exchange occurred after the police performed a safety check:

Maggie: I guess I'm just feeling angry with them because . . . I don't know . . . like I guess at this point I love myself enough to not kill myself . . . I don't understand why they think I'm going to kill myself, like I'm going to be OK, like there's some hope that I can make it through this and that I don't need the [redacted] cops to come ask me how I'm doing, though I guess I'm grateful that someone cares enough to do that for me.

Therapist: That sounds like a powerful experience, especially considering some of the things we've discussed up until now. What is it like for you to be able to say you love yourself and have hope for your future?

Maggie: I don't know . . . it's the first time I've looked at myself and really felt like I'm worthy of anything good. It's different, it just feels different.

At the time, I experienced the conversation as revealing a great irony that Maggie would find the ability to articulate love and hope for herself with great clarity in one of our last sessions during such a tumultuous series of events. Especially since all of this occurred while she was considering taking an extended leave of absence from her academic career, working on coping with a variety of diagnoses without medication for the first time in her life, adjusting to the loss of her longest romantic partner, and a variety of other significant difficulties. Looking back, though, the various factors that changed dramatically in Maggie's life may have also afforded her the opportunity to examine herself and treat herself in novel ways.

In summary, this client who was facing what she had previously considered insurmountable challenges was able to facilitate positive change in her life.

Through GFPP she moved toward her desired states by establishing approach goals; identifying, amplifying, and continuously seeking ways to apply her strengths toward reaching her approach goals; and generating positive emotions in her day-to-day life. Continued practice led Maggie to see herself as worthy of love and provided some personal hope for the future.

Analysis of Case #2

This case example describes a client, Maggie, who was very motivated to discontinue a chronic pattern of depression and suicidal ideation. She demonstrated great resolve to be different! Maggie described a long maladaptive history of coping with suicidal thoughts. The suicidal ideation was particularly worrisome because this client had previously attempted suicide multiple times. Early in the therapy process, the therapist sought to understand when Maggie's problems were less present or absent using the success-finding technique. This illuminated a maladaptive way of coping through the use of marijuana. Maggie was mostly oriented toward avoidance goals and avoidance behaviors (i.e., procrastination and marijuana).

The therapist framed the client's persistent motivation to feel "not this way" as a strength, and used positive empathy to refocus on the client's desired states and approach goals (i.e., feeling centered, autonomous, and self-caring). Initially, the therapist struggled to have hope for a client who described a long litany of concerns occurring consistently over an extended period of time. Many of their sessions focused on crisis intervention and problem-solving. In the early sessions, the client was feeling anything but autonomous, centered, and able to take care of herself.

A significant shift occurred when the therapist pointed out that Maggie used her strengths of kindness and caring for others but not herself. Maggie was ready to hear the message and trusted the authenticity of the therapist. As she engaged in a self-compassion intervention, the positive emotions Maggie experienced broadened her toward attending to her personal needs. The therapist also facilitated Maggie's growth by encouraging her to experience positive emotions during her day-to-day activities. A critical event in helping her to turn the corner on her old destructive patterns of coping occurred when she reacted in anger to the realization that a stranger had called police out of concern for Maggie's safety. The incident helped Maggie realize her self-worth and ability to love herself. The overall outcome of therapy was increased well-being and greater hope for the future.

CASE #3: SEEKING MEANING AND CONNECTION, BY THEODORE T. BARTHOLOMEW

Case Presentation

Rebecca was a 22-year-old, heterosexual, Black woman. She was an engineering major at a large public university and employed full-time in a stressful job.

Rebecca, who had never received mental health care previously, was referred to the university counseling center by a campus physician. During her medical visit, she reported depressed affect and suicidal ideation to her physician. Her physician immediately referred Rebecca to the counseling center, and Rebecca was brought for an urgent session. During the session, she exhibited flat affect— "I don't know" was her most frequent response—and was reluctant to engage in therapy, stating on multiple occasions that she felt "obligated to be there." She was uncertain how long she had been depressed but made it clear that this was an ongoing struggle. Rebecca reported that she had lost meaning in her life, was routinely tired, and often felt isolated. Further, she struggled to identify any moments of joy in the last several months.

She reported intense suicidal ideation, which raised significant concern. Rebecca stated that she had attempted suicide the month prior by trying to consume alcohol to the point of death, and she described an experience in high school of impulsively skiing into a tree. Our session quickly turned to discussing hospitalization when Rebecca indicated that she could not be certain that she would not attempt suicide, though she denied a plan. Prior to this appointment, Rebecca had given away belongings, including bringing her pet ferret to live with her parents. She denied access to any weapons but reported access to prescription medications at her parents' home. However, Rebecca was skeptical of hospitalization, stating that it would interfere and cost too much. After consultation with a staff psychologist, I discussed hospitalization with Rebecca as an opportunity to step away from her daily stressors in order to begin focusing on her well-being. Eventually, Rebecca voluntarily agreed to hospitalization; however, she was not admitted to the hospital because she denied ideation when she arrived. A local suicide prevention agency developed a suicide prevention plan with Rebecca, which included returning for psychotherapy with me at the counseling center.

The following week, Rebecca and I met to begin therapy, which would eventually last 12 sessions and include a referral to psychiatric services. We focused first on her symptoms of depression and her background to begin conceptualizing the onset of her depressed mood. I learned more about Rebecca's family and her role as the person who held their relationships together. She also began to open up more about those things that she had previously enjoyed, including spending time with friends, target shooting, and exercising, despite having discontinued each of these. We spent time focusing on when these activities vanished. In the initial session, however, focusing upon enjoyment in the past elicited minimal reaction as Rebecca's flat affect and relatively unmotivated attitude persisted. Her distress was assessed at each session; assessment revealed that Rebecca's depressive symptoms remained clinically significant, but her suicidal ideation began to decrease.

During the sessions, I gathered information that allowed me to conceptualize a treatment plan with Rebecca that emphasized her assets, focused on what she revealed as meaningful, and balanced concentrating on her well-being with honoring her genuine psychological suffering. My initial intervention strategy with Rebecca was to identify her strengths. Though she was typically dismissive of positive moments, I highlighted and celebrated when she reported going to the gym with a friend or scheduling time with her academic advisor to address her school-related stress. We explored strengths further in the context of her family environment, as she provided a great deal of support to those she cared about. I became increasingly convinced that Rebecca possessed a myriad of strengths and assets that could help unlock positive emotions. Her assessment results began to show noticeably decreased depressive symptoms; however, we agreed that it would be best for her to meet with a psychiatrist and begin medication in conjunction with therapy.

With each session Rebecca became more open to identifying moments during the week when she relied on her own strengths and assets. We began exploring how she felt when she relied on her strengths in these meaningful moments. She reported feeling more content and less distant from friends. While her affect remained relatively flat generally, she began to smile, laugh, and joke much more in our work together. Rebecca also started to reminisce about how her friends had historically seen her as more jovial and engaged. I focused on this perception with Rebecca by asking her what I would see if I were there during these moments. She responded that she just felt happy during those times. Although this was not an emotionally deep response, it allowed me the latitude to begin employing positive empathy. When Rebecca reported feeling disconnected, I could reflect back to her that it sounded like she wanted to have close relationships. When she felt disengaged, I expressed that it seemed like she craved meaningful activities in her life. Informal approach goals were established.

We began to foster hope that Rebecca could be more agentic in her life, and we collaboratively identified approach goals. This led to Rebecca expressing that she was unhappy in engineering and at the university. She identified an alternative career interest, and we explored how she could pursue this line of work. By this point, Rebecca had been in therapy from November until late April, and she informed me that she would be ending her time at the university in May. Her depressive symptoms had fallen below clinical levels and she no longer identified any suicidal thoughts. Just as importantly, Rebecca reported that she was excited about pursuing her newly chosen career. This was something that carried meaning to her and that she was invested in pursuing. She opted to continue medication, but turning attention to her strengths, positive emotional experiences, and desires for her future allowed us to mutually terminate therapy on a hopeful trajectory.

Analysis of Case #3

Rebecca started therapy because of a high level of concern by a physician and her therapist for her suicidal orientation, flat affect, and depressed mood. Rebecca also seemed incapable of experiencing positive emotions and perceived her life as meaningless. She had attempted suicide in her recent past, which heightened the concern. The initial therapy intake session was marked by Rebecca's lack of responsiveness. Her level of depression and suicidal threat were severe enough that the therapist convinced her to seek hospitalization, explaining that she could gain some relief from her problems through hospitalization. She denied suicidal ideation at the hospital and was not admitted, but instead referred to a local suicide prevention agency. The prevention plan that was developed included returning for therapy.

When Rebecca started therapy, the therapist asked about her symptoms of depression and gathered information about her family background. Questions about her family led to Rebecca revealing previously enjoyable activities in her life and a role in her family as the one keeping the family together. The added interest in previously enjoyable activities provided a glimpse at some of the many strengths available to Rebecca. Therapy progress was tracked by session-to-session assessment of psychological functioning, which revealed continuing depressive symptoms but decreasing suicidal ideation.

The therapist concentrated on identifying strengths, meaning in life, and ways to increase well-being. Despite Rebecca's dismissive tendencies, the therapy persistently identified and amplified strengths. The constant attention to strengths resulted in a marked decrease in depressive symptoms in the assessments. Rebecca started to report the use of her strengths outside of therapy. Positive emotions emerged in therapy through capitalization and strength amplification. The therapist used positive empathy when Rebecca demonstrated depressive characteristics to identify the approach goals of gaining desired close relationships and increasing meaningful activities in her life. Rebecca progressed to exercising autonomy by questioning her current academic major and finally choosing a new career direction. At the conclusion of therapy, Rebecca's depression had decreased below clinical levels and her enthusiasm for her new life course was clearly evident.

What is notable about this case is the initial severe level of depression that was met with the therapist's persistent and patient use of positive empathy to counter the client's expressions of hopelessness over the course of an entire academic year. The therapist was able to balance attention to the problem and prevention of harm with efforts to reveal the client's considerable strengths. Initially, the client's lack of hope and high level of despair made progress slow, but eventually well-being was built to a level that allowed for more autonomous acts by the client.

CASE #4: WORRYING ABOUT THE PITFALLS OF BEING TOO HAPPY, BY KATE HAWLEY

Case Presentation

David initially sought treatment at the university counseling center when his marijuana use began to impede his academic success. He indicated that he used marijuana to shield himself from "everything horrible in the world." For the year prior to treatment, David had experienced intense anger and irritability, feelings of worthlessness, low self-esteem, difficulty concentrating, and a general sense that life was meaningless. He felt lonely and longed for social connection but had limited social support and questioned his social competence. David's experiences were consistent with a diagnosis of major depressive disorder without suicidal or homicidal ideation.

David was a 23-year-old, heterosexual, European American man. He had experienced depression since early high school and struggled to maintain close relationships. David experienced a happy childhood until his father passed away very suddenly before he hit puberty. His father's death had been confusing, but David reported that it brought his family closer. At the beginning of treatment, he stated that he had "processed" his father's death and did not want to focus on this during therapy.

David was not experiencing many positive emotions in his life. He had a low sense of well-being, and he did not believe he had the resources to cope with negative experiences or stressors. David's life had changed in an instant at a very young age, and he lived in constant fear of unpredictability, lacking a sense of control. This caused him to avoid anything that could cause him pain, which ultimately prevented him from moving toward his goals.

In our first few sessions together, David stated his belief that "we are all just chemicals on a rock in a universe somewhere . . . and nothing in life really has meaning." He also noted that it was difficult for him to feel happy with so much suffering occurring in the world. I immediately saw many strengths in David: among his intelligence, critical thinking skills, curiosity, and wit was his clear compassion for others. In an early session, after validating and empathizing with David's pain, I reflected this strength back to him. I had hoped to engender positive emotions and a sense of hope, but he initially scoffed at this attempt. He was unable to see himself in a positive light. However, he did begin describing the passion he felt for human rights issues. I worked to reflect this deep passion and the clear meaning he drew from it. He was surprised, but agreed that he did find meaning in some aspects of his life, which led to exploration of other sources of meaning for David. His face lit up as he talked about his love for his pets and family members, and we capitalized on this joy.

Once David had experienced positive emotions in therapy (passion, interest, and joy), he appeared ready to identify goals for treatment. David stated that he wanted to stop relying on marijuana to relieve his emotional pain and wanted to feel less lonely. Utilizing positive empathy to identify approach goals, we determined that David wanted to utilize healthier coping methods for his pain and feel greater social connection in his life.

Near the beginning of treatment, David determined that he was not ready to reduce his marijuana intake and stated that the most important goal for him was to experience more social connection in his life. I encouraged this goal by reflecting the value and meaning David drew from relationships. He and

I explored social activities he could partake in that would also bring joy or meaning, and David decided to become involved in various campus activities. When David reported positive social interactions, I celebrated his successes and facilitated his understanding about how he was able to be successful.

David: Well, I actually, I went to [campus organization] on Saturday. It was, I mean, it was good, surprisingly. I met some people and you know, it was cool, I liked them.

Therapist: Wow! You put yourself out there and it was a success! (Showing enthusiasm for David's experiences and reiterating the positive outcomes of his actions) How does that make you feel about yourself? (Encouraging identification of strengths and positive emotion)

David: Umm . . . I guess, capable. Yeah, capable and proud. I enjoyed myself.

Therapist: You felt capable and proud (reflecting strengths). It sounds like you found that something good happened from the actions you took (reflecting a sense of agency).

David: Yeah . . . Yeah! I mean, I guess you could say that . . . I mean, I felt better. I feel better. It's empowering, I just don't want to hype it up, though.

Therapist: Why not? (Smiling and teasing) We should celebrate that, what a big accomplishment for you! (Celebrating David's positive experiences and reflecting his growth)

David: Well, I guess it doesn't hurt . . .

Throughout treatment, David had trouble acknowledging his strengths and celebrating his accomplishments. He worried that celebrating each new accomplishment would set him up for failure in the future. I worked with him to help him grow more comfortable with celebrating himself and savoring the positive results of his actions. As he revealed accomplishments, I retraced what he did to create the success so he could have more positive interactions in the future (i.e., success-finding).

Once David became more comfortable in social situations and began experiencing more social success and positive emotion, he decided he wanted to return the focus of treatment to his marijuana use. It seemed that he felt he had developed a greater capacity to address this issue. I was not specialized in the treatment of marijuana dependence, but I could help David process the emotions related to it. David understood that he used marijuana to feel safe in an otherwise frightening world. He was incredibly hard on himself when he could not quit immediately, and stated that he felt ashamed and stupid. I introduced self-compassion and reflected the strength that David was motivated to quit, and that he was taking action to accomplish this goal. We then explored other things in David's life that made him feel safe.

Therapist: Are there times when you don't feel the craving as much? (Utilizing success-finding to explore other coping mechanisms in David's life)

David: Yeah, when I'm with my family.

Therapist: Hmm . . . so we know it is not on your mind as much when you are
surrounded by people you care about.
David: Yeah, because then I feel safe . . .
Therapist: Ah . . . so there are things other than marijuana that can contrib-
ute to your sense of safety. (Encouraging and integrating positive coping
strategies)

It was important that David realized that he had a positive and healthy sup-
port system and did not have to rely solely on marijuana to help him feel better.
Once David felt that he might be able to let go of marijuana and retain a sense
of safety, he accepted my referral to a community provider for more focused
substance abuse treatment.

While we worked toward helping David experience positive emotions, he
continued to avoid his negative emotions. He was surprised that he remained
upset or angry when he was trying so hard to push these feelings down.
Together, we discussed the importance of experiencing a range of emotions
and we introduced elements of mindfulness practice. Through observing his
emotions and allowing them to occur, David grew more comfortable with a
spectrum of emotions and indicated that he felt better able to "cope with what
comes up for me."

Toward the end of treatment, David began to discuss deeper issues, such as
the anger he felt regarding his father's death and his deep concern that no one
will be able to love him unconditionally. Once he experienced a greater sense
of well-being, he felt ready to approach topics that he had avoided his entire
life. I reflected David's growth and his strength in bringing up these concerns,
and validated his anger and ambivalence regarding his father. We explored
David's feelings about his relationship with his father and his ideas about love
in general. We also discussed what David learned from his father, and what he
continues to carry with him today as a result of their relationship.

David eventually graduated from the university and planned to move
away, resulting in our mutual decision to end treatment. As therapy termi-
nated, we discussed what he gained from the process. He reported that he had
developed an ability to open up. He gained insight into himself and was able
to experience his emotions rather than discussing them at an intellectual or
conceptual level. He developed new friendships and learned that others cared
for him. Perhaps most importantly, David was able to experience a sense
of meaning in life, which led to more opportunities to experience positive
emotion.

Analysis of Case #4

The client, David, came to therapy dealing with life's unpredictability, marked by
the sudden death of his father when David was young. David's depressive symptoms and maladaptive coping through marijuana contributed to his lack of a sense

of competence and self-efficacy. Additionally, David suffered from an inability to experience happiness. The therapist's emphasis on David's strength of being compassionate toward others and passionate about human rights was effective in getting him to acknowledge some level of meaning in life. The therapist was then able to facilitate David's exploration of other meaningful aspects of his life, namely family and pets. When discussing these, David was able to express joy, interest, and passion, among other positive emotions. These positive emotional events were emphasized. Positive emotions opened the gate to establishing approach goals. The use of positive empathy transformed avoidance goals of feeling lonely and evading emotional pain through marijuana into the approach goals of feeling more connected and finding healthier ways of coping. Approach goals led to action (e.g., joining campus organizations). These successes were capitalized on, leading to broadening, which was identified by David acknowledging that he felt "empowered."

David worried that making progress in therapy would set him up for a fall. It seemed that he was worried about being too happy because this would lead to unforeseen disappointment or loss that would be devastating. His stance of apprehension was probably due to his early experience of his father suddenly dying and his subsequent guardedness toward any future unpredictable losses and downturns. In effect, David was being cautious to not be too happy because the fall from the pedestal of happiness would be too far and presumably could destroy him. David's progress toward well-being was not predicated on knowing what his problem was. His growth occurred through a supportive relationship that emphasized his strengths and successes. Slowly over time in therapy, his positive emotions supported multiple broadening experiences. David was able to build a reservoir of well-being that allowed him to explore scary issues, such as anger over the death of his father.

ASSESSING COMMON THREADS AND DISTINCTIVE QUALITIES OF THE FOUR CASES

A qualitative analysis of the four cases was conducted to uncover the common threads and distinctive features. The phenomena of interest in this investigation were the therapeutic processes in GFPP. Of course, the sample helped define the phenomenon. Each of the four therapists, the authors of the case examples, had been trained in GFPP and expressed enthusiasm for the approach. Each therapist was asked to write a two- to three-page description of one of their past experiences using GFPP. Details of each case were altered to make the clients unidentifiable. No parameters were designated concerning the type of client or issues that the therapists chose to describe. We assumed that each author chose a case that was rich in methods typifying GFPP.

One of the authors of this book performed the qualitative analysis. First, the four cases were read completely. Next the researcher went back through each case and underlined significant statements that described therapy processes. All identified processes were considered to be GFPP processes. Therefore, in addition to the four hallmarks of GFPP (i.e., strengths, positive emotions, goals, and hope), any processes that occurred (e.g., problem identification) were considered to be processes accompanying the core elements of GFPP. Therapy processes included both therapist- and client-initiated events. The 84 significant statements identified in the four case examples were labeled using a shorthand method called invariant constituents. The invariant constituents (i.e., identifiable and understandable factors) were grouped into 17 themes. Table 5-1 lists all themes, invariant constituents, and significant statements produced through the analysis. Themes are listed in order of prevalence of occurrence across the four cases.

As presented in Table 5-1, the most prevalent theme was *Identifying, Amplifying, and Using Client Strengths.* Fifteen occurrences of strength identification, amplification, and use were found. Strengths were used to overcome hesitancy, identify goals, and initiate treatment plans. The therapist of Case #1 wrote that the "first step in treatment was an effort to engage [the client] on his own terms, drawing on his strengths and values to cultivate motivation and meaningful goals for treatment." Capitalization often accompanied strength identification. The therapist in Case #4 wrote, "I worked with him to help him grow more comfortable with celebrating himself and savoring the positive results of his actions. We continued to capitalize on each positive interaction." Working with the client's strengths often was accomplished despite the client initially responding by denying or minimizing the presence of personal strengths. The therapist in Case #3 described this process:

> First, my intervention strategy with Rebecca turned toward identifying what strengths she possessed. Though she was typically dismissive of positive moments, I would highlight and amplify moments when she reported going to the gym with a friend or scheduling time with her academic advisor to address her school-related stress.

Thus, working with client strengths was clearly a common thread of the four cases. Each of the four therapists performed strength-oriented work as a foundational process accompanying the formation of approach goals and experiences of positive emotions. Identifying client strengths also helped to overcome lack of client engagement, and the use of client strengths contextualized therapy to individual clients.

The next most common theme was *Broadening,* with 11 occurrences. Client broadening took various forms, represented by increased flexibility; willingness to discuss problems and negative life events; or feeling empowered, safe, and freed up. Broadening was viewed as both a process and an outcome in the case examples. Broadening also was the client's expression of positive emotions, as noted by the therapist of Case #4: "His face lit up as he talked about his love for his pets and family members, and we capitalized on this joy."

The third area designated as a common thread was *Forming Approach Goals Through Positive Empathy,* with eight occurrences. Again, each of the four

therapists moved to approach goals with their clients. Approach goal formation followed a progression that started with the client expressing dissatisfaction or identifying an avoidance goal. The therapist responded through positive
empathy that included an expression of a client desired state acknowledged by
the client. The desired state was used as a basis for forming the approach goal.
As the therapist in Case #3 reported, "When Rebecca reported feeling disconnected, I could reflect back to her that it sounded like she wanted to have close
relationships." An approach goal then resulted from each of the positive empathy statements.

The fourth common thread demonstrated by each therapist and client dyad was
Attention to Problems. The therapist's attention to the client's presenting problems,
symptoms, and complaints was a strategy of following the energy of the client.
Attention to problems also helped balance the therapist's focus on strengths and
other non-problem areas of the client's life. Another function of having a problem
focus was to join with the client's immediate experience,. As the therapist in Case
#2 explains,

> Our first few sessions were dominated by each previous week's difficulties,
> which included decreasing grades, loss of medical support equating to facing
> (for the first time in many years) her emotional difficulties without familiar
> assistance, and the eventual loss of a romantic relationship that amounted to
> much of her support system.

A fifth common thread reported by three of the four therapists was *Generalizing
Treatment Gains*. Progress was first experienced in therapy and then generalized
to situations outside of therapy that were salient to the client. The process of generalization could be initiated by the client or the therapist. The client employing
treatment gains outside of therapy is characterized as the client exercising autonomy. Generalization of treatment gains usually took place near the conclusion of
therapy. The therapist in Case #1 provided a wonderful and creative example of the
transfer of treatment gains from therapy to the client's life. The client applied something practiced in therapy to the enhancement of the relationship with his partner:

> Peter brought in the lyrics to a song that he had written for Wendy [his part-
> ner], in which he expressed his appreciation for her and communicated his
> hopes for their future together. He subsequently reported that this creation
> was "quite a hit" with Wendy.

Working with Reluctant Clients was a common process in three of the four
cases. Reluctance took the forms of being too depressed to engage in therapy,
challenging the reasons another had for the client coming to therapy, or being
hesitant to revisit past traumas from losses. The clearest example of reluctance
was described by the therapist of Case #1: "[The client] seemed to be attending
"under orders" as a way to placate his partner rather than out of a sincere desire
for change." After reading the case examples, GFPP functioned as an excellent

approach for reluctant clients, because rather than focusing on the problems and difficulties that the clients may wish to avoid, GFPP can start in non-problem areas of strength. By first focusing on positives and strengths, clients more easily move to trusting the therapist, forming an alliance, and eventually discussing areas that are related to reasons the client sought therapy.

Using Capitalization also came up as a common thread process, occurring in three of the four cases. It was also mentioned as an accompaniment to *Forming Approach Goals Through Positive Empathy* and *Identifying, Amplifying, and Using Client Strengths*. Capitalization is the client's sharing of positive occurrences that are met with the therapist's celebration. Celebrating capitalization leads to the client having a higher regard for the event that was shared and experiencing positive emotion, and the relationship with the therapist is enhanced (Gable, Reis, Impett, & Asher, 2004). The therapist typically pursues how the client influenced the occurrence of the positive event. Capitalization can be used to encourage broadening, as shown by the therapist of Case #3.

> . . . but at this point in treatment, she smiled, laughed, and joked much more in our work together. Rebecca also started to talk about how her friends had historically seen her as a more jovial and engaged person. I celebrated her capitalization on this perception with Rebecca by asking her what I would see if I were there during these moments—she responded that she just feels happy at those times.

The following processes were identified in two or fewer cases and occurred three times or less. Included in this list were *Avoidance Goals as a Starting Point; Client Autonomy; Applying Positive Psychology Interventions; Positive Emotions; Approach Behaviors; Collaborating with Psychiatry and Community Resources; Building an Alliance; Positive Reframing;* and *Success-Finding.* Thus, these processes were not classified as common threads but may have been distinctive to the work of one or more therapists with a particular client. This is not to say that this list of processes is not characteristic of the GFPP approach. Instead, we would like these processes to be thought of as applied to specific client situations to contextualize the process with a particular client.

In summary, consistent through each case description was the GFPP orientation toward building the client's well-being. The therapists steadily pursued client strengths and positive emotions to facilitate growth, change, and hope.

Table 5-1 THEMES, INVARIANT CONSTITUENTS, AND SIGNIFICANT STATEMENTS
IN FOUR GFPP THERAPIST CASE EXAMPLES

Theme

Invariant Constituents

Significant Statements[1]

Identifying, amplifying, and using client strengths (15)

Strength identification

she provided a great deal of support to those she cared about.

Using the client's strengths overcomes hesitancy

first step in treatment was an effort to engage him on his own terms, drawing on his strengths and values to cultivate motivation and meaningful goals for treatment.

Strength identification

Through the therapist's facilitation, he identified several meaningful personal strengths, including his affinity for teaching (he had previously served in a variety of temporary tutoring/mentoring positions and described "inspiring the students and connecting with them on a personal level" as a source of satisfaction in previous positions); his appreciation of nature; his creativity and artistic talents as a recreational musician; and a supportive family in which he felt "very lucky" to be a member.

Aligning strengths with goals

He expressed a sense of satisfaction upon discovering that these qualities aligned felicitously with the personal strengths that he and the therapist had explored during earlier sessions.

Suggestion to apply personal strengths with self

how her strengths (e.g., kindness, love, creativity) had primarily been applied with others and rarely to herself.

Identifying strengths to initiate better times

her role as the person who held their relationships together. She also began to open up more about those things that she had previously enjoyed, including spending time with friends, target shooting, and exercising, despite having discontinued each of these.

Strength treatment planning

a treatment plan with Rebecca that could instead emphasize her assets.

Persistent and consistent strength focus

First, my intervention strategy with Rebecca turned toward identifying what strengths she possessed. Though she was typically dismissive of positive moments, I would highlight and amplify moments when she reported going to the gym with a friend or scheduling time with her academic advisor to address her school-related stress.

Strength focus leads to client engagement

Throughout this period of our work, Rebecca became less apathetic toward identifying moments away from therapy when she relied on her own strengths and assets.

Therapist commitment and attention to client strengths

I immediately saw many strengths in David. Among his intelligence, critical thinking skills, curiosity, and wit was his clear compassion for others.

Strength identification: compassion for others than for self

he did begin describing the passion he felt for human rights issues.

(continued)

Table 5-1 CONTINUED

Amplification of strengths

I worked to reflect this deep passion and the clear meaning he drew from it.

Persistent pursuit of strengths and positive emotions

I worked with him to help him grow more comfortable with celebrating himself and savoring the positive results of his actions. We continued to capitalize on each positive interaction.

Amplifying strengths

I reflected David's growth and his strength in bringing up these concerns.

Finding strength and positives amid experiencing loss

We also discussed what David learned from his father, and what he continues to carry with him today as a result of their relationship.

Broadening (11)

Overcoming fears

he disclosed freely for the first time about his fears concerning the relationship, including their lack of communication.

Openness to express negative feelings

including his concerns about his future with Wendy and his apprehensions about communicating his feelings to her, and also his sense of sorrow and loss concerning the deaths of several beloved friends and family members.

Posttraumatic Growth

Peter was able to identify the ways in which the love he felt for the deceased inspired him to "create heartfelt music" and lead "a more real, raw, life." After a brief exploration of posttraumatic growth and an exercise in which he envisioned what he hoped to accomplish before his own passing . . .

Increased flexibility

he was now satisfied to work in a position that fit "the most important criteria" in order to incrementally approach his other goals of contributing financially to his relationship; having enough money to "go on last-minute adventures;" acquiring skills and experience valuable for future enterprises; and saving money in order to build toward the bona fide Dream Job.

Ready to attend to problems/struggles

Looking back on it, though, the various factors that changed dramatically in Maggie's life may have also afforded her the opportunity to interact with herself and her thoughts in novel ways.

Willingness to express dissatisfaction

expressing that she was unhappy in engineering and at the university.

Uncovering life meaning

he *did* find meaning in some aspects of his life.

Feeling safe and freed up to feel negatives and explore loss

David began to discuss deeper issues, such as the anger he felt regarding his father's death and his deep concern that no one will be able to love him unconditionally.

Table 5-1 CONTINUED

Increased flexibility

he was now satisfied to work in a position that fit "the most important criteria" in order to incrementally approach his other goals of contributing financially to his relationship; having enough money to "go on last-minute adventures;" acquiring skills and experience valuable for future enterprises; and saving money in order to build toward the bona fide Dream Job.

Broadening

It appeared that once he experienced a greater sense of well-being, he felt ready to approach topics that he had avoided his entire life.

Broadening and Building

He reported that he had developed an ability to open up, had gained insight into himself, and was able to experience his emotions rather than discussing them at an intellectual or conceptual level. He had developed new friendships and learned that others cared for him. Perhaps most importantly, David was able to experience a sense of meaning in life, which led to more opportunities to experience positive emotion.

Forming Approach Goals Through Positive Empathy (8)

Early approach goals

Thus an early task was to establish client-congruent vocational approach goals.

Positive empathy and success-finding

using positive empathy and success-finding.

Identifying desired states through approach goals

She accomplished this in (and outside of) therapy through re-orienting to her desired states by establishing approach goals.

Using positive empathy

Although this was not an emotionally deep response, it allowed me the latitude to begin employing positive empathy.

Using positive empathy

When Rebecca reported feeling disconnected, I could reflect back to her that it sounded like she wanted to have close relationships.

Using of positive empathy leading to approach goals

When she felt disengaged, I expressed that it seemed like she craved meaningful activities in her life.

Use of positive empathy to support approach goals

Utilizing positive empathy to identify approach goals, we determined that David wanted to utilize healthier coping methods for his pain and feel greater social connection in his life.

Formation of a new approach goal

We then explored other things in David's life that made him feel safe.

Attention to problems (7)

Attention to problems initially

Our first few sessions were dominated by each previous week's difficulties, which included decreasing grades, loss of medical support equating to facing (for the first time in many years) her emotional difficulties without familiar assistance, and the eventual loss of a romantic relationship that amounted to much of her support system.

(continued)

Table 5-1 CONTINUED

Attending to crises

Maggie felt like her life was in perpetual crisis and we mutually agreed that our work together felt at times more like damage control than anything else.

Client narrowly focused on problem

She was uncertain how long she had been depressed but made it clear that this was an ongoing struggle.

Understanding the problem

Rebecca reported that she had lost meaning in her life, was routinely tired, and was often felt isolated. Further, she struggled to identify any moments of joy in the last several months.

Attention to the problem definition

David initially sought treatment at the university counseling center when his marijuana use began to impede his academic success. He indicated that he used marijuana to shield himself from "everything horrible in the world." For the year prior to treatment, David had experienced intense anger and irritability, feelings of worthlessness, low self-esteem, difficulty concentrating, and a general sense that life was meaningless. He felt lonely and longed for social connection but had limited social support and questioned his social competence. David's experiences were consistent with a diagnosis of major depressive disorder without suicidal or homicidal ideation.

Client refusal to focus on negative life event

At the beginning of treatment, he stated that he had "processed" his father's death and did not want to focus on this during therapy.

Therapist using empathy

but I could help David process the emotions related to it.

Working with reluctant clients (6)

Focusing on strengths with reluctant clients

Taking them where they are at. Focusing on strengths and what they want to work on rather than what their partner or you think is the "problem."

Lack of motivation for therapy

seemed to be attending "under orders" as a way to placate his partner rather than out of a sincere desire for change.

Client mistrusts therapist control

established an ongoing therapeutic motif in which he became notably intractable in response to directive or otherwise structured approaches to treatment.

Lack of autonomy

During this session, she exhibited flat affect—"I don't know" was her most frequent response—and was reluctant to engage in therapy, stating on multiple occasions that she felt "obligated to be there."

Client refusal to focus on problem

At the beginning of treatment, he stated that he had "processed" his father's death and did not want to focus on this during therapy.

Focus on strengths as a strategy for client reluctance

I immediately saw many strengths in David. Among his intelligence, critical thinking skills, curiosity, and wit was his clear compassion for others.

Table 5-1 CONTINUED

Common reason for clients failing to commit to a more empowered
and positive perspective

> He worried that celebrating each new accomplishment would set him up for failure in the future.

Using capitalization (5)

Use of capitalization

> Peter and the therapist practiced capitalization by celebrating his job-hunting progress.

Client practicing capitalization

> brought in the lyrics to several songs that he had written (a tactic that predictably elicited considerable positive affect as he proudly shared several of his "favorite pieces" with his therapist).

Use of capitalization/celebration by focusing on better times, strengths,
and positive emotions

> but at this point in treatment, she smiled, laughed, and joked much more in our work together. Rebecca also started to talk about how her friends had historically seen her as a more jovial and engaged person. I celebrated this perception with Rebecca by asking her what I would see if I were there during these moments—she responded that she just feels happy at those times.

Capitalizing on successes in goal pursuit

> social interactions, I helped him capitalize on and celebrate these successes and understand how he was able to be successful.

Capitalization and suggesting broadening to positive emotions

> "Wow! You put yourself out there and it was a success!" (Showing enthusiasm for David's experiences and reiterating the positive outcomes of his actions) "How does that make you feel about yourself?" (Encouraging identification of strengths and positive emotion.)

Promoting hope (5)

Hope for therapy

> The first several sessions focused on identifying and amplifying sources of motivation, in order to instill hope, increase flexibility, and galvanize commitment to treatment.

Hope in moving toward his best-possible-self

> "once I get that Dream Job up and running."

Hope as an outcome

> personal hope for the future.

Solidifying approach goals and hope

> We began to foster hope that Rebecca could be more agentic in her life, and we collaboratively identified approach goals.

Therapist struggling to have hope for the client

> Even though she engaged meaningfully in counseling, it was not clear in the beginning whether our work could have a noticeable impact in her life given the sheer number of concerns she was facing.

(continued)

Table 5-1 CONTINUED

Generalizing treatment gains (5)

Generalization of gains in therapy to life outside of therapy

one incremental step toward these goals would be to purposefully practice capitalization with Wendy, both by sharing his good news and by expressively savoring her good news.

Practicing in therapy and then generalizing outside of therapy

Peter brought in the lyrics to a song that he had written for Wendy, in which he expressed his appreciation for her and communicated his hopes for their future together. He subsequently reported that this creation was "quite a hit" with Wendy.

Generalization of treatment

Just as importantly, Rebecca reported that she was excited about pursuing her newly chosen career.

A tangible behavior and outcome to pursue

David decided to become involved in various campus activities.

Generalization of treatment successes

he reported and retraced how he experienced success so he could have more positive interactions in the future.

Avoidance goals as a starting point (3)

Using negatives, and avoidance goals for an anchor to identify approach goals

The abundance of avoidance goals featured in this litany presented a clear starting point for enhancing positive affect, hope, and motivation.

Moving from an avoidance goal to an approach goal

Peter reoriented his original avoidance goal of "proving that I'm not going to cheat on her again" to "building trust."

Flipping from avoidance goals to approach goals

Shifting to differentiate between feeling "not this way" (an avoidance goal) and wanting to actually feel centered, autonomous, and caring toward herself (an approach goal).

Client Autonomy (3)

Increased autonomy about his goals

he was able to independently tie these sentiments to his increasingly clear goals concerning both his ideal job and his plans to cultivate a warm, trusting, and open relationship with Wendy.

Demonstrated client motivation/autonomy

Maggie's presentation in session was respectful, thoughtful, and engaged. She regularly applied herself with the work of counseling and seemed to feel comfortable guiding the pace and direction of the therapy hour.

Broadening, more autonomy, client motivation

Once David became more comfortable in social situations and began to experience more social success and positive emotion, he decided he wanted to return the focus of treatment to his marijuana use.

Table 5-1 CONTINUED

Applying Positive Psychology interventions (3)

Self-compassion intervention

Much of the later work of our counseling sessions was oriented around finding ways for her to apply her strengths of creativity and love toward herself, and it was a surprising chain of events that led to her finally being able to apply these strengths to her lived experiences.

Self-compassion intervention

introduced self-compassion.

Mindfulness as an intervention

Together, we discussed the importance of experiencing a range of emotions and we introduced elements of mindfulness practice.

Positive emotions (3)

Positive emotions and then goals

David had experienced positive emotions in therapy (passion, interest, and joy), and he appeared ready to identify goals for treatment.

Achieving balance between negative and positive emotions

Through observing his emotions and allowing them to occur, David grew more comfortable with a spectrum of emotions and indicated that he felt better able to "cope with what comes up for me."

Positive emotions, broadening, and capitalization

His face lit up as he talked about his love for his pets and family members, and we capitalized on this joy.

Approach behaviors (3)

Exploring approach behaviors

explored social activities he could partake in that would also bring joy or meaning.

Pathway to the goal or approach behaviors

"recapturing some of the fun and playfulness from when we first started dating."

Encouraging approach behaviors

"Ah . . . so there are things other than marijuana that can contribute to your sense of safety." (Encouraging and integrating positive coping strategies.)

Collaborating with Psychiatry and Community Resources (2)

Working collaboratively with medical issues and medical model (e.g., psychiatry)

The following week, Rebecca and I met to begin therapy, which would eventually last 12 sessions and include a referral to psychiatric services.

Working in collaboration with a problem focused system

he accepted my referral to a community provider for more focused treatment (for marijuana use).

Building an alliance (2)

Evidence of client motivation

. . . he identified as fitting these criteria, including positions at a natural history museum; a native plant nursery, and a local health food co-op.

(continued)

Table 5-1 CONTINUED

Building an alliance and finding enthusiasm for therapy

> This was the first time that Peter had proactively brought clear goals and successes into treatment, and he introduced these materials by exclaiming, "I've been looking forward to showing these to you."

Positive reframing (2)

Reframing hospitalization as an opportunity to gain well-being

> I discussed hospitalization with Rebecca as an opportunity to step away from her daily stressors in order to begin focusing on her well-being.

Positive reframe of the problem as a strength

> reflected the strength that David was motivated to quit, and that he was taking action to accomplish this goal.

Success-finding (1)

Success-finding

> "Hmm . . . so we know it is not on your mind as much when you are surrounded by people you care about."

[1] Several of the quotes (significant statements) in the table do not match the case presentations as presented in the chapter exactly. The quotes in the table were taken from the unedited versions of the case studies.

6

Conclusion and Future Directions

We, the authors, appreciate your reading about Goal Focused Positive Psychotherapy (GFPP). We hope you will pursue practicing and applying the theoretical orientation. Our fondest wish is that you research and contribute to the further development of the model. In this final chapter we present our research examining GFPP and outline ideas for further research and development that could occur. We hope our ideas are catalysts for even better ideas that you will contribute!

RESEARCH SUPPORTING GFPP

Meta-analysis results indicate that psychotherapy models that meet the specifications listed in the Contextual Model are not statistically different from one another in helping clients accomplish their outcome goal (e.g., Wampold et al., 1997). There is a detailed presentation of the analyses and logic in *The Great Psychotherapy Debate* by Wampold and Imel (2015). As presented in Chapter 1 of this book, Wampold's cogent arguments support GFPP. The support examined here is regarding psychotherapy results or outcome. When comparing the outcomes of two or more psychotherapies meeting the criteria of the Contextual Model, no difference between the effectiveness of any two models is apparent (Wampold et al., 1997). A psychotherapy model cannot be chosen based upon superior effectiveness. Based upon the multitude of studies, GFPP could claim equivalence to any other psychotherapy model.

However, we wanted to be certain of this result by doing our own study. Also, we believed that clients would find GFPP to be more attractive. As you know from the synopsis of the three-year study in Chapter 1, the research supported our claims.

The Three-Year Study of GFPP

The effectiveness of the GFPP model as an integrated psychotherapy treatment is based upon a three-year treatment comparison study. The purpose of the research was to examine the therapeutic effectiveness of GFPP compared to empirically supported psychotherapy as performed in a clinic. The three-year effectiveness study examined what the clients thought of the psychotherapy sessions (i.e., the process) and how effective the psychotherapy was (i.e., the outcome). The study took place at a community clinic that trained doctoral counseling and clinical psychologists. GFPP was compared with a treatment-as-usual group, which included cognitive-behavioral and interpersonal psychodynamic therapy. All therapists received supervision from a professor who practiced the psychotherapy that he supervised. Three hour-long weekly supervision sessions for the therapists included video review of therapy. The clients were assigned to therapists as therapists had openings in their caseload, so the assignment was not random. The design was a field study, quasi-experimental design comparing two treatment groups with three pretreatment and posttreatment measures.

The sample included 91 adult clients between the ages of 18 and 65 (mean age 27). Sixty-six percent of clients identified as female. The primary self-identified ethnic makeup of the clients was 54% European American, 16% Latino/a, and 9% Asian American, and the rest were "other" or declined to identify their ethnicity. The clinic accepted clients with all diagnoses except active psychosis and drug/alcohol dependence. Twenty-four GFPP and 67 treatment-as-usual cases were included in the study.

The hypothesis was that GFPP would function as well as empirically supported treatments as assessed by three outcome measures.

MEASURES

Three measures were used to assess the treatments. Two measures, the Outcome Questionnaire (OQ; Lambert, Hansen, Umpress, Lunnen, Okiishi, Burlingame, & Reisinger, 1996) and the Outcome Rating Scale (ORS; Miller et al., 2003), were used to examine outcome by assessing the client's self-reported functioning level. The Session Rating Scale (SRS; Duncan et al., 2003) was used to assess the session process by measuring the clients' evaluation of the therapy sessions.

The OQ, a 45-item questionnaire assessing psychological distress, was one measure of client level of functioning. The OQ assesses symptomatic functioning (anxiety, depression, substance abuse), interpersonal problems (quality of interpersonal relationships), and social role adjustment (problems with family, work, and leisure). The validity of the OQ has been evaluated as strong. Its test–retest and internal consistency results are moderate to high (Lambert et al., 1996). Convergent validity and discriminant validity for the OQ have been supported by a large number of studies (as reported by Lambert & Finch, 1999).

The ORS, a four-item questionnaire, was the second measure of client functioning. The ORS measures three areas of client functioning (the individual, relational, and social domains) and provides an overall measure of client functioning. The items assess a client's self-rating for the last week's well-being. The items ask, "How are you doing" overall (general sense of well-being), individually (personal well-being), interpersonally (family, close relationships), and socially (work, school, friendships). The validity of the ORS is considered strong. Its reliability was high, with a Cronbach's coefficient alpha of .93 (Miller et al., 2003). Miller et al. (2003) reported a correlation between the ORS and the OQ of .58.

The SRS, a four-item measure assessing the therapeutic alliance, was used to evaluate the client's perception of the therapy sessions. Based on more than 1,000 studies, the client's assessment of the therapeutic alliance has been shown to serve as the best predictor of therapy outcome or success (Orlinsky, Rønnestad, & Willutzki, 2004). The four items of the SRS ask the client to rate the relationship with the therapist (i.e., did the client feel heard, understood, and respected), the significance of goals and topics discussed in the session, the extent to which the approach or method the therapist used in the session fit the client, and the quality of the session overall. Taken together, the items can be viewed as the client's beliefs about how therapy is progressing based upon the occurrences in the just-concluded session.

PROCEDURE

The level-of-functioning measures (OQ and ORS) were given prior to every session. The measure of therapeutic alliance and relationship (SRS) was given at the end of every session. The pretherapy and posttherapy coefficients were created for each of the measures by calculating the mean of the measures from the first three sessions and the mean of the last three sessions. Cases were included if there were seven or more sessions.

RESULTS

The pretherapy measures revealed no statistical differences between the scores for the GFPP clients and the treatment-as-usual clients on any of the measures. There were differences initially for the OQ and the ORS measures (Figs. 6-1 and 6-2); therefore, the statistical analyses controlled for pretreatment differences for the GFPP and treatment-as-usual clients.

The two therapy outcome dependent variables, the OQ and the ORS, were analyzed initially in a MANCOVA with the first three session averages for each measure used as a covariate and referred to as the pre-measures. The use of covariates adjusted the analysis to correct for the beginning differences between groups. The overall MANCOVA was not significant: $F(2, 87) = .85$; $p = .43$; partial eta squared $= .02$; power $= .19$. The MANCOVA indicated that the outcome measures revealed no difference between the two therapy approaches. Examination of the individual ANCOVAs confirmed that no statistically significant differences existed between the GFPP and treatment-as-usual groups on the ORS and OQ measures of therapy outcome. The pre- and post-measure means for the ORS and OQ are presented in Figures 6-1 and 6-2.

The second set of analyses examined the session process measure. Using an analysis of covariance, the SRS revealed a statistically significant difference

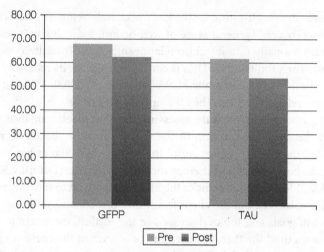

Figure 6-1 Pretreatment and posttreatment client distress means from the OQ-45. The *lower* OQ-45 scores indicate better mental health.

between the GFPP and treatment-as-usual approach: $F(1, 88) = 6.55$; $p = .01$; partial eta squared = .07; power = .72. An analysis of covariance allows the pretreatment levels of the SRS to be controlled. The clients rated GFPP as significantly more favorable on the therapeutic alliance measure. Since the overall measure of therapeutic alliance was significant, a post hoc examination of the relationship, goals, and approach of therapy questions was done to determine which areas of the therapeutic alliance were important to the clients. Because there are multiple measures of the same phenomenon, a MANCOVA was employed. The results of the MANCOVA were not statistically significant, but the effect size was judged

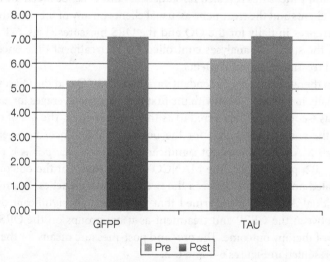

Figure 6-2 Pretreatment and posttreatment client well-being means from the ORS. The *higher* ORS scores indicate better mental health.

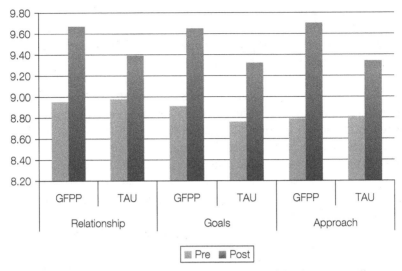

Figure 6-3 Pretreatment and posttreatment client ratings of the therapeutic alliance score means from the SRS.

sufficient to examine the individual analyses at the corrected degrees of freedom: $F(4, 82) = 1.99$; $p = .10$; partial eta squared = .09; power = .57. Then the individual items were examined. Each of the individual analyses of covariance was significant, indicating that all of the therapeutic alliance domains were rated higher in the GFPP treatment. The clients' opinion of the relationship indicated that they believed the relationship was significantly better in GFPP than treatment as usual: $F(1, 85) = 6.45$; $p = .01$; partial eta squared = .07; power = .71. Similarly, the goals focused on in therapy were rated significantly better in GFPP than treatment as usual: $F(1, 85) = 5.31$; $p = .02$; partial eta squared = .06; power = .62. And the approach that the therapist was using in therapy was rated significantly better in GFPP than treatment as usual: $F(1, 85) = 6.28$; $p = .01$; partial eta squared = .07; power = .70. Finally, the overall experience of the session's worth revealed that GFPP was significantly better than treatment as usual: $F(1, 85) = 7.15$; $p = .009$; partial eta squared = .08; power = 0.75. The averaged first three ratings of therapy and the averaged last three ratings of therapy for each of the three therapeutic alliance domains are shown in Figure 6-3. The higher scores on the therapeutic alliance (SRS) ratings mean that the client thought the alliance was better.

DISCUSSION OF THE THREE-YEAR STUDY
The results of this initial evaluation of GFPP are quite favorable. The hypothesized non-difference between the GFPP and treatment-as-usual clients on the outcome measures was correct. The difference that was expected did occur. The GFPP clients rated their therapy sessions more positively that the treatment-as-usual clients. Obviously, we are pleased by these results.

The outcome measures indicated that GFPP was no more helpful than treatment as usual on the OQ and ORS. The decades of research on therapy outcome substantiate that complete psychotherapy models that have the allegiance of the therapist enacting the psychotherapy will have similar outcomes (Wampold & Imel, 2015). This three-year study substantiates that GFPP performs as well as the empirically supported psychotherapies.

The area of superiority of GFPP over treatment as usual was that clients rated the GFPP sessions more positively. The SRS assessment indicated that the GFPP sessions were significantly superior when compared to treatment as usual. The clients reported a greater liking of the relationship with the therapist, the goals and topics talked about in the session, and the approach or method the therapist used in the GFPP than the treatment-as-usual sessions. The SRS measure addresses the heart of our argument for using the GFPP, which is that clients like the process of focusing upon their strengths, positive emotions, and goals, and this leads to the benefits measured by the SRS.

The demonstration of superior results for GFPP on the SRS is particularly notable because the SRS measures the therapeutic alliance. As discussed earlier, the quality of the therapeutic alliance is highly predictive of successful outcomes in psychotherapy of any theory (Horvath & Bedi, 2002). A significantly stronger therapeutic alliance was found for the GFPP model, which predicts reduced client dropout (Sharf, Primavera, & Diener, 2010). Future research should explore GFPP's possible advantage in helping more clients than treatment as usual.

We hypothesize that the superior therapeutic alliance may best be explained by the GFPP techniques that facilitate the therapist's expression of the client's attractive characteristics. Research indicates that the therapist, not the client, makes a larger difference in whether a client rates the therapeutic alliance high or low (Baldwin, Wampold, & Imel, 2007). Certain therapists consistently receive higher scores from their clients regarding the therapeutic alliance, while others consistently receive lower alliance scores.

We attribute the higher therapeutic alliance scores for GFPP compared to treatment as usual to the GFPP techniques that promote the therapists' expression of the characteristics and techniques that the literature describes as facilitating the alliance. A literature review by Ackerman and Hilsenroth (2003) specified the therapist attributes and techniques that have contributed to strong alliances. The therapist's personal attributes include being flexible, respectful, trustworthy, interested, friendly, warm, and open. The techniques include exploration; reflection; supportive statements; noting past therapy success; accurate interpretation; facilitating expression of affect; actively affirming, understanding, and attending to clients' experiences; and interpreting what the clients want. The GFPP model structures most of the techniques and characteristics known for facilitating the therapeutic alliance into the process of therapy. Although not enumerated by Ackerman and Hilsenroth, GFPP adds additional techniques that identify strengths, positive emotions, and approach goals, and these surely enhance the therapeutic alliance. We contend that GFPP elicits the therapist characteristics that clients value by means of its techniques and attitudes.

In conclusion, the first effectiveness study of GFPP supported the theory's benefits when compared to treatment as usual. GFPP was as good at producing the client outcome scores as treatment as usual and was better at achieving higher therapeutic alliance scores.

WHERE TO GO FROM HERE?

A central focus of this book has been to present an orientation toward psychotherapy based upon what clients are able to accomplish when attending to and employing their positive emotions, strengths, and goals. The emphasis is upon how therapists can support the client's abilities through positive psychology and typical psychotherapy principles. The reader is urged to develop a GFPP orientation— that is, a conviction that each client has a wealth of healthy strengths and desires that can incrementally move him or her toward greater well-being. The therapist's GFPP orientation includes the assumption that the client has been imbued with or accumulated healthy attributes through being human, as well as learning from culture, family, school, work . . . everywhere. We believe the GFPP orientation toward the client is therapeutic. However, the GFPP orientation is only a first step; the therapist must be able to enact the orientation. Future research needs to examine the benefits to both the client and the therapist of a GFPP orientation and the helpfulness of the therapeutic techniques and interventions as well. Adding new ways of communicating to clients how they can use their abilities to create a meaningful, enjoyable life will create new pathways and therefore hope.

THE CONTEXTUAL MODEL FRAMEWORK

In structuring the possible future research on GFPP, we offer a framework based upon the Contextual Model. The Contextual Model is a meta-theory that describes psychotherapy from a philosophical vantage point. The Contextual Model's basic premise is that "the benefits of psychotherapy accrue through social processes and that the relationship, broadly defined, is the bedrock of psychotherapy effectiveness" (Wampold & Imel, 2015, p. 50). GFPP is a psychotherapy model that fits within the domain of the Contextual Model meta-theory for psychotherapy because of the centrality of a psychological model. Therefore, exploring psychotherapy research through the lens of the Contextual Model and psychological metaphor may be productive in avoiding the pitfalls of studies guided by the physical science metaphor.

Research Allegiance Versus Treatment Integrity

Clarifying the meta-theory or philosophical background of a theory is imperative when claiming that a psychotherapy model was properly carried out. When researching psychotherapy models such as GFPP, a study must be able to demonstrate that the specific psychotherapy model was enacted in the study if the results of the study are to be trusted. The current gold standard for justifying the claim that a psychotherapy model was properly carried out is treatment integrity or treatment fidelity. *Treatment integrity* describes the degree to which an intervention was implemented as proposed by the psychotherapy model (Perepletchikova, Treat, & Kazdin, 2007). The problem with treatment integrity is that the definition focuses upon the implementation of the interventions by the therapist. Treatment integrity includes (a) the therapist's inclusion of the correct procedures; (b) the therapist's competence with the procedures; (c) and whether or not the examined procedures differ as required by theory from another, different set of procedures (Waltz, Addis, Koerner, & Jacobson, 1993). Treatment integrity assumes a physical science, cause-and-effect model. The assumption underlying the concept of treatment integrity is that if the treatment action occurs as described, then the therapist was competent and the client should respond in a certain manner that leads to successful therapy outcome.

When leaving the physical science metaphor (i.e., the medical model), an alternative to treatment integrity that fits with a psychological metaphor is therapist allegiance. *Therapist allegiance* is defined as the therapist believing in the value of the therapeutic approach being used with the client (Wampold & Imel, 2015). The therapist's belief in or allegiance to the therapy model being used increases the potency of the therapy (Luborsky et al., 1999; Munder, Brutsch, Leonhart, Gerger, & Barth, 2013; Wampold & Imel, 2015). The therapist allegiance is similar to the therapist's orientation toward therapy and the therapist's intent[1] during psychotherapy. The intent and the belief of the therapist are critical in psychotherapy because of the persuasive nature of the relationship between the client and therapist in creating change. When the therapist believes in the client and the therapy, then the client tends to believe in, engage in, and benefit from therapy. As presented in Chapter 4, when the therapist has hope, the client is more likely to have hope too. Therefore, future research needs to measure the therapist's allegiance to GFPP.

Second, the assessment of competence as an ability to facilitate the experiences for the client that a GFPP orientation describes is also important. A measure of competence should assess how the client responded since the change theory is the positive emotion of the client, tied to the Broaden-and-Build phenomenon.

Third, future research should capture the phenomenon of Broaden-and-Build in measureable terms, since Broaden-and-Build is the way change is conceptualized in GFPP. Fitzpatrick and Stalikas (2008) suggest that perhaps all psychotherapies should conceptualize positive change as Broaden-and-Build. If Broaden-and-Build is a central concept of positive change through psychotherapy, then how should broadening be identified as a therapeutic change process through research and in practice? Besides using electrodes to measure a client's cardiovascular reactions (as Fredrickson did in her foundational research of Broaden-and-Build), is there a behavioral indicator that captures the broadening process of clients? Perhaps client responses to positive cues from the therapist can be studied to understand the essence of broadening for clients in therapy. Maybe measures of broadening that clients complete at the conclusion of a session can be validated.

If a valid measure of broadening can be developed, then the next step of research could be to uncover links between broadening and well-being, and between broadening and client problem states. The complete state model of mental health conceptualizes mental health and mental illness on two different continua, yet we do not have sufficient empirical evidence of the relationship between mental illness and mental health (i.e., well-being). Is Fredrickson accurate in theorizing the undoing hypothesis? Can broadening in whatever form undo symptoms of mental illness? Does well-being over time diminish mental illness? Keyes (2007) provides evidence through the complete state model of mental health of the coexistence of a human being's problem states and his or her well-being. Can we assume in the context of psychotherapy that individuals can flourish *and* suffer from some form of mental illness at the same time? We pose these questions for the future research of GFPP and as accessible measures of broadening are developed.

The Contextual Model Pathways

The Contextual Model describes a meta-theory of psychotherapy consisting of three pathways that contribute to client growth that build upon an initial bond that begins the relationship between the therapist and client. (For an in-depth description of the Contextual Model, see Wampold & Budge, 2012.)

1. The first pathway to client change is the formation of a real relationship between the therapist and client.
2. The second pathway consists of the client's expectations of benefit that are created through therapeutic techniques.
3. The final pathway is the client's change through participating in the therapy interventions.

INITIAL BOND RESEARCH

The initial bond is formed by the client's expectations of what therapy and the therapist will be like, as well as past experiences with people whom the client may view as similar to the therapist. The initial bond can be influenced, but the attribution of trustworthiness occurs almost immediately upon meeting a person (Benedetti, 2011). As reviewed in Chapter 3, trust can be enhanced by the décor of the therapy office, the dress of the therapist, and the website presentation fitting the client's expectations. Even before arriving for the first therapy session, the client's expectations could be adjusted by receiving preparatory information. Clients with discrepant expectations about what they expect and experience in psychotherapy will have a weaker therapeutic alliance and will be at higher risk for prematurely dropping out of therapy (Frankl, Philips, & Wennberg, 2014). Future GFPP development and research could focus upon the initial bond that the client experiences upon arriving at the first GFPP session. Perhaps a specifically designed intake or pre-intake contact could help the client trust the therapist and the GFPP therapy process to a greater extent than the typical process. Researching the initial bond and dropout rates is important because psychotherapy has a 33% to 50% dropout rate that needs to be remedied (Sharf, Primavera, & Diener, 2010). Perhaps GFPP's initial focus upon client strengths will engage clients and reduce the dropout rate. A remedy to the high dropout problem for services to minority populations and economically disadvantaged people is especially needed (Barrett et al., 2008). Perhaps altering the traditional intake process to be more strength-focused would decrease the large dropout rate as well. We hope researchers will further investigate the issues of client expectations, the initial bond, and therapy attendance as these issues relate to GFPP.

FIRST PATHWAY: REAL RELATIONSHIP

The first pathway to client change in the meta-theoretical Contextual Model consists of forming a real relationship between the therapist and client (Wampold & Budge, 2012). An essential GFPP therapy orientation and skill is to engage the client in a *real* and *therapeutic* relationship based upon the client's abilities and desires. In Chapter 5, we presented four cases in which therapists worked to form a relationship with their clients based upon what the clients needed to focus on when they came to therapy. Client abilities, strengths, and desires were considered at the start of therapy rather than narrowly working toward a problem definition or applying a certain method based upon a particular diagnostic category.

Engaging the client in a *real* relationship in therapy refers to the genuine personal relationship that exists between the therapist and client, based upon "the ability and willingness to be what one truly is in the relationship—to be authentic, open and honest" (Gelso & Carter, 1994, p. 297). Wampold and Imel (2015) point to research from many areas that supports the centrality of real human connection: attachment (Bowlby, 1980), belongingness (Baumeister, 2005), social support (Cohen & Syme, 1985), and Carl Rogers' therapy (1951). Loneliness, the opposite of experiencing a real relationship, is an influential factor in mortality, at least as harmful as smoking, obesity, or alcoholism (Luo, Hawkley, Waite, & Cacioppo, 2012). A healthy real relationship is fundamentally therapeutic and provides a solid foundation for psychotherapy. As the therapist, you must be willing and able to form a real relationship with your client, one in which you reveal your personhood and react to the client in an authentic way. The therapist must genuinely believe that forming a real relationship with the client is essential.

A real relationship has central importance in therapy because humans have an innate propensity to cooperate with a person when in a good relationship such as psychotherapy (Wampold & Budge, 2012). The design of human brains encourages influence through relationships (Lieberman, 2013).

Therefore, an area to focus upon in researching GFPP is examining the real relationship. What does the client experience in GFPP? As the therapist attempts to highlight the client's strengths, promote positive affect, explore goals, and increase hope, does the client increasingly experience the therapy relationship as a real relationship that is healthy? Is the GFPP therapist viewed as more genuine in the hope for therapy because of the focus on client strengths, positive affect, and goals? Can the therapist genuinely portray hope for the client and the GFPP process? Does having a GFPP orientation toward client growth facilitate the real relationship?

We assume that a therapist can be facilitative in forming a real relationship by having a GFPP orientation because the therapist's belief and hope can authentically engage the client. A real relationship includes an appreciation and openness to all that has contributed to the client's development, both the strengths and the problems. The therapist's ability to be authentic, open, and honest with a client in a therapeutic manner should promote trust, openness, hope, and growth in the client. The real relationship for a GFPP therapist includes honestly believing in the client having strengths and important desires associated with healthy values that will reveal the client's ability to have a meaningful life. GFPP's orientation toward therapy is more than a treatment or set of techniques. We look forward to research supporting our contention that from the perspectives of both the client and the therapist, the relationship of the therapist with the client is enhanced by the skilled application of the GFPP orientation.

The GFPP orientation recognizes the importance of culture (Hook, Farrell, Davis, DeBlaere, Van Tongeren, & Utsey, 2016). It includes valuing the distinctiveness of each person's rich and unique life. Meeting the client with cultural humility, the "ability to maintain an interpersonal stance that is other-oriented (or open to the other) in relation to aspects of cultural identity that are most important to the client" (Hook, Davis, Owen, Worthington, & Utsey, 2013, p. 354) is a component of cultural competence that can contribute to the development of a real relationship. Cultural humility leads to therapeutic humility. Prized in GFPP, therapeutic humility means being actively curious about the client as representing more than the presenting problem or psychopathology. The therapist explores the client's world in order to reveal strengths and desires, as well as to know the client more broadly. The therapist must be comfortable and skillful in discussing the client's world. As the therapist, you contribute a lifetime of learning about cultures, happiness, family issues, death, goals, loss, success, pain, and so many other issues. This wisdom allows you greater empathy and ease of communicating about personal experiences.

Future GFPP development and research can further our knowledge of how to focus upon positive emotions, values, strengths, and hope. It would be important to know if the real relationship is enhanced by focusing upon strengths, positive emotions, and goals developed in a genuine manner. Also, will GFPP-oriented therapists be viewed as more culturally competent because of their orientation toward the client? The research on capitalization suggests that the positive focus will enhance the relationships in therapy (Gable, Reis, Impett, & Asher, 2004).

SECOND PATHWAY: CLIENT EXPECTATIONS

The second pathway in the Contextual Model meta-theory consists of the client's expectations of benefit that are created through the therapeutic techniques. The real relationship creates the client's openness to accepting the therapist's explanation of therapy. However, the expectation of therapy success increases when the client believes the therapist's explanation of the value of the treatment approach and the therapeutic tasks (Wampold & Budge, 2012). The focus of GFPP on the generation of client hope is very similar to the Contextual Model's second pathway of enhancing the client's expectation for success. Client expectations are influenced by both the therapist's self-presentation and the rationale given for the treatment (Devilly & Borkovec, 2000; Horvath, 1990; Hoyt, 1996; Ilardi & Craighead, 1994; Kazdin & Krouse, 1983). The therapeutic rationale is most acceptable to the client when it fits the client's beliefs (Conoley et al., 1994; Scheel et al., 1999). As the therapist understands the client's views, a rationale that fits the client can be employed. Therefore, the client's expectation of success rests on the openness of the client, the therapist's ability, and the believability or acceptability of the therapeutic rationales. Future research could focus on whether hope is generated when the therapist matches the therapy rationale with the client's beliefs.

THIRD PATHWAY: CLIENT PARTICIPATION

The third pathway in the Contextual Model meta-theory is the client changing through participating in the therapy interventions. The client must figure out how to adjust the therapist's ideas into a workable intervention. Bohart and Tallman (2010) maintain that in order to participate in the therapy intervention, the client must actively consider the intervention, adjust the suggested intervention to personally fit, and then engage in the suggested intervention. They assert that the client factor is the most important and most underappreciated common factor in psychotherapy. Psychotherapists too often disrespect clients when they "only see clients contributing by (a) hoping therapy will help, (b) being distressed, and (c) coming to seek help" (Bohart & Tallman, 2010, p. 129). When the client factor is emphasized, the therapist supplies the support and structure, but the client is the major contributor to change.

At times the therapist supplies the support and structure for an intervention, but the client does not implement a suggested intervention. At such times, the therapist should reflect on the reasons for the client's non-acceptance and revise the intervention strategy to be more acceptable to the client. When clients decide not to participate in an intervention, it may be that the interventions were applied without considering the client. Therefore, the client's response to the intervention can be seen as providing information about the client's beliefs or strengths, not as resistance. Perhaps either the therapist's presentation of the intervention or the intervention itself should be revised. The goal would be to gain the client's approval of a change strategy. Fitting an intervention to the client's context is paramount.

When the client is understood to be an active agent, the research focus should include the client's perceptions of the interventions. Did the client believe the intervention was workable before attempting it—that is, was the rationale for engaging in the intervention convincing? Acceptable? Was the description of the intervention clear?

ADDING SYSTEMS THEORY

A systems theory perspective is not yet well integrated into GFPP. Systems theory adds an appreciation of a client's complexity as well as providing a guide for examining a client's environment. Urie Bronfenbrenner's Bioecological Systems Theory has been extremely helpful in examining a person's environmental influences at the internal, micro-, meso-, and macro-systemic levels (Bronfenbrenner & Bronfenbrenner, 2009). The person's interaction with biological maturation, family, community, culture, and society can provide many opportunities for discovering strengths. Systems theories predict that changes in one level will affect other areas, so intervention possibilities are increased. Future development of the GFPP model could better explicitly integrate a systems perspective.

While positive psychology and family therapy have incorporated systems theory into a family therapy model (Conoley & Conoley, 2009), perhaps the GFPP orientation could further inform the practice of family therapy. Additionally, translating GFPP into business and school settings could enhance the group dynamics. Individuals could act as active agents in identifying strengths derived from interactions, support positive emotions as building blocks of change, and facilitate hope. Approach goals could focus upon intrinsic values that would be mutually beneficial. The original aspiration of positive psychology was the betterment of individuals and society.

NEW STRIDES IN POSITIVE PSYCHOLOGY

Advancements in positive psychology will continue to develop, which will increase the pathways for clients to achieve well-being through a meaningful life. There are many research initiatives exploring exciting ideas. One area that may develop is the extra helpfulness of some strengths or values. For example, the research in self-affirmation reveals that reflecting upon kindnesses performed in the past has more therapeutic influence than reflecting upon some other values (Jessop, Simmonds, & Sparks, 2009). Does kindness hold some special characteristic? Or perhaps kindness is a pro-social strength, and that is why loving-kindness meditation is becoming more recommended in psychotherapy. Similarly, the expression of gratitude appears to hold more promise than is fully understood or employed (Wood, Froh, & Geraghty, 2010). However, there might be an interaction of endorsed values and the strengths being expressed. Perhaps the Values in Action (VIA) strengths research will develop toward a more sophisticated understanding of people and values.

Another area of positive psychology that is currently blossoming is the growth mindset that focuses on the incremental implicit theory of change (see Chapter 2). Educational interventions using the growth mindset are redefining the limits imposed by negative stereotypes, bigotry, and low expectations. Indeed, growth mindset is beginning to change personality. Accomplishments that seemed impossible may become achievable as psychology attends more to growth (Dweck, 2008).

Finally, positive psychology is being applied to many fields. Articles appear each month about applying positive psychology to classroom learning, sports, fitness, substance abuse prevention and treatment, mentoring, youth development, and personal coaching, among many other areas. Across the world interest is expressed in positive psychology. Will positive psychology become part of mainstream psychology or grow as a different discipline? Perhaps more exciting insights will be forthcoming soon. We look forward to the future!

CHAPTER 1

1. *Happiness, subjective well-being*, and *well-being* will be used interchangeably.
2. In all likelihood Aristotle's definition of happiness will not be similar to modern definitions. However, no original texts exist of Aristotle's writings; only second-, third-, or fourth-hand reports exist of what Aristotle originally said, and therefore accounts of his meaning disagree.
3. Sometimes the physical science metaphor is referred to as the *medical model* of psychotherapy.
4. When writing about client idiosyncrasies, we mean to communicate the client's strengths, immediate and past life experiences, and immediate and long-term goals. Included in a client's strengths and past life experiences are culture, education, relationship history, and many other issues that make all of us distinctive individuals.
5. In our writing, we will use *happiness, subjective well-being*, and *well-being* interchangeably. Later in the book distinctions will be made between these terms and psychological well-being.
6. Positive empathy is intuiting what the client wants based upon the present content and context. Further definition occurs in subsequent chapters.
7. For a full presentation of Wampold's analyses and argument see Wampold & Imel (2015).

CHAPTER 2

1. The video of the original film with Carl Rogers, Fritz Perls, and Albert Ellis can be found on YouTube and is worth your time.
2. Self-compassion and incremental change are described in Chapter 3.

CHAPTER 3

1. *Common factors* are the processes that reside in all bona fide psychotherapies.
2. See later in this chapter for descriptions of these interventions.
3. Mindfulness will be further described later in the chapter. The psychological applications of mindfulness typically use only a small part of the Buddhist tradition.

CHAPTER 4

1. The small, incremental steps are consistent with the growth mindset described in Chapter 3.
2. Many resources for PCOMS are available on the internet at no cost.

CHAPTER 6

1. Intent was presented in Chapter 3.

REFERENCES

Aberg, M. A., Pedersen, N. L., Toren, K., Svartengren, M., Backstrand, B., Johnsson, T., . . . Kuhn, H. G. (2009). Cardiovascular fitness is associated with cognition in young adulthood. *Proceedings of the National Academy of Science U S A, 106*, 20906–20911.

Ackerman, S. J., & Hilsenroth, M. J. (2003). A review of therapist characteristics and techniques positively impacting the therapeutic alliance. *Clinical Psychology Review, 23*, 1–33.

Adams, J. F., Piercy, F. P., & Jurich, J. A. (1991). Effects of Solution Focused Therapy's "formula first session task" on compliance and outcome in family therapy. *Journal of Marital and Family Therapy, 17*, 277–290.

Aiken, G. A. (2006). The potential effect of mindfulness meditation on the cultivation of empathy in psychotherapy: A qualitative inquiry. *Dissertation Abstracts International, Section B: Sciences and Engineering, 67*, 2212.

Alarcon, G. M., Bowling, N. A., & Khazon, S. (2013). Great expectations: A meta- analytic examination of optimism and hope. *Personality and Individual Differences, 54*(7), 821–827.

American Psychiatric Association. (2013). *Diagnostic and statistical manual of mental disorders* (5th ed.). Arlington, VA: American Psychiatric Publishing

American Public Media. Podcast—A Prairie Home Companion. Retrieved September 29, 2016, from https://www.prairiehome.org/listen/podcast/.

Anderson, H. D. (1995). Collaborative language systems: Toward a postmodern therapy. In R. H. Mikesell, D-D. Lusterman, & S. H. McDaniel (Eds.), *Integrating family therapy: handbook of family psychology and systems theory* (pp. 27–44). Washington, DC: American Psychological Association.

Arciniega, G. M., Anderson, T. C., Tovar-Blank, Z. G., & Tracey, T. J. G. (2008). Toward a fuller conception of machismo: development of a traditional machismo and caballerismo scale. *Journal of Counseling Psychology, 55*, 19–33.

Aronson, J., Cohen, G. L., & Nail, P. R. (1999). Self-affirmation theory: an update and appraisal. In E. Harmon-Jones & J. Mills (Eds.), *Cognitive dissonance: progress on a pivotal theory in social psychology*. Washington, DC: American Psychological Association.

Aubuchon-Endsley, N. L., Callahan, J. L., González, D. A., Ruggero, C. J., & Abramson, C. I. (2015). The impact of hope in mediating psychotherapy expectations and outcomes: a study of Brazilian clients. *International Journal of Integrative Psychotherapy, 6*, 63–80.

Baer, R. A., Fischer, S., & Huss, D. B. (2005). Mindfulness-based cognitive therapy applied to binge eating: a case study. *Cognitive and Behavioral Practice*, *12*(3), 351–358.

Baldwin, S. A., Wampold, B. E., & Imel, Z. E. (2007). Untangling the alliance–outcome correlation: exploring the relative importance of therapist and patient variability in the alliance. *Journal of Consulting and Clinical Psychology*, *75*(6), 842.

Bandura, A. (1997). *Self-efficacy: the exercise of control*. New York: W.H. Freeman.

Barrett, M. S., Chua, W. J., Crits-Christoph, P., Gibbons, M. B., & Thompson, D. (2008). Early withdrawal from mental health treatment: implications for psychotherapy practice. *Psychotherapy: Theory, Research, Practice, Training*, *45*(2), 247–267.

Bartholomew, T. T., Scheel, M. J., & Cole, B. P. (2015). Development and validation of the hope for change through counseling scale. *The Counseling Psychologist*, *43*(5), 671–702.

Bateson, C. (2011). *Altruism in humans*. New York: Oxford University Press.

Baumeister, R. F. (2005). *The cultural animal: human nature, meaning, and social life*. New York: Oxford University Press.

Baumeister, R. F., Vohs, K. D., Aaker, J. L., & Garbinsky, E. N. (2013). Some key differences between a happy life and a meaningful life. *The Journal of Positive Psychology*, *8*(6), 505–516.

Beck, J. T., & Strong, S. R. (1982). Stimulating therapeutic change with interpretations: A comparison of positive and negative connotation. *Journal of Counseling Psychology*, *29*(6), 551–559.

Bell-Tolliver, L., Burgess, R., & Brock, L. J. (2009). African American therapists working with African American families: an exploration of the strengths perspective in treatment. *Journal of Marital and Family Therapy*, *35*(3), 293–307.

Beltzer, M. L., Nock, M. K., Peters, B. J., & Jamieson, J. P. (2014). Rethinking butterflies: the affective, physiological, and performance effects of reappraising arousal during social evaluation. *Emotion*, *14*(4), 761–768.

Benedetti, F. (2011). *The patient's brain: The neuroscience behind the doctor–patient relationship*. New York: Oxford University Press.

Benish, S. G., Imel, Z. E., & Wampold, B. E. (2008). The relative efficacy of bona fide psychotherapies for treating post-traumatic stress disorder: a meta-analysis of direct comparisons. *Clinical Psychology Review*, *28*(5), 746–758.

Benton, J. M., & Overtree, C. E. (2012). Multicultural office design: a case example. *Professional Psychology: Research and Practice*, *43*(3), 265–269.

Berg, I. K. (1994). *Family-based services: a solution-focused approach*. New York: W. W. Norton & Co.

Berg, I. K., & Miller, S. D. (1992). Working with Asian American clients: one person at a time. *Families in Society*, *73*(6), 356–363.

Bernard, J. M., & Goodyear, R. K. (2014). *Fundamentals of clinical supervision* (5th ed.). Boston, MA: Pearson.

Bernieri, F. (1988). Coordinated movement and rapport in teacher–student interactions. *Journal of Nonverbal Behavior*, *24*, 120–138.

Bernieri, F. J., Davis, J. M., Rosenthal, R., & Knee, C. R. (1994). Interactional synchrony and rapport: measuring synchrony in displays devoid of sound and facial affect. *Personality and Social Psychology Bulletin*, *20*, 303–311.

Birkett, M. (2014). Self-compassion and empathy across cultures: comparison of young adults in China and the United States. *International Journal of Research Studies in Psychology*, *3*(3), 25–34.

Biswas-Diener, R. (2012). *The courage quotient*. San Francisco, CA: Jossey-Bass.

Biswas-Diener, R., Kashdan, T. B., & Minhas, G. (2011). A dynamic approach to psychological strength development and intervention. *The Journal of Positive Psychology*, *6*(2), 106–118.

Bohart, A. C., & Greenberg, L. S. (1997). *Empathy reconsidered: new directions in psychotherapy*. Washington, DC: American Psychological Association.

Bohart, A. C., & Tallman, K. (2010). Clients: the neglected common factor in psychotherapy. In B. L. Duncan, S. D. Miller, B. E. Wampold, & M. A. Hubble (Eds.), *The heart and soul of change: delivering what works in therapy* (2nd ed., pp. 83–111). Washington, DC: American Psychological Association.

Bordin, E. S. (1979). The generalizability of the psychoanalytic concept of the working alliance. *Psychotherapy: Theory, Research, and Practice*, *16*, 252–260.

Bordin, E. S. (1994). Theory and research on the therapeutic working alliance: new direction. In A. O. Horvath & L. S. Greenberg (Eds.), *The working alliance: theory, research, and practice* (pp. 13–37). New York: Wiley.

Bowlby, J. (1980). *Attachment and loss, Volume 3: Loss, sadness and depression*. New York: Basic Books.

Bronfenbrenner, U., & Bronfenbrenner, U. (2009). *The ecology of human development: experiments by nature and design*. Cambridge, MA: Harvard University Press.

Bryant, F B. (2003). Savoring Beliefs Inventory (SBI): a scale for measuring beliefs about savouring. *Journal of Mental Health*, *12*(2), 175–196.

Buckner, J. D., Cromer, K. R., Merrill, K. A., Mallott, M. A., Schmidt, N. B., Lopez, C. (2009). Pretreatment intervention increases treatment outcomes for patients with anxiety disorders. *Cognitive Therapy and Research*, *33*, 126–137.

Burnette, J. L., O'Boyle, E. H., VanEpps, E. M., Pollack, J. M., & Finkel, E. J. (2013). Mind-sets matter: a meta-analytic review of implicit theories and self-regulation. *Psychological Bulletin*, *139*(3), 655–701.

Buschor, C., Proyer, R. T., & Ruch, W. (2013). Self- and peer-rated character strengths: how do they relate to satisfaction with life and orientations to happiness? *The Journal of Positive Psychology*, *8*(2), 116–127.

Carkhuff, R. R. (1969). *Helping and human relations (Vol. 1)*. New York: Holt, Rinehart, & Winston.

Carmody, J., Baer, R. A., Lykins, E. L. B., & Olendzki, N. (2009). An empirical study of the mechanisms of mindfulness in a mindfulness-based stress reduction program. *Journal of Clinical Psychology*, *65*(6), 613–626.

Carver, C. S. (2004). Negative affects deriving from the behavioral approach system. *Emotion*, *4*(1), 3–22.

Carver, C. S., & Scheier, M. (1990). *Principles of self-regulation: action and emotion*. New York: Guilford Press.

Chang, J. H., Huang, C. L., & Lin, Y. C. (2015). Mindfulness, basic psychological needs fulfillment, and well-being. *Journal of Happiness Studies*, *16*(5), 1149–1162.

Chao, R. K., & Tseng, V. (2002) Parenting of Asians. In M. H. Bornstein (Ed.), *Handbook of parenting: social conditions and applied parenting* (pp. 59–93). Mahwah, NJ: Erlbaum.

Chiesa, A., Serretti, A., & Jakobsen, J. C. (2013). Mindfulness: top-down or bottom-up emotion regulation strategy? *Clinical Psychology Review*, *33*(1), 82–96.

Chirkov, V., Ryan, R. M., Kim, Y., & Kaplan, U. (2003). Differentiating autonomy from individualism and independence: a self-determination theory perspective on internalization of cultural orientations and well-being. *Journal of Personality and Social Psychology*, *84*(1), 97–110.

Cohen, G. L., Aronson, J., & Steele, C. M. (2000). When beliefs yield to evidence: reducing biased evaluation by affirming the self. *Personality and Social Psychology Bulletin*, *26*, 1151–1164.

Cohen, G. L., & Sherman, D. K. (2014). The psychology of change: self-affirmation and social psychological intervention. *Annual Review of Psychology*, *65*, 333–371.

Cohen, G. L., Sherman, D. K., Bastardi, A., Hsu, L., McGoey, M., & Ross, L. (2007). Bridging the partisan divide: self-affirmation reduces ideological closed-mindedness and inflexibility in negotiation. *Journal of Personality & Social Psychology*. *93*. 415–430.

Cohen, J. (1988). *Statistical power analysis for the behavioral sciences* (2nd ed.). New Jersey: Lawrence Erlbaum.

Cohen, S. E., & Syme, S. (1985). *Social support and health*. Academic Press.

Cohn, M. A., Fredrickson, B. L., Brown, S. L., Mikels, J. A., & Conway, A. M. (2009). Happiness unpacked: positive emotions increase life satisfaction by building resilience. *Emotion*, *9*(3), 361–368.

Collett, P. (1971). Training Englishmen in the non-verbal behaviour of Arabs. *International Journal of Psychology*, *6*(3), 209–215.

Comas-Diaz, L., & Griffith, E. E. (Eds.). (1988). *Clinical guidelines in cross-cultural mental health*. New York: Wiley.

Conoley, C. W., & Conoley, J. C. (2009). *Positive psychology and family therapy: creative techniques and practical tools for guiding changing and enhancing growth*. Hoboken, NJ: John Wiley and Sons Inc.

Conoley, C. W., Conoley, J. C., Ivey, D., & Scheel, M. (1991). The effects of matching rationales on the acceptability of consultation interventions. *Journal of Counseling and Development*, *69*(6), 546–549.

Conoley, C. W., & Garber, R. A. (1985). Effects of reframing and self-control directives on loneliness, depression, and controllability. *Journal of Counseling Psychology*, *32*(1), 139–142.

Conoley, C. W., Morgan-Consoli, M. L., Zetzer, H., Hernandez, E., & Hernandez, R. (2016). Examining basic helping skills in cross-cultural counseling between European American counselors and Mexican American clients. *Revista Interamericana de Psicologia/Interamerican Journal of Psychology*, *49*(3), 382–403.

Conoley, C. W., Padula, M. A., Payton, D. S., & Daniels, J. A. (1994). Predictors of client implementation of counselor recommendations: match with problem, difficulty level, and building client strengths. *Journal of Counseling Psychology*, *41*, 3–7.

Conoley, C. W., Pontrelli, M. E., Oromendia, M. F., Bello, B. D. C., & Nagata, C. M. (2015). Positive empathy: a therapeutic skill inspired by positive psychology. *Journal of Clinical Psychology*, *71*(6), 575–583.

Conoley, C. W., Vasquez, E., Bello, B., Oromendia, M. F., & Jeske, D. R. (2015). Celebrating the accomplishments of others: mutual benefits of capitalization. *The Counseling Psychologist*, *43*(5), 734–751.

Cook, J. E., Purdie-Vaughns, V., Garcia, J., & Cohen, G. L. (2012). Chronic threat and contingent belonging: protective benefits of values affirmation on identity development. *Journal of Personality and Social Psychology*, *102*(3), 479–496.

Coppock, T. E., Owen, J. J., Zagarskas, E., & Schmidt, M. (2010). The relationship between therapist and client hope with therapy outcomes. *Psychotherapy Research*, *20*(6), 619–626.

Corrigan, P. W., Rafacz, J., & Ruesch, N. (2011). Examining a progressive model of self-stigma and its impact on people with serious mental illness. *Psychiatry Research, 189*(3), 339–343.

Cosmides, L., & Tooby, J. (2000) Evolutionary psychology and the emotions. In M. Lewis & J. M. H. Jones (Eds.), *Handbook of emotions.* (pp. 91–115). New York: Guilford.

Crawford, J. (1999). *Bilingual education: history, politics, theory, and practice* (4th ed.). Los Angeles: Bilingual Educational Services.

Csikszentmihalyi, M. (1990). *Flow: the psychology of optimal experience.* New York: Harper Perennial.

Cummins, J. (1994). Knowledge, power, and identity in teaching ESL. In F. Genesee (Ed.), *Educating second language children.* New York: Press Syndicate of the University of Cambridge.

Davidson, R. J. (2000). Affective style, psychopathology, and resilience: brain mechanisms and plasticity. *American Psychologist, 55*(11), 1196–1214.

Davidson, R. J., Kabat-Zinn, J., Schumacher, J., Rosenkranz, M., Muller, D., Santorelli, S. F., . . . Sheridan, J. F. (2003). Alterations in brain and immune function produced by mindfulness meditation. *Psychosomatic Medicine, 65*(4), 564–570.

Davis, D. M., & Hayes, J. A. (2011). What are the benefits of mindfulness? A practice review of psychotherapy-related research. *Psychotherapy, 48*(2), 198–208.

Deci, E. L., & Ryan, R. M. (2000). The "what" and "why" of goal pursuits: human needs and the self-determination of behavior. *Psychological Inquiry, 11*(4), 227–268.

Deci, E. L., & Ryan R. M. (2008). Self-determination theory: a macro-theory of human motivation, development, and health. *Canadian Psychology, 49*(3) 182–185.

De Jong, P., & Berg, I. K. (2008). *Interviewing for solutions* (3rd ed.). Belmont, CA: Thomson Brooks/Cole Publishing Co.

Del Re, A. C., Flückiger, C., Horvath, A. O., Symonds, D., & Wampold, B. E. (2012). Therapist effects in the therapeutic alliance–outcome relationship: a restricted-maximum likelihood meta-analysis. *Clinical Psychology Review, 32*(7), 642–649.

de Shazer, S. (1988). *Clues: investigating solutions in brief therapy.* New York: Norton.

de Shazer, S., Dolan, Y., Korman, H., McCollum, E., Trepper, T., & Berg, I. K. (2007). *More than miracles: the state of the art of solution-focused brief therapy.* New York: Haworth Press.

Devilly, G. J., & Borkovec, T. D. (2000). Psychometric properties of the credibility/ expectancy questionnaire. *Journal of Behavior Therapy and Experimental Psychiatry, 31*(2), 73–86.

Devlin, A. S., Borenstein, B., Finch, C., Hassan, M., Iannotti, E., & Koufopoulos, J. (2013). Multicultural art in the therapy office: community and student perceptions of the therapist. *Professional Psychology: Research and Practice, 44*(3), 168–176.

Devos, T., & Banaji, M. R. (2003). Implicit self and identity. In M. R. Leary & J. P. Tangney (Eds.), *Handbook of self and identity* (pp. 153–175). New York: Guilford Press.

Dew, S. E., & Bickman, L. (2005). Client expectancies about therapy. *Mental Health Services Research, 7*, 21–33.

Diedrich, A., Grant, M., Hofmann, S. G., Hiller, W., & Berking, M. (2014). Self-compassion as an emotion regulation strategy in major depressive disorder. *Behaviour Research and Therapy, 58*, 43–51.

Diedrich, A., Hofmann, S. G., Cuijpers, P., & Berking, M. (2016). Self-compassion enhances the efficacy of explicit cognitive reappraisal as an emotion regulation strategy in individuals with major depressive disorder. *Behaviour Research and Therapy, 82*, 1–10.

Diener, E. (1984). Subjective well-being. *Psychological Bulletin*, *95*, 542–575.

Diener, E., Oishi, S., & Ryan, K. (2013). Universal and cultural differences in the causes and structure of "happiness"—a multilevel review. In C. Keyes (Ed.), *Mental well-being: international contributions to the study of positive mental health* (pp. 153–176). Dordrecht, Netherlands: Springer.

Diener, E., Sandvik, E., & Pavot, W. (1991). Happiness is the frequency, not the intensity, of positive versus negative affect. *Subjective Well-Being: An Interdisciplinary Perspective*, *21*, 119–139.

Dimidjian, S., & Linehan, M. M. (2003). Defining an agenda for future research on the clinical application of mindfulness practice. *Clinical Psychology: Science and Practice*, *10*(2), 166–171.

Dittmar, H., Bond, R., Hurst, M., & Kasser, T. (2014). The relationship between materialism and personal well-being: a meta-analysis. *Journal of Personality and Social Psychology: Personality Processes and Individual Differences*, *107*(5), 879–924.

Duncan, B. L., Miller, S. D., Sparks, J. A., Claud, D. A., Reynolds, L. R., Brown, J., & Johnson, L. D. (2003). The Session Rating Scale: preliminary psychometric properties of a "working" alliance measure. *Journal of Brief Therapy*, *3*(1), 3–12.

Duncan, B. L., & Reese, R. J. (2015). The Partners for Change Outcome Management System (PCOMS): revisiting the client's frame of reference. *Psychotherapy*, *52*(4), 391–401.

Dweck, C. S. (1999). *Self-theories: their role in motivation, personality, and development. Essays in social psychology*. New York: Psychology Press.

Dweck, C. (2008). *Mindset: the new psychology of success*. New York: Ballantine Books.

Edwards, M., Adams, E. M., Waldo, M., Hadfield, O. D., & Biegel, G. M. (2014). Effects of a mindfulness group on Latino adolescent students: examining levels of perceived stress, mindfulness, self-compassion, and psychological symptoms. *Journal for Specialists in Group Work*, *39*(2), 145–163.

Elliot, A. J. (2008). Approach and avoidance motivation. In A. J. Elliot (Ed.), *Handbook of approach and avoidance motivation*. New York: Taylor & Francis.

Elliot, A. J., & Church, M. A. (2002). Client articulated avoidance goals in the therapy context. *Journal of Counseling Psychology*, *49*(2), 243–254.

Elliot, A. J., & Niesta, D. (2009). Goals in the context of the hierarchical model of approach—avoidance motivation. In G. B. Moskowitz, & H. Grant (Eds.), *The psychology of goals* (pp. 56–76). New York: Guilford Press.

Elliott, R., Bohart, A. C., Watson, J. C., & Greenberg, L. S. (2011). Empathy. *Psychotherapy*, *48*(1), 43–49.

Emmons, R. A. (2003). Personal goals, life meaning, and virtue: wellsprings of a positive life. In C. L. M. Keyes & J. Haidt (Eds.), *Flourishing: positive psychology and the life well-lived* (pp. 105–128). Washington, DC: American Psychological Association.

Emmons, R. A., & McCullough, M. E. (2003). Counting blessings versus burdens: an experimental investigation of gratitude and subjective well-being in daily life. *Journal of Personality and Social Psychology*, *84*(2), 377–389.

Emmons, R. A., & Shelton, C. M. (2002). Gratitude and the science of positive psychology. In C. R. Snyder & S. J. Lopez (Eds.), *Handbook of positive psychology* (pp. 459–471). Oxford: Oxford University Press.

Enriquez, V. G. (1993). Developing a Filipino psychology. In U. Kim & J. W. Berry (Eds.), *Indigenous psychologies: research and experience in cultural context* (pp. 152–169). Thousand Oaks, CA: Sage Publications, Inc.

Erdley, C. A., Cain, K. M., Loomis, C. C., Dumas-Hines, F., & Dweck, C. S. (1997). Relations among children's social goals, implicit personality theories, and responses to social failure. *Developmental Psychology, 33*, 263–272.

Esquivel, G. B., & Keitel, M. A. (1990). Counseling immigrant children in schools. *Elementary School Guidance and Counseling, 24*, 213–218.

Evans, S., Ferrando, S., Findler, M., Stowell, C., Smart, C., & Haglin, D. (2008). Mindfulness-based cognitive therapy for generalized anxiety disorder. *Journal of Anxiety Disorders, 22*(4), 716–721.

Falicov, C. J. (2010). Changing constructions of machismo for Latino men in therapy: "The devil never sleeps." *Family Process, 49*, 309–329.

Fitzpatrick, M. R., & Stalikas, A. (2008). Positive emotions as generators of therapeutic change. *Journal of Psychotherapy Integration, 18*(2), 137.

Flaskerud, J. H. (1986). The effects of culture-compatible intervention on the utilization of mental health services by minority clients. *Community Mental Health Journal, 22*, 127–141.

Flückiger, C., & Grosse Holtforth, M. (2008). Focusing the therapist's attention on the patient's strengths: a preliminary study to foster a mechanism of change in outpatient psychotherapy. *Journal of Clinical Psychology, 64*(7), 876–890.

Fowler, J. H., & Christakis, N. A. (2008). Dynamic spread of happiness in a large social network: longitudinal analysis over 20 years in the Framingham Heart Study. *British Medical Journal, 337*(2338), 1–9.

Frank, J. D., & Frank, J. B. (1991). *Persuasion and healing: a comparative study of psychotherapy* (3rd ed.). Baltimore, MD: Johns Hopkins University Press.

Frankl, M., Philips, B., & Wennberg, P. (2014). Psychotherapy role expectations and experiences: discrepancy and therapeutic alliance among patients with substance use disorders. *Psychology and Psychotherapy: Theory, Research and Practice, 87*(4), 411–424.

Frankl, V. E. (1984). *Man's search for meaning*. New York: Simon and Schuster.

Fredrickson, B. L. (1998). What good are positive emotions? *Review of General Psychology, 2*(3), 300–319.

Fredrickson, B. L. (2001). The role of positive emotions in positive psychology: the broaden-and-build theory of positive emotions. *American Psychologist, 56*(3), 218–226.

Fredrickson, B. L. (2013a). Updated thinking on positivity ratios. *American Psychologist, 68*(9), 814–822.

Fredrickson, B. L. (2013b). Positive emotions Broaden-and-Build. In E. Ashby Plant & P. G. Devine (Eds.), *Advances in experimental social psychology* (vol. 47, pp. 1–53). Burlington, VT: Academic Press.

Fredrickson, B. L., Cohn, M. A., Coffey, K. A., Pek, J., & Finkel, S. M. (2008). Open hearts build lives: positive emotions, induced through loving-kindness meditation, build consequential personal resources. *Journal of Personality and Social Psychology, 95*(5), 1045.

Frederickson, B. L., Tugade, M. M., Waugh, C. E., & Larkin, G. R. (2003). What good are positive emotions in crises? A prospective study of resilience and emotions following the terrorist attacks on the United States on September 11th, 2001. *Journal of Personality and Social Psychology, 84*(2), 365–376.

Friedman, R. S., & Förster, J. (2001). The effects of promotion and prevention cues on creativity. *Journal of Personality and Social Psychology: Attitudes and Social Cognition*, *81*(6), 1001–1013.

Frijda, N. H. (1986). *The emotions*. Cambridge, England: Cambridge University Press.

Fuller, F., & Hill, C. E. (1985). Counselor and helpee perceptions of counselor intentions in relation to outcome in a single counseling session. *Journal of Counseling Psychology*, *32*(3), 329–338.

Gable, S. L. (2006). Approach and avoidance social motives and goals. *Journal of Personality*, *74*(1), 175–222.

Gable, S. L., & Haidt, J. (2005). What (and why) is positive psychology? *Review of General Psychology*, *9*(2), 103–110.

Gable, S. L., Reis, H. T., Impett, E. A., & Asher, E. R. (2004). What do you do when things go right? The intrapersonal and interpersonal benefits of sharing positive events. *Journal of Personality and Social Psychology*, *87*(2), 228–245.

Garfield, J. L. (2011) *The meaning of life: perspectives from the world's great intellectual traditions. Course guidebook*. The Teaching Company, USA.

Garland, E. L., Fredrickson, B., Kring, A. M., Johnson, D. P., Meyer, P. S., & Penn, D. L. (2010). Upward spirals of positive emotions counter downward spirals of negativity: insights from the Broaden-and-Build Theory and affective neuroscience on the treatment of emotion dysfunctions and deficits in psychopathology. *Clinical Psychology Review*, *30*(7), 849–864.

Gaser, C., & Schlaug, G. (2003). Brain structures differ between musicians and non-musicians. *Journal of Neuroscience*, *23*(27), 9240–9245.

Gaston, L. (1990). The concept of the alliance and its role in psychotherapy: theoretical and empirical considerations. *Psychotherapy*, *27*, 143–152.

Gelso, C. J. (2004). *A theory of the real relationship in psychotherapy*. Paper presented at the International Conference of the Society for Psychotherapy Research, Rome, Italy.

Gelso, C. J., & Carter, J. A. (1994). Components of the psychotherapy relationship: their interaction and unfolding during treatment. *Journal of Counseling Psychology*, *41*(3), 296.

Gelso, C. J., Nutt Williams, E., & Fretz, B. R. (2014). *Counseling psychology* (3rd ed.). Washington, DC: American Psychological Association.

Gerber, Z., Tolmacz, R., & Doron, Y. (2015). Self-compassion and forms of concern for others. *Personality and Individual Differences*, *86*, 394–400.

Geschwind, N., Peeters, F., Drukker, M., vas Os, J., & Wichers, M. (2011). Mindfulness training increases momentary positive emotions and reward experience in adults vulnerable to depression: a randomized control trial. *Journal of Consulting and Clinical Psychology*, *79*, 618–628.

Gilbert, P. (2010). An introduction to compassion-focused therapy in cognitive behavior therapy. *International Journal of Cognitive Therapy*, *3*, 97–112.

Glass, J., & Owen, J. (2010). Latino fathers: the relationship among machismo, acculturation, ethnic identity, and paternal involvement. *Psychology of Men & Masculinity*, *11*, 251–261.

Gopaul-McNicol, S., & Thomas-Presswood, T. (1998). *Working with linguistically and culturally different children: innovative clinical and educational approaches*. Boston: Allyn & Bacon.

Graves, J. R., & Robinson, J. D. (1976). Proxemic behavior as a function of inconsistent verbal and nonverbal messages. *Journal of Counseling Psychology, 23*, 333–338.

Greenberg, L. S., & Watson, J. C. (2006). Change process research. In J. C. Norcross, L. E. Beutler, & R. F. Levant (Eds.), *Evidence-based practice in mental health: debate and dialogue on the fundamental questions* (pp. 81–89). Washington, DC: American Psychological Association.

Greenberg, L. S., Watson, J. C., Elliott, R., & Bohart, A. C. (2001). Empathy. *Psychotherapy: Theory, Research, Practice, Training, 38*(4), 380–384.

Greenberg, R. P., Constantino, M. J., & Bruce, N. (2006). Are patient expectations still relevant for psychotherapy process and outcome? *Clinical Psychology Review, 26*(6), 657–678.

Grencavage, L. M., & Norcross, J. C. (1990). Where are the commonalities among the therapeutic common factors? *Professional Psychology: Research and Practice, 21*(5), 372.

Haase, R. F., & Tepper, D. T. (1972). Nonverbal components of empathic communication. *Journal of Counseling Psychology, 19*, 417–424.

Hanh, N. (1998). *Interbeing: fourteen guidelines for engaged Buddhism.* Berkeley, CA: Parallax Press.

Hansen, J., & Wänke, M. (2010). Truth from language and truth from fit: The impact of linguistic concreteness and level of construal on subjective truth. *Personality and Social Psychology Bulletin, 36*(11), 1576–1588.

Harber, K. D., Yeung, D., & Iacovelli, A. (2011). Psychosocial resources, threat, and the perception of distance and height: support for the resources and perception model. *Emotion, 11*(5), 1080–1090.

Harbin, J. M., Gelso, C. J., & Rojas, A. E. P. (2014). Therapists' work with client strengths: the development of a measure. *The Counseling Psychologist, 42*(3), 345–373.

Hatcher, R. L., & Barends, A. W. (2006). How a return to theory could help alliance research. *Psychotherapy: Theory, Research, Practice, Training, 43*(3), 292–299.

Hayes, S. C., Follette, V. M., & Linehan, M. (Eds.). (2004). *Mindfulness and acceptance: expanding the cognitive-behavioral tradition.* New York: Guilford Press.

Henderson, V. P., Clemow, L., Massion, A. O., Hurley, T. G., Druker, S., & Hebert, J. R. (2012). The effects of mindfulness-based stress reduction on psychosocial outcomes and quality of life in early-stage breast cancer patients: a randomized trial. *Breast Cancer Research and Treatment, 131*, 99–109.

Hernandez, R. (2002). *Fatherwork in the crossfire: Chicano teen fathers struggling to take care of business.* East Lansing, MI: Michigan State University, Julian Samora Research Institute. (ERIC Document Reproduction Service No. ED471926).

Higgins, E. T., Shah, J., & Friedman, R. (1997). Emotional responses to goal attainment: strength of regulatory focus as moderator. *Journal of Personality and Social Psychology: Attitudes and Social Cognition, 72*(3), 515–525.

Hill, C. E. (1992). An overview of four measures developed to test the Hill process model: therapist intentions, therapist response modes, client reactions, and client behaviors. *Journal of Counseling & Development, 70*(6), 728–739.

Hill, C. E., Siegelman, L., Gronsky, B. R., Sturniolo, F., & Fretz, B. R. (1981). Nonverbal communication and counseling outcome. *Journal of Counseling Psychology, 28*(3), 203–212.

Hill, R. B. (1999). *The strengths of African American families: twenty-five years later.* New York: University Press of America.

Hodges, T. D., & Clifton, D. O. (2004). Strengths-based development in practice. In P. A. Linley & S. Joseph (Eds.), *Positive psychology in practice* (pp. 256–268). Hoboken, NJ: Wiley.

Hofstede, G. (1980). Culture and organizations. *International Studies of Management & Organization, 10*(4), 15–41.

Hook, J. N., Davis, D. E., Owen, J., Worthington, E. L., Jr., & Utsey, S. O. (2013). Cultural humility: measuring openness to culturally diverse clients. *Journal of Counseling Psychology, 60*(3), 353–366.

Hook, J. N., Farrell, J. E., Davis, D. E., DeBlaere, C., Van Tongeren, D. R., & Utsey, S. O. (2016). Cultural humility and racial microaggressions in counseling. *Journal of Counseling Psychology, 63*(3), 269–277.

Horvath, A. O., & Bedi, R. P. (2002). The alliance. In J. C. Norcross (Ed.), *Psychotherapy relationships that work* (pp. 37–70). New York: Oxford University Press.

Horvath, A. O., & Greenberg, L. S. (1994). *The working alliance: theory, research, and practice* (Vol. 173). New York: John Wiley & Sons.

Horvath, A. O., & Luborsky, L. (1993). The role of the therapeutic alliance in psychotherapy. *Journal of Consulting and Clinical Psychology, 61*(4), 561–573.

Horvath, P. (1990). Treatment expectancy as a function of the amount of information presented in therapeutic rationales. *Journal of Clinical Psychology, 46*, 636–642.

Hovey, J. D., & King, C. A. (1996). Acculturative stress, depression, and suicidal ideation among immigrant and second-generation Latino adolescents. *Journal of the American Academy of Child Adolescent Psychiatry, 35*, 1183–1192.

Hoyt, W. T. (1996). Antecedents and effects of perceived therapist credibility: a meta-analysis. *Journal of Counseling Psychology, 43*, 430–447.

Hubble, M. A., & Gelso, C. J. (1978). Effect of counselor attire in an initial interview. *Journal of Counseling Psychology, 25*(6), 581–584.

Hwang, K.K. (1999) Filial piety and loyalty: two types of social identification in Confucianism. *Asian Journal of Social Psychology, 2*(1), 163–183.

Ilardi, S. S., & Craighead, W. E. (1994). The role of nonspecific factors in cognitive-behavior therapy for depression. *Clinical Psychology: Science and Practice, 1*, 138–156.

Ilies, R., Keeney, J., & Scott, B. A. (2011). Work–family interpersonal capitalization: Sharing positive work events at home. *Organizational Behavior and Human Decision Processes, 114*(2), 115–126.

Ireland, M. E., & Pennebaker, J. W. (2010). Language style matching in writing: synchrony in essays, correspondence, and poetry. *Journal of Personality and Social Psychology, 99*, 549–571.

Izard, C. E. (1977). *Human emotions.* New York: Plenum.

Jain, S., Shapiro, S. L., Swanick, S., Roesch, S. C., Mills, P. J., Bell, I., & Schwartz, G. E. (2007). A randomized controlled trial of mindfulness meditation versus relaxation training: effects on distress, positive states of mind, rumination, and distraction. *Annals of Behavioral Medicine, 33*(1), 11–21.

Jenkins, A. H. (1985). Attending to self-activity in the Afro-American client. *Psychotherapy, 22*, 335–341.

Jessop, D. C., Simmonds, L. V., & Sparks, P. (2009) Motivational and behavioural consequences of self-affirmation interventions: a study of sunscreen use among women. *Psychology & Health, 24*(5), 529–544.

Johnson, E. J., & Tversky, A. (1983). Affect, generalization, and the perception of risk. *Journal of Personality and Social Psychology, 45,* 20–31.

Jordan, K. B., & Quinn, W. H. (1994). Session two outcome of the formula first session task in problem- and solution-focused approaches. *American Journal of Family Therapy, 22,* 3–16.

Kabat-Zinn, J. (1982). An outpatient program in behavioral medicine for chronic pain patients based on the practice of mindfulness meditation: theoretical considerations and preliminary results. *General Hospital Psychiatry, 4*(1), 33–47.

Kabat-Zinn, J. (1994). *Wherever you go, there you are: mindfulness meditation in everyday life.* New York: Hyperion.

Kanter, J. W., Santiago-Rivera, A. L., Rusch, L. C., Busch, A. M., & West, P. (2010). Initial outcomes of a culturally adapted behavioral activation for Latinas diagnosed with depression at a community clinic. *Behavior Modification, 34*(2), 120–144.

Karni, A., Meyer, G., Rey-Hipolito, C., Jezzard, P., Adams, M. M., Turner, R., & Ungerleider, L. G. (1998). The acquisition of skilled motor performance: fast and slow experience-driven changes in primary motor cortex. *Proceedings of the National Academy of Science U S A, 95,* 861–868.

Karwowski, M. (2014). Creative mindsets: measurement, correlates, consequences. *Psychology of Aesthetics, Creativity, and the Arts, 8*(1), 62.

Kasser, T. (2002). *The high price of materialism.* Cambridge, MA: MIT Press.

Kasser, T., & Ryan, R. M. (1996). Further examining the American dream: differential correlates of intrinsic and extrinsic goals. *Personality and Social Psychology Bulletin, 22*(3), 280–287.

Kazdin, A. E., & Krouse, R. (1983). The impact of variations in treatment rationales on expectancies for therapeutic change. *Behavior Therapy, 14,* 657–671.

Kelly, A. C., & Garavan, H. (2005). Human functional neuroimaging of brain changes associated with practice. *Cerebral Cortex, 15*(8), 1089–1102.

Kempermann, G., Fabel, K., Ehninger, D., Babu, H., Leal-Galicia, P., Garthe, A., & Wolf, S. (2010). Why and how physical activity promotes experience-induced brain plasticity. *Frontiers in Neuroscience, 4,* 189.

Keyes, C. L. M. (2002). The mental health continuum: from languishing to flourishing. *Journal of Health and Social Behaviour, 43,* 207–222.

Keyes, C. L. M. (2005). Mental illness and/or mental health? Investigating axioms of the complete state model of health. *Journal of Consulting and Clinical Psychology, 73,* 539–548.

Keyes, C. L. M. (2007). Promoting and protecting mental health as flourishing: a complementary strategy for improving national mental health. *American Psychologist, 62,* 95–108.

Keyes, C. L. M., & Lopez, S. J. (2002). Toward a science of mental health: Positive directions in diagnosis and intervention. In C. R. Snyder & S. J. Lopez (Eds.), *Handbook of positive psychology* (pp. 45–62). New York: Oxford University Press.

Keysers, C., & Perrett, D. I. (2004). Demystifying social cognition: a Hebbian perspective. *Trends in Cognitive Sciences, 8*(11), 501–507.

Khoury, B., Lecomte, T., Fortin, G., Masse, M., Therien, P., Bouchard, V., . . . Hofmann, S. G. (2013). Mindfulness-based therapy: a comprehensive meta-analysis. *Clinical Psychology Review, 33,* 763–771.

Kiselica, M. S., & Englar-Carlson, M. (2010). Identifying, affirming, and building upon male strengths: the positive psychology/positive masculinity model of psychotherapy with boys and men. *Psychotherapy: Theory, Research, Practice, Training, 47*, 276–287.

Kivlighan, D. M. (1989). Changes in counselor intentions and response modes and in client reactions and session evaluation after training. *Journal of Counseling Psychology, 36*(4), 471–476.

Klimecki, O. M., Leiberg, S., Ricard, M., & Singer, T. (2014). Differential pattern of functional brain plasticity after compassion and empathy training. *Social Cognitive and Affective Neuroscience, 9*(6), 873–879.

Kok, B. E., Coffey, K. A., Cohn, M. A., Catalino, L. I., Vacharkulksemsuk, T., Algoe, S. B., . . . Fredrickson, B. L. (2013). How positive emotions build physical health: perceived positive social connections account for the upward spiral between positive emotions and vagal tone. *Psychological Science, 24*(7), 1123–1132.

Kolb, B., & Whishaw, I. Q. (1998). Brain plasticity and behavior. *Annual Review of Psychology, 49*, 43–64.

Koole, S. L., Smeets, K., Van Knippenberg, A., & Dijksterhuis, A. (1999). The cessation of rumination through self-affirmation. *Journal of Personality and Social Psychology, 77*(1), 111–125.

Kratz, L. M., Wong, Y. J., & Vaughan, E. L. (2013). Health behaviors among pregnant women: the influence of social support. In S. Chen (Ed.), *Social support: theory, role of gender and culture and health* (pp. 109–122). Hauppauge, NY: Nova Science.

Kristeller, J. L., & Hallett, C. B. (1999). An exploratory study of a meditation-based intervention for binge eating disorder. *Journal of Health Psychology, 4*(3), 357–363.

Ladany, N., Friedlander, M. L., & Nelson, M. L. (2005). *Critical events in psychotherapy supervision: an interpersonal approach.* Washington, DC: American Psychological Association.

Lambert, M. (1992). Psychotherapy outcome research. In J. C. Norcross & M. R. Goldfried (Eds.), *Handbook of psychotherapy integration* (pp. 94–129). New York: Basic.

Lambert, M. J., & Bergin, A. E. (1994). The effectiveness of psychotherapy. In A. E. Bergin & S. L. Garfield (Eds.), *Handbook of psychotherapy and behavior change* (4th ed., pp. 143–189). New York: Wiley.

Lambert, M. J., & Finch, A. E. (1999). The Outcome Questionnaire. In M. E. Maniish (Ed.), *The use of psychological testing for treatment planning and outcomes assessment* (2nd ed., pp. 831–869). Mahwah, NJ: Lawrence Erlbaum.

Lambert, M. J., Hansen, N. B., Umpress, V., Lunnen, K., Okiishi, J., Burlingame, G. M., & Reisinger, C. W. (1996). *Administration and scoring manual for the OQ-45.2.* American Credentialing Services.

Langston, C. A. (1994). Capitalizing on and coping with daily-life events: expressive responses to positive events. *Journal of Personality and Social Psychology, 67*(6), 1112–1125.

Layous, K., Nelson, K. S., & Lyubomirsky, S. (2013). What is the optimal way to deliver a positive activity intervention? The case of writing about one's best possible selves. *Journal of Happiness Studies, 14*(2), 635–654.

Lench, H. C., & Levine, L. J. (2008). Goals and responses to failure: knowing when to hold them and when to fold them. *Motivation and Emotion, 32*(2), 127–140.

Lewin, K. (1951). *Field theory in social science; selected theoretical papers* (D. Cartwright, ed.). New York: Harper & Row.

Lewis, M. (1993). Self-conscious emotions: embarrassment, pride, shame, and guilt. In M. Lewis & J. M. Haviland (Eds.), *Handbook of emotions* (pp. 563–573). New York: Guilford Press.

Lieberman, M.D. (2013). *Social: why our brains are wired to connect.* New York: Crown Publishing Group.

Linley, P. A. (2008a). *Average to A+: realising strengths in yourself and others.* Coventry, UK: CAPP Press.

Littrell, M. A., & Littrell, J. M. (1983). Counselor dress cues: Evaluations by American Indians and Caucasians. *Journal of Cross-Cultural Psychology, 14*(1), 109–121.

Lopez, S. J., Edwards, L. M., Pedrotti, J. T., Prosser, E. C., LaRue, S., Spalitto, S. V., & Ulven, J. C. (2006). Beyond the DSM-IV: assumptions, alternatives, and alterations. *Journal of Counseling and Development, 84*, 259–287.

Luborsky, L., Diguer, L., Seligman, D. A., Rosenthal, R., Krause, E. D., Johnson, S., . . . Schweizer, E. (1999). The researcher's own therapy allegiances: a "wild card" in comparisons of treatment efficacy. *Clinical Psychology: Science and Practice, 6*, 95–106.

Luo, Y., Hawkley, L. C., Waite, L. J., & Cacioppo, J. T. (2012). Loneliness, health, and mortality in old age: a national longitudinal study. *Social Science & Medicine, 74*(6), 907–914.

Lyubomirsky, S. (2007). *The how of happiness.* London: Sphere Books.

Lyubomirsky, S., Sheldon, K. M., & Shchkade, D. (2005). Pursuing happiness: the architecture of sustainable change. *Review of General Psychology, 9*(2), 111–131.

MacBeth, A., & Gumley, A. (2012). Exploring compassion: a meta-analysis of the association between self-compassion and psychopathology. *Clinical Psychology Review, 32*, 545–552.

Maguire, E., Woollett, K., & Spiers, H. (2006). London taxi drivers and bus drivers: a structural MRI and neuropsychological analysis. *Hippocampus, 16*, 1091–1101.

Magyar-Moe, J. L. (2009). *Therapist's guide to positive psychological interventions.* Burlington, MA: Academic Press.

Magyar-Moe, J. L., Owens, R. L., & Scheel, M. J. (2015). Applications of positive psychology in the work of counseling psychologists: current status and future directions. *The Counseling Psychologist, 43*(4), 494–507.

Major, B., & O'Brien, L. T. (2005). The social psychology of stigma. *Annual Review of Psychology, 56*, 393–421.

Malan, D. H. (1973). The outcome problem in psychotherapy research. *Archives of General Psychiatry, 29*, 719–729.

Maramba, G. G., & Nagayama Hall, G. C. (2002). Meta-analyses of ethnic match as a predictor of dropout, utilization, and level of functioning. *Cultural Diversity and Ethnic Minority Psychology, 8*(3), 290–297.

Markus, H. R., & Kitayama, S. (1991). Culture and the self: implications for cognition, emotion, and motivation. *Psychological Review, 98*(2), 224–253.

Marlatt, G. A. (2003). Buddhist philosophy and the treatment of addictive behavior. *Cognitive and Behavioral Practice, 9*(1), 44–50.

Martin, D. J., Garske, J. P., & Davis, M. K. (2000). Relation of the therapeutic alliance with outcome and other variables: a meta-analytic review. *Journal of Consulting and Clinical Psychology, 68*(3), 438–450.

May, A., & Gaser, C. (2006). Magnetic resonance-based morphometry: a window into structural plasticity of the brain. *Current Opinion in Neurology, 19*(4), 407–411.

Mazzucchelli, T., Kane, R., & Rees, C. (2009). Behavioral activation treatments for depression in adults: a meta-analysis and review. *Clinical Psychology: Science and Practice, 16*(4), 383–411.

McCarn, S. R., & Fassinger, R. E. (1996). Revisioning sexual minority identity formation: a new model of lesbian identity and its implications for counseling and research. *The Counseling Psychologist, 24*(3), 508–534.

Mechelli, A., Crinion, J. T., Noppeney, U., O'Doherty, J., Ashburner, J., Frackowiak, R. S., & Price, C. J. (2004). Neurolinguistics: structural plasticity in the bilingual brain. *Nature, 431*(7010), 757–757.

Meevissen, Y. M. C., Peters, M. L., & Alberts, H. J. E. M. (2011). Become more optimistic by imagining a best possible self: effects of a two-week intervention. *Journal of Behavior Therapy and Experimental Psychiatry, 42*, 371–378.

Melidonis, G. G., & Bry, B. H. (1995). Effects of therapist exceptions questions on blaming and positive statements in families with adolescent behavior problems. *Journal of Family Psychology, 9*, 451–457.

Messer, S. B., & Wampold, B. E. (2002). Let's face facts: common factors are more potent than specific therapy ingredients. *Clinical Psychology: Science and Practice, 9*(1), 21–25.

Miller, J. G., Kahle, S., & Hastings, P. D. (2015). Roots and benefits of costly giving: children who are more altruistic have greater autonomic flexibility and less family wealth. *Psychological Science, 26*(7), 1038–1045.

Miller, S. D., & Duncan, B. L. (2000). *The Outcome Rating Scale.* Chicago, IL: Authors.

Miller, S. D., & Duncan, B. L. (2004). *The Outcome and Session Rating Scales: Administration and scoring manual.* Chicago, IL: Authors.

Miller, S. D., Duncan, B. L., Brown, J., Sparks, J. A., & Claud, D. A. (2003). The Outcome Rating Scale: a preliminary study of the reliability, validity, and feasibility of a brief visual analog measure. *Journal of Brief Therapy, 2*(2), 91–100.

Miller, S. D., Duncan, B. L., & Johnson, L. D. (2000). *The Session Rating Scale 3.0.* Chicago, IL: Authors.

Miller, S. L., Duncan, B. L., Sorrell, R., & Brown, G. S. (2005). The Partners for Change Outcome Management System. *Journal of Clinical Psychology, 61*, 199–208.

Molden, D. C., & Dweck, C. S. (2006). Finding "meaning" in psychology: a lay theories approach to self-regulation, social perception, and social development. *American Psychologist, 61*, 192–203. doi:10.1037/0003-066X.61.3.192

Munder, T., Brütsch, O., Leonhart, R., Gerger, H., & Barth, J. (2013). Researcher allegiance in psychotherapy outcome research: an overview of reviews. *Clinical Psychology Review, 33*(4), 501–511.

Neacsiu, A. D., Rizvi, S. L., & Linehan, M. M. (2010). Dialectical behavior therapy skills use as a mediator and outcome of treatment for borderline personality disorder. *Behaviour Research and Therapy, 48*(9), 832–839.

Neff, K. D. (2003). Self-compassion: an alternative conceptualization of a healthy attitude toward oneself. *Self and Identity, 2*, 85–101.

Neff, K. D. (2009). Self-compassion. In M. R. Leary & R. H. Hoyle (Eds.), *Handbook of individual differences in social behavior* (pp. 561–573). New York: Guilford Press.

Neff, K. D. (2011). Self-compassion, self-esteem, and well-being. *Social and Personality Psychology Compass, 5*(1), 1–12.

Neff, K. D. (2012). The science of self-compassion. In C. Germer & R. Siegel (Eds.), *Compassion and wisdom in psychotherapy* (pp. 79–92). New York: Guilford Press.

Neff, K. D. (2015). *Self-compassion: the proven power of being kind to yourself.* New York: Harper Collins.

Neff, K. D., Pisitsungkagarn, K., & Hsieh, Y. P. (2008). Self-compassion and self-construal in the United States, Thailand, and Taiwan. *Journal of Cross-Cultural Psychology, 39,* 267–285.

Newsome, S., Christopher, J. C., Dahlen, P., & Christopher, S. (2006). Teaching counselors self-care through mindfulness practices. *Teachers College Record, 108,* 1881–1990.

Nolen-Hoeksema, S. (2000). The role of rumination in depressive disorders and mixed anxiety/depressive symptoms. *Journal of Abnormal Psychology, 109*(3), 504–511.

Norcross, J. C. (2010). The therapeutic relationship. In B. L. Duncan, S. D. Miller, B. E. Wampold, & M. A. Hubble (Eds.), *The heart & soul of change: delivering what works in therapy* (2nd ed., pp. 113–141). Washington, DC: American Psychological Association.

Nurmi, J. E. (1993). Adolescent development in an age-graded context: the role of personal beliefs, goals, and strategies in the tackling of developmental tasks and standards. *International Journal of Behavioral Development, 16*(2), 169–189.

Nyklicek, I., & Kuijpers, K. F. (2008). Effects of mindfulness-based stress reduction intervention on psychological well-being and quality of life: is increased mindfulness indeed the mechanism? *Annals of Behavior Medicine, 35,* 331–340.

O'Sullivan, M. J., Peterson, P. D., Cox, G. B., & Kirkeby, J. (1989). Ethnic populations: community mental health services ten years later. *American Journal of Community Psychology, 17,* 17–30.

Odou, N., & Bella-Brodrick, D. A. (2013). The efficacy of positive psychology interventions to increase well-being and the role of mental imagery ability. *Social Indicators Research, 110*(1), 111–124.

Orlinsky, D. E., Rønnestad, M. H., & Willutzki, U. (2004). Fifty years of process-outcome research: continuity and change. In M. J. Lambert (Ed.), *Bergin and Garfield's handbook of psychotherapy and behavior change* (5th ed., pp. 307–390). New York: Wiley.

Orzech, K. M., Shapiro, S. L., Brown, K. W., & McKay, M. (2009). Intensive mindfulness training-related changes in cognitive and emotional experience. *Positive Psychology, 4,* 212–222.

Owen, J. J., Tao, K., Leach, M. M., & Rodolfa, E. (2011). Clients' perceptions of their psychotherapists' multicultural orientation. *Psychotherapy, 48*(3), 274–282.

Oyserman, D., & Fryberg, S. (2006). The possible selves of diverse adolescents: content and function across gender, race and national origin. *Possible Selves: Theory, Research, and Applications, 2*(4), 17–39.

Padilla, A. M., & Salgado De Snyder, N. (1985). Counseling Hispanics: strategies for effective intervention. In P. Pedersen (Ed.), *Handbook of cross-cultural counseling and therapy* (pp. 157–164). Westport, CT: Greenwood Press.

Park, N., Peterson, C., & Seligman, M. E. (2004). Strengths of character and well-being. *Journal of Social and Clinical Psychology, 23*(5), 603–619.

Parkinson, B. (2011). Interpersonal emotion transfer: contagion and social appraisal. *Social and Personality Psychology Compass, 5*(7), 428–439.

Pearson, M., O'Brien, P., & Bulsara, C. (2015). A multiple intelligences approach to counseling: enhancing alliances with a focus on strengths. *Journal of Psychotherapy Integration, 25*(2), 128–142.

Pedrotti, J. T., & Edwards, L. M. (2010). The intersection of positive psychology and multiculturalism. In J. G. Ponterotto, J. M. Casas, L. A. Suzuki, & C. M. Alexander (Eds.), *Handbook of multicultural counseling* (3rd ed., pp. 165–174). Thousand Oaks, CA: Sage Publications.

Perepletchikova, F., Treat, T. A., & Kazdin, A. E. (2007). Treatment integrity in psychotherapy research: analysis of the studies and examination of the associated factors. *Journal of Consulting and Clinical Psychology, 75*(6), 829–841.

Peters, M. L., Meevissen, Y. M., & Hanssen, M. M. (2013). Specificity of the Best Possible Self intervention for increasing optimism: comparison with a gratitude intervention. *Terapia Psicologica, 31*(1), 93–100.

Peterson, C., & Seligman, M. E. (2004). *Character strengths and virtues: a handbook and classification.* New York: Oxford University Press.

Pham, L. B., & Taylor, S. E. (1999). From thought to action: effects of process- versus outcome-based mental simulations on performance. *Personality and Social Psychology Bulletin, 25*, 250–260.

Pipes, R. (2016). Psychotherapist Self-Disclosure with Complications—Personal Problems, Sex, "Me-Too." Symposium presented at the annual meeting of the American Psychological Association, Denver, CO.

Pomerantz, E. M., & Kempner, S. G. (2013). Mothers' daily person and process praise: implications for children's theory of intelligence and motivation. *Developmental Psychology, 49*(11), 2040.

Post, S. G. (2005). Altruism, happiness, and health: it's good to be good. *International Journal of Behavioral Medicine, 12*(2), 66–77.

Qin, D. B., Way, N., & Mukherjee, P. (2008). The other side of the model minority story: the familial and peer challenges faced by Chinese American adolescents. *Youth & Society, 39*(4), 480–506.

Rahula, W. (2007). *What the Buddha taught.* New York: Grove/Atlantic, Inc.

Ramseyer, F., & Tschacher, W. (2014). Nonverbal synchrony of head and body movement in psychotherapy: different signals have different associations with outcome. *Frontiers in Psychology, 5*, 979.

Ranney, R. M., Bruehlman-Senecal, E., & Ayduk, O. (2016). Comparing the effects of three online cognitive reappraisal trainings on well-being. *Journal of Happiness Studies* [E-pub before print, July 25].

Ratcliff, C. D., Czuchry, M., Scarberry, N. C., Thomas, J. C., Dansereau, D. F., & Lord, C. G. (1999). Effects of directed thinking on intentions to engage in beneficial activities: actions versus reasons. *Journal of Applied Social Psychology, 29*, 994–1009.

Reese, R. J., Norsworthy, L. A., & Rowlands, S. R. (2009). Does a continuous feedback system improve psychotherapy outcome? *Psychotherapy: Theory, Research, Practice, Training, 46*(4), 418.

Reis, H. T., Smith, S. M., Carmichael, C. L., Caprariello, P. A., Tsai, F., Rodrigues, A., & Maniaci, M. R. (2010). Are you happy for me? How sharing positive events with others provides personal and interpersonal benefits. *Journal of Personality and Social Psychology, 99*, 311–329.

Renner, F., Schwarz, P., Peters, M. L., & Huibers, M. J. (2014). Effects of a best-possible-self mental imagery exercise on mood and dysfunctional attitudes. *Psychiatry Research, 215*(1), 105–110.

Ressel, V., Pallier, C., Ventura-Campos, N., Díaz, B., Roessler, A., Ávila, C., & Sebastián-Gallés, N. (2012). An effect of bilingualism on the auditory cortex. *Journal of Neuroscience, 32*(47), 16597–16601.

Richie, B. S., Fassinger, R. E., Linn, S. G., Johnson, J., Prosser, J., & Robinson, S. (1997). Persistence, connection, and passion: a qualitative study of the career development of highly achieving African American–Black and White women. *Journal of Counseling Psychology, 44*(2), 133–148.

Riggle, E. D., & Rostosky, S. S. (2011). *A positive view of LGBTQ: embracing identity and cultivating well-being.* Lanham, MD: Rowman & Littlefield Publishers.

Riggle, E. D. B., Whitman, J. S., Olson, A., Rostosky, S. S., & Strong, S. (2008). The positive aspects of being a lesbian or gay man. *Professional Psychology: Research and Practice, 39*, 210–217.

Risen, J. L., & Critcher, C. R. (2011). Visceral fit: while in a visceral state, associated states of the world seem more likely. *Journal of Personality and Social Psychology, 100*, 777–793.

Rogers, C. (1951). *Client-centered therapy: its current practice, implications and theory.* Boston: Houghton Mifflin.

Rogers, C. R. (1957). The necessary and sufficient conditions of therapeutic personality change. *Journal of Consulting Psychology, 22*, 95–103.

Rogers, C. (1961). *On becoming a person: a therapist's view of psychotherapy.* Boston: Houghton Mifflin.

Rowe, G., Hirsh, J. B., & Anderson, A. K. (2007). Positive affect increases the breadth of attentional selection. *Proceedings of the National Academy of Sciences U S A, 104*(1), 383–388.

Ryan, R. L., & Deci, E. L. (2000). Self-determination theory and the facilitation of intrinsic motivation, social development, and well-being. *American Psychologist, 55*, 68–78.

Ryan, R., Lynch, M., Vansteenkiste, M., & Deci, E. (2011). Motivation and autonomy in counseling, psychotherapy, and behavior change. *The Counseling Psychologist, 39*, 193–260.

Ryff, C. D. (1989). Happiness is everything, or is it? Explorations on the meaning of psychological well-being. *Journal of Personality and Social Psychology, 57*(6), 1069.

Sandage, S. J., Hill, P. C., & Vang, H. C. (2003). Toward a multicultural positive psychology: indigenous forgiveness and Hmong culture. *Counseling Psychologist, 31*, 564–592.

Santiago-Rivera, A., Arredondo, P. M., & Gallardo-Cooper, M. (2002). *Counseling Latinos and la familia: a practical guide.* Thousand Oaks, CA: Sage.

Scheel, M. J., Conoley, C. W., & Ivey, D. C. (1998). Using client positions as a technique for increasing the acceptability of marriage therapy interventions. *American Journal of Family Therapy, 26*(3), 203–214.

Scheel, M. J., Klentz Davis, C., & Henderson, J. D. (2013). Therapist use of client strengths: a qualitative study of positive processes. *The Counseling Psychologist, 41*, 392–427.

Scheel, M. J., Seaman, S., Roach, K., Mullin, T., & Blackwell-Mahoney, K. (1999). Client implementation of therapist recommendations: predicted by client perception of fit, difficulty of implementation, and therapist influence. *Journal of Counseling Psychology, 46*, 308–316.

Schmitz, T. W., De Rosa, E., & Anderson, A. K. (2009). Opposing influences of affective state valence on visual cortical encoding. *Journal of Neuroscience, 29*(22), 7199–7207.

Schroder, H. S., Dawood, S., Yalch, M. M., Donnellan, M. B., & Moser, J. S. (2015). The role of implicit theories in mental health symptoms, emotion regulation, and hypothetical treatment choices in college students. *Cognitive Therapy and Research, 39*(2), 120–139.

Schure, M. B., Christopher, J., & Christopher, S. (2008). Mind-body medicine and the art of self-care: teaching mindfulness to counseling students through yoga, meditation and qigong. *Journal of Counseling and Development, 86*, 47–56.

Seligman, M. E. P., Steen, T., Park, N., & Peterson, C. (2005). Positive psychology progress: empirical validations of interventions. *American Psychologist, 60*, 410–421.

Shapira, L. B., & Mongrain, M. (2010). The benefits of self-compassion and optimism exercises for individuals vulnerable to depression. *Journal of Positive Psychology, 5*(5), 377–389.

Shapiro, S. L., Astin, J. A., Bishop, S. R., & Cordova, M. (2005). Mindfulness-based stress reduction for health care professionals: results from a randomized trial. *International Journal of Stress Management, 12*(2), 164–176.

Shapiro, S. L., Brown, K. W., & Biegel, G. M. (2007). Teaching self-care to caregivers: effects of mindfulness-based stress reduction on the mental health of therapists in training. *Training and Education in Professional Psychology, 1*, 105–115.

Shapiro, S. L., Schwartz, G. E., & Bonner, G. (1998). Effects of mindfulness-based stress reduction on medical and premedical students. *Journal of Behavioral Medicine, 21*, 581–599.

Sharf, J., Primavera, L. H., & Diener, M. J. (2010). Dropout and therapeutic alliance: a meta-analysis of adult individual psychotherapy. *Psychotherapy: Theory, Research, Practice, Training, 47*(4), 637–645.

Sheldon, K. M., & King, L. (2001). Why positive psychology is necessary. *American Psychologist, 56*(3), 216–217.

Sheldon, K. M., & Lyubomirsky, S. (2006). How to increase and sustain positive emotion: the effects of expressing gratitude and visualizing best possible selves. *The Journal of Positive Psychology, 1*(2), 73–82.

Sheldon, K. M., Ryan, R. M., & Reis, H. T. (1996). What makes for a good day? Competence and autonomy in the day and in the person. *Personality and Social Psychology Bulletin, 22*, 1270–1279.

Sherman, D. K., & Cohen, G. L. (2006). The psychology of self-defense: self-affirmation theory. In M. P. Zanna (Ed.), *Advances in experimental social psychology.* San Diego, CA: Academic Press.

Sherman, D. K., Nelson, L. D., & Steele, C. M. (2000). Do messages about health risks threaten the self? Increasing the acceptance of threatening health messages via self-affirmation. *Personality & Social Psychology Bulletin, 26*, 1046–1058.

Sideridis, G. D., & Kaplan, A. (2011). Achievement goals and persistence across tasks: the roles of failure and success. *Journal of Experimental Education, 79*(4), 429–451.

Sin, N. L., & Lyubomirsky, S. (2009). Enhancing well-being and alleviating depressive symptoms with positive psychology interventions: a practice-friendly meta-analysis. *Journal of Clinical Psychology, 65*(5), 467–487.

Snyder, C. R. (2002). Hope theory: rainbows of my mind. *Psychological Inquiry, 13*(4), 249–275.

Soysa, C. K., & Wilcomb, C. J. (2015). Mindfulness, self-compassion, self-efficacy, and gender as predictors of depression, anxiety, stress, and well-being. *Mindfulness, 6*(2), 217–226.

Stahl, B., & Goldstein, E. (2010). *A mindfulness-based stress reduction workbook*. Oakland, CA: New Harbinger Publications.

Stanley, B., Brown, G. K., Karlin, B., Kemp, J. E., & VonBergen, H. A. (2008). *Safety plan treatment manual to reduce suicide risk: veteran version*. Washington, DC: United States Department of Veterans Affairs.

Steele, C. M. (1988). The psychology of self-affirmation: sustaining the integrity of the self. In L. Berkowitz (Ed.), *Advances in experimental social psychology*. New York: Academic Press.

Stinson, D. A., Logel, C., Shepherd, S., & Zanna, M. P. (2011). Rewriting the self-fulfilling prophecy of social rejection: self-affirmation improves relational security and social behavior up to 2 months later. *Psychological Science, 22*(9), 1145–1149.

Stoltenberg, C. D., & McNeill, B. W. (2010). *IDM supervision: an integrative development model for supervising counselors and therapists* (3rd ed.). New York: Routledge.

Strupp, H. H. (1973). Foreword. In D. J. Kiesler (Ed.), *The process of psychotherapy: empirical foundations and systems of analysis*. Chicago: Aldine.

Sung, B. L. (1987). *The adjustment experience of Chinese immigrant children in New York City*. New York: Center for Migration Studies.

Swift, J. K., Whipple, J. L., & Sandberg, P. (2012). A prediction of initial appointment attendance and initial outcome expectations. *Psychotherapy, 49*, 549–556.

Taylor, S. E., Pham, L. B., Rivkin, I. D., & Armor, D. A. (1998). Harnessing the imagination: mental simulation, self-regulation, and coping. *American Psychologist, 53*, 429–439.

Taylor, V. J., & Walton, G. M. (2011). Stereotype threat undermines academic learning. *Personality & Social Psychology Bulletin, 37*, 1055–1067.

Teasdale, J. D., Segal, Z. V., Williams, J. M., Ridgeway, V. A., Soulsby, J. M., & Lau, M. A. (2000). Prevention of relapse/recurrence in major depression by mindfulness-based cognitive therapy. *Journal of Consulting and Clinical Psychology, 68*(4), 615–623.

Ten Eyck, L. L., Gresky, D. P., & Lord, C. G. (2008). Effects of directed thinking on exercise and cardiovascular fitness. *Journal of Applied Biobehavioral Research, 12*, 237–285

Thomas, C., & Baker, C. I. (2013). Teaching an adult brain new tricks: a critical review of evidence for training-dependent structural plasticity in humans. *Neuroimage, 73*, 225–236.

Tomkins, S. S. (1962). *Affect, imagery, consciousness: Vol. 1, The positive affects*. New York: Springer.

Tse, S., Tsoi, E. W., Hamilton, B., O'Hagan, M., Shepherd, G., Slade, M., . . . Petrakis, M. (2016). Uses of strength-based interventions for people with serious mental illness: a critical review. *International Journal of Social Psychiatry, 62*(3), 281–291.

Vansteenkiste, M., Neyrinck, B., Niemiec, C. P., Soenens, B., Witte, H., & Broeck, A. (2007). On the relations among work value orientations, psychological need satisfaction and job outcomes: a self-determination theory approach. *Journal of Occupational and Organizational Psychology, 80*(2), 251–277.

Vansteenkiste, M., Simons, J., Lens, W., Sheldon, K. M., & Deci, E. L. (2004). Motivating learning, performance, and persistence: the synergistic effects of intrinsic goal contents and autonomy-supportive contexts. *Journal of Personality and Social Psychology: Personality Processes and Individual Differences, 87*(2), 246–260.

Wade, J. C., & Jones, J. E. (2015). *Strength-based clinical supervision: a positive psychology approach to clinical training*. New York: Springer Publishing Company.

Wadlinger, H. A., & Isaacowitz, D. M. (2006). Positive mood broadens visual attention to positive stimuli. *Motivation and Emotion, 30*(1), 87–99.

Waltz, J., Addis, M. E., Koerner, K., & Jacobson, N. S. (1993). Testing the integrity of a psychotherapy protocol: assessment of adherence and competence. *Journal of Consulting and Clinical Psychology*, 61(4), 620–630.

Wampold, B. E. (2007). Psychotherapy: the humanistic (and effective) treatment. *American Psychologist*, 62, 857–873.

Wampold, B. E., Ahn, H. N., & Coleman, H. L. (2001). Medical model as metaphor: old habits die hard. *Journal of Counseling Psychology*, 48(3), 268–273.

Wampold, B. E., & Budge, S. L. (2012). The 2011 Leona Tyler Award Address: The relationship—and its relationship to the common and specific factors of psychotherapy. *The Counseling Psychologist*, 40(4), 601–623.

Wampold, B. E., & Imel, Z. E. (2015) *The great psychotherapy debate: the evidence for what makes psychotherapy work* (2nd ed.). New York: Routledge.

Wampold, B. E., Mondin, G. W., Moody, M., Stich, F., Benson, K., & Ahn, H. N. (1997). A meta-analysis of outcome studies comparing bona fide psychotherapies: empirically," all must have prizes." *Psychological Bulletin*, 122(3), 203.

Wang, S. J. (2007). Mindfulness meditation: its personal and professional impact on psychotherapists. *Dissertation Abstracts International: Section B: Science and Engineering*, 67, 4122.

Watkins, P. C., Grimm, D. L., & Kolts, R. (2004). Counting your blessings: positive memories among grateful persons. *Current Psychology*, 23(1), 52–67.

Watkins, P. C., Van Gelder, M., & Frias, A. (2009). Furthering the science of gratitude. In C. R. Snyder & S. J. Lopez (Eds.), *Oxford handbook of positive psychology* (pp. 437–445). New York: Oxford University Press.

Watzlawick, P., Weakland, J. H., & Fisch, R. (1974). *Change: principles of problem formation and problem resolution*. New York: W.W. Norton & Company.

Weinberg, R. (2008). Does imagery work? Effects on performance and mental skills. *Journal of Imagery Research in Sport and Physical Activity*, 3(1), 1–21.

Williams, J. M. G., & Kuyken, W. (2012). Mindfulness-based cognitive therapy: a promising new approach to preventing depressive relapse. *FOCUS*, 10(4), 489–491.

Willroth, E. C., & Hilimire, M. R. (2016). Differential effects of self-and situation-focused reappraisal. *Emotion*, 16(4), 468–474.

Winter Plumb, E. I., Hawley, K. J., & Conoley, C. W. (2015). *Constructing pathways to the best possible self: a quasi-experimental study of psycho-educational interventions in an undergraduate college class*. Poster presentation at the annual convention of the American Psychological Association, Toronto, Canada.

Wong, Y. J. (2006). Strength-centered therapy: a social constructionist, virtues-based psychotherapy. *Psychotherapy*, 43, 133–146.

Wong, Y. J. (2015). The psychology of encouragement: theory, research, and applications. *The Counseling Psychologist*, 43(2), 178–216.

Wood, A. M., Froh, J. J., & Geraghty, A. W. (2010). Gratitude and well-being: a review and theoretical integration. *Clinical Psychology Review*, 30(7), 890–905.

Wood, A. M., Linley, P. A., Maltby, J., Kashdan, T. B., & Hurling, R. (2011). Using personal and psychological strengths leads to increases in well-being over time: a longitudinal study and the development of the strengths use questionnaire. *Personality and Individual Differences*, 50(1), 15–19.

World Health Organization. (2004). *Promoting mental health: Concepts, emerging evidence, practice (Summary report)*. Geneva: WHO.

Wynn, R., & Wynn, M. (2006). Empathy as an interactionally achieved phenomenon in psychotherapy: characteristics of some conversational resources. *Journal of Pragmatics*, *38*(9), 1385–1397.

Yang, X. (2016). Self-compassion, relationship harmony, versus self-enhancement: different ways of relating to well-being in Hong Kong Chinese. *Personality and Individual Differences*, *89*, 24–27.

Yarnell, L. M., & Neff, K. D. (2013). Self-compassion, interpersonal conflict resolutions, and well-being. *Self and Identity*, *12*(2), 146–159.

Yeager, D. S., & Dweck, C. S. (2012). Mindsets that promote resilience: when students believe that personal characteristics can be developed. *Educational Psychologist*, *47*(4), 302–314.

Yeager, D. S., Johnson, R., Spitzer, B. J., Trzesniewski, K. H., Powers, J., & Dweck, C. S. (2014). The far-reaching effects of believing people can change: implicit theories of personality shape stress, health, and achievement during adolescence. *Journal of Personality and Social Psychology*, *106*(6), 867.

Yeager, D. S., Miu, A., Powers, J., & Dweck, C. S. (2013). Implicit theories of personality and attributions of hostile intent: a meta-analysis, an experiment, and a longitudinal intervention. *Child Development*, *84*, 1651–1667.

Yeager, D. S., Trzesniewski, K. H., & Dweck, C. S. (2013). An implicit theories of personality intervention reduces adolescent aggression in response to victimization and exclusion. *Child Development*, *84*(3), 970–988.

Yeager, D. S., Trzesniewski, K., Tirri, K., Nokelainen, P., & Dweck, C. S. (2011). Adolescents' implicit theories predict desire for vengeance after remembered and hypothetical peer conflicts: correlational and experimental evidence. *Developmental Psychology*, *47*, 1090–1107.

Yeager, D. S., & Walton, G. (2011). Social-psychological interventions in education: they're not magic. *Review of Educational Research*, *81*, 267–301.

Zessin, U., Dickhäuser, O., & Garbade, S. (2015). The relationship between self-compassion and well-being: a meta-analysis. *Applied Psychology: Health and Well-Being*, *7*(3), 340–364.

ABOUT THE AUTHORS

Collie W. Conoley, PhD, is a Professor in the Department of Counseling, Clinical and School Psychology at the University of California, Santa Barbara and Director of the Carol Ackerman Positive Psychology Center at the University of California, Santa Barbara. In addition to academe, he has worked in community mental health, private practice, inpatient hospital, day treatment center, and university counseling center. His research interests include positive psychology, psychotherapy process and outcome research, multicultural psychology, as well as individual, couple, and family psychology. Collie received his doctorate from the University of Texas at Austin.

Michael J. Scheel, PhD, ABPP, is a Professor in the Department of Educational Psychology at the University of Nebraska-Lincoln (UNL) and the Director of Training of the UNL graduate program in counseling psychology. He is the associate editor of *The Counseling Psychologist* and an American Psychological Association Fellow of Division 17. He was the 2014 recipient of the Shane Lopez Distinguished Contributions to Positive Psychology Award and the 2016 Outstanding Training Director Award. His primary research interest is applications of positive psychology in psychotherapy and in prevention of high school dropout. He teaches courses and speaks on leading happier and healthier lives and on psychotherapy from a strength perspective. He also is the director of the high school dropout prevention program, Building Bridges, which has served over 500 high school students.

DISCARD